Catholic Universities in Church and Society: A Dialogue on *Ex corde Ecclesiae*

Origins
2-17-94

Contributors

Rev. Michael J. Buckley, S.J., is Professor of Systematic Theology at Boston College.

Philip Burling, Esq., is Senior Partner at Foley, Hoag & Elliott in Boston, Massachusetts.

Sr. Sharon Euart, R.S.M., is Associate General Secretary of the National Conference of Catholic Bishops.

Philip Gleason is Professor of History at the University of Notre Dame.

Rev. J. Bryan Hehir is Professor of the Practice in Religion and Society at the Harvard Divinity School.

Rev. David Hollenbach, S.J., is Margaret O'Brien Flatley Professor of Catholic Theology at Boston College.

Elizabeth Topham Kennan is the President of Mount Holyoke College.

Rev. Joseph A. Komonchak is Associate Professor in the Department of Religion and Religious Education at The Catholic University of America.

Michael J. Lacey is Director of the Division of United States Studies at the Woodrow Wilson International Center for Scholars of the Smithsonian Institution.

Rev. John P. Langan, S.J., is Rose Kennedy Professor of Christian Ethics at Georgetown University.

David Thomas Link, Esq., is Joseph A. Matson Dean and Professor at Notre Dame Law School.

Gregory T. Moffatt is an Associate at Foley, Hoag & Elliott in Boston, Massachusetts.

Rabbi David Novak is Edgar M. Bronfman Professor of Modern Judaic Studies at the University of Virginia.

David J. O'Brien is Loyola Professor of Roman Catholic Studies at the College of the Holy Cross.

Rev. Leo J. O'Donovan, S.J., is the President of Georgetown University.

Rev. Ladislas Orsy, S.J., is Professor of Canon Law at The Catholic University of America.

Jaroslav Pelikan is Sterling Professor of History at Yale University.

Rev. James H. Provost is Professor of Canon Law at The Catholic University of America.

Rev. George H. Tavard, A.A., is Distinguished Professor of Theology at Marquette University.

Charles H. Wilson, Esq., is a Washington, D.C. attorney who has litigated church-state issues for a number of years.

Catholic Universities in Church and Society:
A Dialogue on *Ex corde Ecclesiae*

Edited by JOHN P. LANGAN, S.J.

Foreword by LEO J. O'DONOVAN, S.J.

GEORGETOWN UNIVERSITY PRESS / WASHINGTON, D.C.

Georgetown University Press, Washington, D.C. 20057-1079
© 1993 by Georgetown University Press. All rights reserved.
Printed in the United States of America
10 9 8 7 6 5 4 3 2 1   1993
THIS VOLUME IS PRINTED ON ACID-FREE OFFSET BOOK PAPER.

Library of Congress Cataloging-in-Publication Data

Catholic universities in church and society : a dialogue on Ex corde
    Ecclesiae / foreword by Leo J. O'Donovan ; edited by John P. Langan.
        p.   cm.
    Papers from a symposium held at Georgetown University in April
1993.
    1. Catholic Church. Pope (1978–   : John Paul II). Ex corde
Ecclesiae—Congresses.   2. Universities and colleges (Canon law)—
Congresses.   3. Christian education (Canon law)—Congresses.
I. Langan, John, 1940–   .
LAW <CANON Cath 1993>
377'.82—dc20
ISBN 0-87840-544-5   93-22154

Contents

Foreword   vii
Rev. Leo J. O'Donovan, S.J.

Acknowledgements   ix

**The American Background of *Ex corde Ecclesiae:*
A Historical Perspective**   1
Philip Gleason

> COMMENT: *David J. O'Brien*   20
> COMMENT: *Rev. J. Bryan Hehir*   28
> DISCUSSION: 32

The Catholic University in the Church   35
Rev. Joseph A. Komonchak

> COMMENT: *Rev. John P. Langan, S.J.*   56
> COMMENT: *Rev. George H. Tavard, A.A.*   63
> DISCUSSION: 69

**The Catholic University and the Promise Inherent
in Its Identity**   74
Rev. Michael J. Buckley, S.J.

> COMMENT: *Rev. David Hollenbach, S.J.*   90
> COMMENT: *Rabbi David Novak*   95
> DISCUSSION: 101

A Canonical Commentary on *Ex corde Ecclesiae*   105
    Rev. James H. Provost

    COMMENT: *Sr. Sharon A. Euart, R.S.M*   137
    COMMENT: *Rev. Ladislas Orsy, S.J.*   146
    DISCUSSION: 150

Notes from the Other Side of the Wall:
A University Counsel's Reflections on Potential Interactions
between the Civil Law and the Apostolic Constitution   153
    Philip Burling, Esq. and Gregory T. Moffatt

    COMMENT: *Charles H. Wilson, Esq.*   176
    COMMENT: *David Thomas Link, Esq.*   187
    DISCUSSION: 193

Ex corde Universitatis: Reflections on the Significance of Newman's
"Insisting Solely on Natural Theology"   196
    Jaroslav Pelikan

    COMMENT: *Elizabeth Topham Kennan*   210
    COMMENT: *Michael J. Lacey*   214
    DISCUSSION: 223

GENERAL WRAP-UP DISCUSSION   226

    APPENDIX A:
Apostolic Constitution, *Ex corde Ecclesiae,* of the Supreme Pontiff,
John Paul II, on Catholic Universities   229

    APPENDIX B:
Draft Ordinances: National Conference of Catholic Bishops
Committee to Implement the Apostolic Constitution,
Ex corde Ecclesiae,   255

Foreword

In August 1990 Pope John Paul II issued the apostolic constitution, *Ex corde Ecclesiae,* on Catholic universities. This is a document that expresses the pope's deep interest in the development of Catholic intellectual life in the university setting and also his care for the role of religious faith as a dialogical, integrating element in shaping modern culture more generally. The constitution offers both a theological understanding of the Catholic university and a set of general norms for its governance. It thus provokes reflection on such important theological themes as the relations between faith and reason and between the church and culture. But it also raises practical questions about the implications of its norms for the situation of the university in canon law and in civil law.

The university is a complex and valuable institution. A Catholic university has a special complexity arising from its religious character and mission. It embodies a fundamental dimension of our response to ultimate values. It is thus easy to conclude that a document such as *Ex corde Ecclesiae* requires the careful reading and respectful attention that it is a particular function of a university to supply. The purpose of the Georgetown University Symposium on *Ex corde Ecclesiae,* held at the end of April 1993, was precisely to provide an opportunity for scholarly reading, interpretation, and discussion of this important document and to assist others in pondering its implications for the American context.

The papers, comments, and discussion summaries included in this volume are intended to serve as the record of one scholarly dialogue about the Apostolic Constitution and about the issues it raises for educators, theologians, lawyers, and the members of the academy. The approach taken is interdisciplinary and ecumenical. The volume also reflects the conviction of the participants that the Catholic character of universities bearing the Catholic name is a precious *vii* legacy from the generations that built and staffed them, often at great sacrifice, and is also an invaluable resource for the future of American society and of world Catholicism.

LEO J. O'DONOVAN, S.J.
Georgetown University

Acknowledgments

We are grateful to Marilyn P. & Thomas J. Donnelly, to the Loyola Foundation, and to others for their generous support of the symposium. Special thanks to Michael Kelly, university vice president of Georgetown University, for summarizing the discussions. Our gratitude goes also to the participants in the symposium for a lively and thoughtful discussion.

PHILIP GLEASON, *University of Notre Dame*

The American Background of
Ex corde Ecclesiae:
A Historical Perspective

Many factors contributed to the issuance of *Ex corde Ecclesiae* in August 1990, but changes in American Catholic higher education since the 1960s were surely among the more important. These changes are not only important in themselves; they are essential to our understanding of the American context in which the general guidelines set forth in *Ex corde Ecclesiae* are to be given local application. Unfortunately, little historical work has been done on this period of American Catholic history, and still less has been devoted to the development of Catholic colleges and universities. However, a set of documents has recently been brought together in a volume that is highly germane to the topic and that also provides a useful point of departure for certain historical observations.

The volume in question is *American Catholic Higher Education: Essential Documents, 1967-1990,* edited by Alice Gallin, O.S.U. The documents collected here are, broadly speaking, of two sorts—statements drawn up by Catholic educators, mostly from the United States, and statements drawn up by Roman authorities. Taken together, they number about two dozen. The first section of the book contains four successive efforts to define the nature of a Catholic university worked out under the auspices of the International Federation of Catholic Universities between 1967 and 1972. Part 2 covers the beginning of a "bilateral dialogue" between Rome and American Catholic educators in the mid- and late-1970s, while part 3 reproduces the exchanges that led up to the issuance of the Revised Code of Canon Law (1983), which included eight new canons dealing with Catholic universities. Part 4, the longest section of the book, reproduces the "point and counterpoint" of drafts and responses that preceded the issuance of *Ex corde Ecclesiae,* the text of which brings the volume to its conclusion.[1]

Since all of these documents bear on the nature of the Catholic university and its place in the church and in society, and since they cover the three decades from Vatican II to *Ex corde Ecclesiae,* they allow us to identify several recurring concerns in that crucial epoch. My method in the following discussion will be to comment on what seem to me the most prominent of these recurring themes in the light of what I know about the history of American Catholic higher education. After taking note of two preliminary points, I will first treat themes that can be thought of as dealing primarily with the Catholic university in relation to the church, and second, themes that involve the Catholic university in relation to the world more broadly considered.

The first of the preliminary points calls attention to the theme of *novelty.* Again and again, the editor—who as executive director of the Association of Catholic Colleges and Universities from the late 1970s until 1992 was actively involved in the formulation of several of the most important of these documents—notes that the item in question was the first of its kind.[2] Thus the so-called "Land O'Lakes Statement" of 1967 was the first official effort ever made by a broadly representative group of Catholic educators to define the nature of the Catholic university. Proposing canons (in 1976) to cover Catholic universities in the Revised Code of Canon Law was a first; the establishment of a committee of bishops and representatives from the Association of Catholic Colleges and Universities in 1974 was a first; the bishops' pastorals on Catholic universities (1980) and on campus ministry (1985) were firsts. These "firsts"— which were on occasion objected to as "innovations"[3]—testify to the newness of the situation to which they were responses.

Second, the documents drawn up from the late sixties through the late eighties were all—as Sister Alice points out—phases of an "in-dialogue" process. The parties involved in this dialectical process were, broadly speaking, ecclesiastical authorities on the one hand, and academic representatives on the other. The latter led the dialogue up through the statement on "The Catholic University in the Modern World," which was drawn up by the International Federation of Catholic Universities in 1972, and they would have been quite content had the conversation ended there. That statement did not, however, satisfy Roman authorities on two points: the explicitness with which the Catholic identity of Catholic institutions was affirmed, and the adequacy of the provisions aimed at maintaining that identity. From then on, the dialogue consisted, for the most part, of Roman authorities proposing more stringent measures to secure those two points, and academic representatives attempting to moderate Rome's proposals. The final document—*Ex corde Ecclesiae* itself— could perhaps be called a happy synthesis in that it avoids what the academics found most objectionable in earlier Roman initiatives, while embodying papal encouragement, challenge, and admonition.

THE CATHOLIC UNIVERSITY'S RELATION
TO THE CHURCH

Turning now to the first of our two broad divisions of commentary, we begin with a point that is frequently adverted to in the documents, namely, the diversity that characterizes Catholic higher education.

Diversity

Diversity is usually mentioned in the documents in connection with the difficulty—not to say impossibility—of formulating uniform policies for, much less legislating for, Catholic universities all over the world, despite the differences they must accommodate in terms of political regimes, state of economic development, cultural characteristics of the area, and so on.[4] We are concerned here, however, with diversity in the strictly American (i.e., U.S.) context, which is sufficient in itself to boggle the mind and more than sufficient to guarantee that the coming changes would impact quite differently upon different kinds of institutions.

Fortunately, a careful study made in 1964-65 gives us a good picture of the situation just as change was preparing to shift into high gear.[5] At that time, some 457 Catholic institutions of higher education enrolled about 280,000 full-time students. All but 20,500 of these students attended the institutions for lay persons that we usually think of as "colleges and universities"; but 200 of the total number of institutions were for clerics or religious only. More specifically, 54 were diocesan seminaries; 72 were houses of study for religious men; and 74 catered strictly to women religious. Two-thirds of the latter— the so-called "Sister Formation colleges"—had been established since 1950 and were regarded in that decade as an exciting reform; they were, however, to prove very vulnerable to change because they were quite small (37 full-time students was the median for the group), academically weak (88 percent being unaccredited), and wholly dependent for their existence on the continued flourishing of their parent communities of religious women. By the early 1960s, they were a source of serious concern to Catholic educators.[6]

Among the institutions for lay students, colleges for women were the most numerous. There were 142 such schools, enrolling some 69,000 students, just over a quarter of the total number of lay students. Fourteen were junior colleges; two-thirds of the remaining 128 were strictly baccalaureate-level colleges, but 22 offered masters-level work, and 1 offered a doctorate. As a group, women's colleges were relatively small, four-fifths of them having 750 or fewer students, but 3 out of 4 were accredited, and competent observers (such as Monsignor John Tracy Ellis) considered the better ones academically the best Catholic education had to offer. Religious still predominated on the faculties of these schools, constituting 60 percent of the total faculty of 5,350; and although a quarter had lay persons on their governing boards, women's colleges tended to have closer juridical links to the sponsoring religious community than men's or coeducational institutions.

Their heavy dependence on religious as faculty made them vulnerable when change hit the sisterhoods in the late sixties; and some of the lay presidents who began to appear about the same time found themselves unduly constrained by governing boards dominated by religious, who sometimes gave higher education a lower priority than hospitals or other works their communities had undertaken.[7] In any case, colleges for women were to suffer greater attrition than men's or coeducational schools. By 1976 the College and University Department of the National Catholic Educational Association (NCEA) counted only fifty women's colleges; but the decline was not as great as it appeared, since many had simply become coeducational.[8]

The fifty-two Catholic men's colleges, with their total enrollment of eighty-two thousand, were on the average larger than the women's colleges, a quarter of them having two thousand or more students. Nearly all (nine out of ten) were accredited. More than half were strictly undergraduate institutions, but nineteen offered the masters, and two had doctoral programs. Men's colleges had a markedly higher proportion of lay faculty (69 percent) than women's colleges, and half already had lay persons on their governing boards, although the great shift in this matter was still to come.

Coeducational institutions—sixty-three in number, with a total enrollment of 109,000—varied widely among themselves. Eight were junior colleges, and a higher percentage than the men's colleges had fewer than 750 students. However, graduate work was concentrated in these institutions, since they harbored 70 percent of the full-time graduate students in Catholic universities. They also depended more than others on lay professors: 73 percent of the full-time faculty of 6,700 were lay persons, and the percentage was even higher in the larger institutions.

Obviously the Catholic higher educational universe of 1964-65 was very diverse internally. And while the changes that were coming affected all, one can, in hindsight, readily appreciate that the impact of those changes would not be uniform. That is important to keep in mind, because we tend to think primarily in terms of the biggest institutions, whose presidents were the most visible leaders, and whose inherent complexity fed an inexorable demand for greater autonomy than seemed available under the old ecclesiastical framework. Yet the smaller institutions—the women's colleges and especially the Sister Formation colleges—were the most exposed to the shattering effects of internal change in the religious communities.

Role of Religious Communities

This brings us to a second recurring theme: the role of religious communities in American Catholic higher education. This is a point frequently mentioned in the documents leading up to *Ex corde Ecclesiae,* usually by American Catholic educators who responded to Roman proposals for closer episcopal oversight of higher education by pointing out that most American Catholic colleges were founded by religious communities, are not now, and have not historically been, under the direct administrative control of the bishops.[9] It is an important and complex point, with which we must deal here in schematic fashion.

1. First of all, we should note that this point is connected with the diversity already discussed, since their different religious-order connections constitute a partial explanation for the existence of so much diversity among American Catholic institutions of higher education. Thus, to give but one example, two dozen different religious congregations were involved in the operation of the thirty Catholic colleges and universities in New York State in the late 1960s.[10]

2. The same factor goes far toward accounting for the oft-lamented "proliferation" and "duplication of effort" that has militated against academic excellence in Catholic higher education.[11] But the reason for so much college-founding by the different religious orders was not simply misguided emulation. In the nineteenth century, establishing a "college" commended itself, not only because it filled a genuine social need and thereby gave the religious community meaningful work to do, but also because it brought in income, served as a recruiting agency for the order, and in general constituted a nucleus from which the community could grow. And despite the changed situation in more recent times, much the same applied to the growth of Catholic women's colleges in the twentieth century—a development that proceeded both by upgrading existing academies and by founding wholly new institutions. Because religious orders must make their own way by their own efforts—both in respect to monetary income and recruitment of new blood—schools and colleges were essential to their continued existence. On that account, it is pointless to bemoan "proliferation" without realistically confronting the fact that the Catholic church in the United States has neither the administrative nor fiscal institutions that would make it possible to "consolidate" our super-abundance of Catholic colleges and universities.

3. We have also to consider religious communities in connection with the change-over to lay boards of trustees pioneered in the midsixties by Webster College, St. Louis University, and Notre Dame, and thereafter extended to virtually all Catholic institutions. This development has been called by a specialist in educational administration "a positive movement" that gave Catholic colleges access to "new sources of expertise, finances, and human resources" without diluting their "Catholic mission or institutional purpose."[12] This may very well be true, but it requires two qualifications. The first is that precisely because religious communities played such a crucial role in the past, and because they had historically constituted the main institutional link between Catholic higher education and "the church," the recent change to autonomous lay boards has necessarily *distanced* "the church" from that activity. The laicization of governing

boards must therefore be considered as much an "innovation" as the new juridical relationship with the hierarchy that Rome has tried to promote, but which American Catholic educators pointed out had almost never existed in the past. Second, it is well to recall that the displacement of ministers as the dominant group on the governing boards of American Protestant institutions was part and parcel of the larger movement of secularization that undoubtedly *did* affect the religious character of those institutions.[13]

4. We should also note that religious communities themselves have undergone a revolution since Vatican II. Thus the Jesuits—the order that has always dominated American higher education in numbers of institutions, students, and university-level activity—suffered stunning losses of personnel (a 38 percent decline between 1965 and 1990, according to Peter McDonough), and even seemed to question the worthwhileness of their commitment to education as an apostolate.[14] Much the same thing happened in most other communities, and these and related changes reduced the effective presence of religious on Catholic campuses to a shadow of what it had been in the immediate preconciliar era. That development, perhaps even more than the shift to autonomous lay boards, means that religious communities are no longer in a position to play the same role that was theirs historically—that is, as the chief institutional link between higher education and the church considered as an organized ecclesiastical entity.

5. Finally, the influence of the women's movement and feminism enters as a radically novel element in the historical experience of religious orders of women. As noted above, Catholic women's colleges were especially vulnerable because of their relatively small enrollments and heavy dependence on religious as faculty members. The movement toward coeducation in the sixties and early seventies presented further challenges. Continuing changes in the understanding of, and attitudes toward, gender roles and relationships since then (i.e., the early 1970s) have undoubtedly been a major factor in the development of women's religious communities and their colleges, but to the best of my knowledge the resultant changes have not been studied systematically.

Relations with the Hierarchy

This matter is closely linked to the role of religious communities and usually comes up in the documents when American Catholic educators argue the inappropriateness to this country of Roman proposals for some sort of juridical link between bishops and Catholic universities.[15] This objection is quite well founded, but the historical situation is more complex than simple nonconnection. Again the treatment will have to be very general.

Actually, the bishops *were* very much involved in founding Catholic colleges in the early days of the American church. After all, John Carroll founded Georgetown in his capacity as bishop; it was only turned over to the Jesuits after their official restoration.[16] In fact, many if not most of the colleges founded in the first half of the nineteenth century owed their original impulse to episcopal rather than religious-order initiatives. Moreover, even after these schools were turned over to religious orders, and when the latter founded others on their own, the goodwill of the bishops was recognized as essential to the success of a college. Negative evidence for this assertion—that is, difficulties between religious authorities and bishop—punctuates the history of most Catholic colleges.[17]

It is true that the original closeness of bishops to the colleges dropped off sharply when the bishops were able to establish free-standing seminaries— for their interest in recruiting and preparing priests was what made the "mixed" college-seminary of the early years an institution with which they were vitally concerned. This happened at different times in different parts of the country, but the middle decades of the nineteenth century witnessed the transition to free-standing seminaries in the older settled regions.[18] The development of parochial schools, which took place in the same era, also operated to divert the bishops' educational attention from the colleges.

The Catholic University of America (est. 1889) was, of course, an episcopal undertaking, and its overall impact on Catholic higher education was immense—not least in the role played by its rectors in organizing in 1904 the National Catholic Educational Association (NCEA), which served as the vehicle by which Catholic educators could undertake the modernization of their second-ary and collegiate work.[19] By that time, higher education was overwhelmingly in the hands of the religious orders, many representatives of which were uneasy about the dangers of centralization resulting from undue influence on the part of the hierarchy. Father Francis W. Howard, the NCEA's long-term secretary (who later became a bishop himself), was a determined foe of centralization in all forms, who feared that it might come through the National Catholic Welfare Conference or even from the Catholic University itself.[20]

One of the chief complaints of the "college men" (and Howard believed in keeping women at a distance, even after their colleges multiplied in the twentieth century) was that the bishops were undercutting the colleges by providing pastoral care for Catholic students on secular campuses. What some of them (the college men) wanted was a collective episcopal statement compara-ble to that issued on the subject of parochial schools by the Third Plenary Council of Baltimore in 1884—in other words, they wanted the bishops to *mandate* attendance at Catholic colleges. Though bruited on two occasions (1907 and 1932), this was never a realistic hope, because (among other reasons) the bishops were unwilling to require the faithful to patronize institutions whose quality they (the bishops) could neither guarantee nor effectively influence.

The point of all this is to suggest that the relationship between the hierarchy and higher education has never been one of absolute separation. On the contrary, informal links have always existed; and Catholic educators have always known that they could not take lightly the importance of good relations with the hierarchy generally and with their local ordinaries in particular.[21]

Autonomy

Concern for the autonomy of the academic institution, which runs as a leitmotiv in the documents that lead up to *Ex corde Ecclesiae,* is obviously closely connected with the foregoing discussion of religious communities and bishops.[22] Here four observations based on history suggest themselves.

1. The desire and the need for institutional autonomy might be considered a sort of built-in inertial force that gathers momentum inexorably with the growing size and complexity of a university (and here we really are speaking more of universities than of colleges). In other words, as a place grows bigger, more complex, more internally differentiated, requiring more and more specialists of various sorts (administrative as well as academic), it simply *has* to be freer of nonacademic external controls or it will be unable to function effectively.

The operation of this law of academic organizational development is vividly illustrated in the relations between Jesuit universities and the Jesuit Educational Association. This body was created in 1934 to unify and coordinate Jesuit education at every level and exerted a very positive influence in the thirties and forties. But by the late 1950s, the presidents of major Jesuit universities began to chafe at the efforts of the executive secretary of the Jesuit Educational Association to exert even an indirect coordinating influence. The reason was not that they felt no concern for the overall good of Jesuit higher education. No doubt they did, but they were much more concretely concerned about the good of the institutions for which they were immediately responsible. By 1970 they were able to throw off the oversight of the association, substituting for it an informal conference of Jesuit university presidents who consulted together but had no obligation whatever to coordinate their activities toward some suprainstitutional Jesuit educational goal.[23]

2. It is essential to note that, in this context, "autonomy" means freedom from external *ecclesiastical* control, not all sorts of external controls, since no university is "autonomous" with respect to the requirements established by accrediting associations, governmental agencies, philanthropic institutions, and accepted academic procedures.[24] The progressive sloughing off of external religious controls, while continuing to accommodate to the latter sort, can legitimately be spoken of as secularization. Indeed, it was regarded in precisely that light by conservative Catholic educators when accrediting agencies began their work and state governments established new teacher certification and other requirements in the early years of the twentieth century.[25]

3. Concern for autonomy is closely linked with the issue of academic freedom in Catholic colleges and universities which did not really become a live issue until the 1960s. Only a decade earlier, at the height of McCarthyism,

Catholic academics in the sensitive area of the social sciences expressed less concern about academic freedom than any comparable group among American educators.[26] In contrast, the academic freedom crisis set off when Saint John's University (New York) summarily dismissed some two dozen dissident faculty members in December 1965 was the most spectacular early symptom of the seismic upheaval that was to shake the foundations of Catholic higher education.[27]

4. The new concern for autonomy must be seen against the backdrop of Vatican II and the cultural revolution that took place in American society in the 1960s. Vatican II made "freedom in the church" a different kind of issue than it had ever been before, while "freedom now" and "liberation" were the watchwords of the civil rights/black movement, the women's movement, anti-Vietnam protesters, student rebels, and prophets of the counterculture. In the context of the radical antiauthoritarianism of the 1960s, Catholic institutions of higher learning could not continue in the old ways and remain immune to the "dissent" that had become a powerful symbol of positive values.

The Role of Theology

Theology was one of the neuralgic points so far as academic freedom is concerned. It is also, of course, a central issue so far as the preservation of an institution's Catholic identity is concerned, and as such it is frequently mentioned in the various statements dealing with Catholic higher education from Land O'Lakes to *Ex corde Ecclesiae.*[28]

I am not equipped to comment on the intellectual dimensions of this theme—that is, on the content and quality of the theology done in Catholic colleges and universities since Vatican II. As matters appear to a nonprofessional (and not very systematic) observer, I would say that developments worthy of attention are: the collapse of "sacred theology" as previously understood, the development of many "theologies," the new biblical orientation of theology; the partial displacement of theology by "religious studies," with the latter being understood not merely as ecumenical but as an "academic subject" just like any other subject in the sense that competence to teach it had nothing to do with the personal religious commitments of the teacher.

Developments of this sort are nicely illustrated in the history of the College Theology Society, formed in 1954 as a professional association of teachers of undergraduate religion (or theology) classes. The needs and interests of this group differed from those of the seminary professors of theology who dominated the Catholic Theological Society of America (est. 1946). The new association was first called the Society of Catholic College Teachers of Sacred Doctrine, and its adoption in 1967 of the more aseptically academic name, College Theology Society, reflected the kind of changes sketched in the preceding paragraph. This kind of academic neutralization of the specifically Catholic quality of theological study in Catholic universities has recently aroused expressions of concern on the part of Catholic theologians, some of whom speak of it in terms of "secularization."[29]

From the institutional viewpoint, several historical developments stand out as important. The first is that, except at the Catholic University of America, theology was a seminary, not university, subject until after World War II. Indeed, it amounted to very little on any other Catholic campus until the 1960s. Even the pioneering graduate program in theology for women at Saint Mary's College, Notre Dame, Indiana, testifies to this point. It was established in 1943 precisely because sisters, who taught religion in parochial and high schools, could not study the subject anywhere else.[30]

Indeed, "religion" developed very slowly as an academic subject in Catholic colleges—as late as 1937, only three colleges out of eighty-four surveyed offered an undergraduate major in religion, and two more years passed before a movement got under way to make "theology," rather than scholastic philosophy, the integrating core of Catholic undergraduate education. Through the forties and well into the fifties, Catholic academics disagreed confusedly over whether the subject to be taught to undergraduates should be called "religion" or "theology." In fact, this controversy was one of the reasons the mouth-filling title Society of Catholic College Teachers of Sacred Doctrine was adopted by those who felt the need for a professional association in the early fifties.[31]

The academic upgrading of theology in the 1960s, and the launching of regular academic-year graduate programs, coincided in certain cases (e.g., at the University of Notre Dame) with the relocation to the university of the religious community's candidates for the priesthood. This was primarily intended to bring the seminarians into closer contact with the intellectual life of the university, but it also created a kind of instant clientele for the instructional wares of the graduate departments in question. One might speculate that it also tended to awaken new interest in the universities on the part of the bishops, since instruction in theology, some of it given to candidates for the priesthood, was now a much more visible and important activity on Catholic campuses than it had been since the development of free-standing seminaries in the middle decades of the nineteenth century.

THE CATHOLIC UNIVERSITY'S RELATION TO THE LARGER WORLD

The second major category of themes selected for commentary from the documents leading up to *Ex corde Ecclesiae* can be subdivided into those having to do primarily with the academic world and those having to do with the culture and the larger world. Under the first heading, we begin with accreditation.

Accreditation

Accreditation is referred to a number of times in the documents, usually in explaining the educational and legal context in which Catholic universities operate in the United States.[32] Historically, accreditation has been a crucial factor in requiring Catholic institutions to conform to the educational norms of this country and as a collective bulwark protecting all educational institutions (not just Catholic ones) against purely governmental regulation. The story of accreditation as it affects Catholic institutions is long and complicated, punctuated by fears of secularization from the very beginning, but generally recognized by Catholic educators as having played an immensely positive role in improving academic standards.[33]

The influence of accreditation was greatest, and its positive contribution to Catholic institutions most vital, in the early decades of the century. Known in those days as "standardization," it played a key role in the organizational modernization of Catholic undergraduate education that took place between 1900 and the early 1920s. It was also a crucial factor in stimulating American teaching sisters to launch the professional upgrading venture that evolved into the Sister Formation Movement. Catholic seminaries also began to get seriously interested in accreditation in the post-World War II years.

By establishing standards to which institutions must conform, accrediting bodies perform a quasi-legal function and constitute a voluntary substitute for, or form of partnership with, public law. The recent attempt by the Middle States Association to enforce a "diversity" standard illustrates the range and complexity of these interactions, their potential impact on the religious dimension, and, in this case, the adverse reaction from public authority they can arouse. This brings us to a different facet of the Catholic university's relation to the larger world.

The Legal Dimension

The legal dimension is referred to several times in our documents in the same kind of context as accreditation—that is, in explaining to Rome the kind of requirements American Catholic institutions must conform to.[34] I will do little more than take note of the topic here, since it is a quite technical field, both in respect to administrative regulations and norms established by court rulings, and because it will be dealt with elsewhere in this volume. With respect to rulings by the courts, however, it is worthwhile to emphasize how recently activity in this sphere began to affect Catholic colleges and universities in a significant way. The main body of Supreme Court decisions dealing with the Establishment Clause dates from the 1940s, but the earliest case whose relevance to higher education is noted in the 1976 "position paper" of the NCEA's College and University Department is *Tilton* v. *Richardson* (1971).[35] The so-called "Bundy money" situation in New York—that is, state aid for private institutions of higher education that are held to be "constitutionally eligible"—best illustrates the importance state legislative measures can have.[36] The ramifications of federal policies on student aid, ROTC-type programs, and governmental funding of research—all of which have mushroomed since World War II, and especially since the 1960s—are far too extensive for discussion here.[37]

In general, one might say that the legal context within which Catholic colleges and universities exist is ambivalent. On the one hand, the American polity has unquestionably encouraged religious groups by affording protection for freedom of action, in higher education and elsewhere. On the other hand, the stringency with which anything "sectarian" is handled by public authorities sets up a countervailing pressure in the general direction of secularization, which becomes more pronounced as institutions of higher education become more deeply entangled with governmental programs.

Although accreditation and the legal situation are noted here primarily as institutional forces operating on Catholic universities in the academic world, they also carry ideological implications. As we turn now to our second subdivision of themes—those having to do with the relation of Catholic universities to the larger world—the broadly ideological issues move front and center.

One such theme that recurs frequently in the documents, especially *Ex corde Ecclesiae* and its Roman preliminaries, has to do with the Catholic university's role in the evangelization of culture; another, implicit throughout, has to do with secularization.[38] These are too broad and diffuse to discuss in detail, but the history of Catholic higher education in this country suggests some sketchy observations about the general topics of culture, Catholic culture, ghettoism, and secularization.

Catholic Universities and Culture

First of all, it can be said emphatically that attention to, and the desire to influence, the general culture is not new to American Catholic educators.[39] It was very a prominent theme in the 1930s and 1940s. Inspired by the Catholic intellectual and cultural revival of that era, and particularly by Christopher Dawson's notion of culture as animated by religion, Catholic educators aspired to convey to their students an "integral Catholic culture," and ultimately to convert the larger world to that culture. In 1935, for example, the College and University Department of the NCEA formally approved the report of its Committee on Educational Policy and Program, which included the following language:

> The Catholic college will not be content with presenting Catholicism as a creed, a code, or a cult. Catholicism must be seen as a culture; hence, the graduates of the Catholic college of liberal arts will go forth not

merely trained in Catholic doctrine, but they will have seen the whole
sweep of Catholicism, its part in the building up of our western civilization,
past and present . . . They will have before them not merely the facts
in the natural order but those in the supernatural order also, those facts
which give meaning and coherence to the whole of life.[40]

That earlier effort at evangelizing the national culture did not attain its
ultimate goal. It did, however, take its place within, and contribute to the
creation of, a vibrant American Catholic subculture that had its own distinctive
institutions, norms, and outlook on the world. Though this subculture constituted a highly visible and quite vigorous element in the cultural pluralism of
American society, Catholics themselves came to be dissatisfied with it, those
most dissatisfied calling it a "ghetto." This process of internal detachment
from the Catholic subculture seems to have been set in motion by World War
II. It was unquestionably reinforced by criticism from outsiders like Paul
Blanshard, which Catholics could not help being influenced by, even though
they accused the critics of bigotry. The resulting dissatisfaction manifested
itself in the "self-criticism" that erupted after Monsignor Ellis's epoch-making
critique of Catholic intellectual life in 1955, and that helped prepare the way
for the wholesale repudiation of the "preconciliar church" that took place in
the aftermath of Vatican II and the general cultural upheaval of the 1960s.

This earlier attempt at evangelizing the culture by means of mobilizing
Catholics into their own organizations in every field of activity—each of which
was supposed to contribute to the desired "restoration of all things in Christ"—
had the ironic practical effect of cutting Catholics off from their culture more
than many of them wanted to be cut off. In other words, the effort to evangelize
culture by that mode was dialectically related to the "ghettoism" that came
to be despised by progressive Catholics.

How will the new evangelization of culture avoid that peril and at the
same time avoid the contrary peril—that is, the danger of losing group identity
by total absorption into the surrounding culture, the culture one wishes to
evangelize without being so different one loses contact with it?[41] This is another
way of putting the question of secularization. Certainly the main tendency
since Vatican II—in Catholic higher education, as elsewhere in the Catholic
world—has been toward embracing the world in a positive way, deprecating
the peril of secularization, and treating dismissively the "prophets of gloom"
who warn against it. But the danger of total absorption is there if what is
distinctive to Catholicism has been so much weakened by self-criticism and
repudiation of the "outdated" that it is rendered exiguous. Observers of Catholic
higher education began talking about an "identity crisis" almost thirty years
ago; that expression is no longer in vogue, but the assimilation of Catholic
institutions to secular norms has, if anything, gathered momentum. In other
words, the danger has not lessened but increased.

The drafters of the series of statements on the nature of the Catholic university from Land O'Lakes in 1967 up through the 1972 document approved by the International Federation of Catholic Universities surely represented the progressive, liberal school of thought. They were moderate, to be sure, and ostensibly confident that none of the changes over which they presided were really weakening the "Catholic character" of their institutions. But the response from Rome indicated uncertainty from the top on this point, and it was doubtless fed by reports from conservative Catholics in this country who felt the same way.[42] If nothing else, the process of dialogue thereupon initiated served the salutary purpose of making the participants more sensitively aware of the perceptions of the other.

One of the points of agreement between the two major parties to the dialogue—that is, educators and Roman authorities—is the positive emphasis both give to the theme of *peace and justice*.[43] The prominence of this theme accords with my belief that it has been tacitly understood by its promoters as serving the important latent function of providing a new raison d'être for Catholic institutions of higher education, and, by so doing, constituting a new way to preserve their Catholic identity. Thus, after noting the danger of secularization, Joseph A. Tetlow, S.J., asked, "Is it possible that the work of faith for justice, expressed in concrete matters for research and praxis, might supply the questions of ultimate social and moral importance?" Another Jesuit, Father Peter Henriot, suggested that launching into peace-and-justice work would amount to a "second founding" for Catholic colleges. And in her role as executive director of the Association of Catholic Colleges and Universities, Alice Gallin, O.S.U., called attention to Henriot's suggestion, adding that justice is central to Catholics' self-understanding and is relevant to higher education.[44]

The peace-and-justice theme is certainly in line with some of the newer trends in theology and brings faith actively into life. One may, however, question whether it is not losing its dynamism. To the degree that it has been associated with liberation theology and general intellectual leftism, it would seem almost certain to decline in vitality as a result of the collapse of formerly communist regimes and the overall discrediting of revolutionary socialism.

Peace-and-justice is also handicapped by the fact that most faculty members tend—if I have assessed their collective reaction accurately—to regard it as "activism," which is acceptable as an extracurricular, but which is too far removed from the properly academic realm to be a satisfactory center or anchorage for a university's distinctiveness.

This brings us to a matter that, though frequently mentioned, is not given great emphasis in the documents: the crucial role of the *faculty* in maintaining, or not maintaining, an institution's Catholic character.[45] Different observers assess the situation quite diversely, but my own view is that the attenuation of commitment to this goal on the part of the faculty has already gone very far. Not simply on peace-and-justice, but on the Catholic character issue as such.

A careful study of the situation at Marquette University singled out changes taking place in the make-up and outlook of the faculty as the most significant factor eroding the Catholic character of the institution. These changes resulted from the devolution to departmental search committees of the primary responsibility for faculty hiring and the tendency on the part of such committees to ignore religious considerations in selecting prospective new faculty members. The resulting *de facto* adoption of religiously neutral criteria for hiring at Marquette led this investigator to predict in 1977 that "If observable patterns continue, by 1998 Catholicity will not merely have changed but will have lost its significance as a distinctive characteristic of some institutions of American, Catholic higher education."[46]

At my own university, maintaining a preponderance on the faculty of committed Catholics has been affirmed as an institutional goal since the early 1970s. At the present, however, an ongoing self-study has, for the first time, raised a considerable rumble of uneasiness among the faculty about the emphasis given to the Catholic character of Notre Dame and what implications that commitment might have for faculty hiring and promotion. Indeed, the issue has become a divisive one within the faculty, for there are others who believe that something must be done now to stem the tide running against preservation of Notre Dame's Catholic character as a result of changes in the religious composition of the faculty.

It is, I suspect, in this difficult and delicate area that we will encounter the greatest challenge to successfully carrying forward the work toward which *Ex corde Ecclesiae* and all the documents that led up to it are oriented.

NOTES

1. Alice Gallin, O.S.U., ed., *American Catholic Higher Education: Essential Documents, 1967-1990* (Notre Dame, Ind.: University of Notre Dame Press, 1992).

2. For Gallin's commentary, see *American Catholic Higher Education: Essential Documents,* pp. 1-6, 63-64, 153-54, 189-90. For another retrospective review by a participant in much of the dialogue, see Ann Ida Gannon, B.V.M., "Some Aspects of Catholic Higher Education since Vatican II," *CCICA Annual, 1987,* pp. 11-32.

3. See, for example, Gallin, *American Catholic Higher Education: Essential Documents,* pp. 168, 171, 267.

4. For example, Gallin, *American Catholic Higher Education: Essential Documents,* pp. 266-67.

5. Unless otherwise indicated, the following discussion is based on data provided in Charles E. Ford and Edgar L. Roy, *The Renewal of Catholic Higher Education* (Washington, D.C.: National Catholic Educational Association, 1968).

6. See M. Patrice Noterman, S.C.C., "An Interpretive History of the Sister Formation Conference, 1954-1964" (Ph.D. diss., Loyola University [Chicago], 1988), pp. 132-34.

7. On this point see the "stunningly candid" remarks of Dr. Edward L. Henry, then president of Saint Mary's College, Notre Dame, Indiana, in *College Newsletter* 36 (June 1974): 5-8. (*College Newsletter* was the publication of the College and University Department of the NCEA.)

8. The 1976 figure of fifty is given in the "position paper" reproduced in Gallin, *American Catholic Higher Education: Essential Documents,* p. 72. (The NCEA's College and University Department was reorganized as the Association of Catholic Colleges and Universities in 1978.)

9. See, for example, Gallin, *American Catholic Higher Education: Essential Documents,* pp. 266, 276.

10. Edward Michael O'Keefe, "The Influence of New York State Aid to Private Colleges and Universities (1968) on the Process of Change Taking Place in Catholic Institutions of Higher Learning" (Ph.D. diss., State University of New York at Buffalo, 1974), p. 15.

11. For a recent example of this lament, see William P. Leahy, S.J., *Adapting to America: Catholics, Jesuits, and Higher Education in the Twentieth Century* (Washington, D.C.: Georgetown University Press, 1991), esp. pp. 137-41.

12. Martin J. Stamm, "The Emerging Guardianship of American Catholic Higher Education," *Occasional Papers on Catholic Higher Education* 5 (Summer 1979): 25-29. Alice Gallin, O.S.U., is presently engaged in a historical study of this process.

13. See Richard Hofstadter and Walter P. Metzger, *The Development of Academic Freedom in the United States* (New York: Columbia University Press, 1955), pp. 344-63.

14. Peter McDonough, *Men Astutely Trained: A History of the Jesuits in the American Century* (New York: Free Press, 1992), p. 5; Joseph A. Tetlow, S.J., "The Jesuits' Mission in Higher Education: Perspectives and Contexts," *Studies in the Spirituality of Jesuits* 15-16 (November 1983, January 1984), esp. 106, note 169.

15. Gallin, *American Catholic Higher Education: Essential Documents,* pp. 266-67, 277, 280, 311.

16. See Philip Gleason, "The Main Sheet Anchor: John Carroll and Catholic Higher Education," *Review of Politics* 38 (October 1976): 576-613.

17. For general discussion, see Edward J. Power, *Catholic Higher Education in America: A History* (New York: Appleton-Century-Crofts, 1972), pp. 42-45; for two examples, see Edward Sorin, C.S.C., *Chronicles of Notre Dame du Lac,* trans. John M. Toohey, C.S.C., ed. and annot. James T. Connelly, C.S.C. (Notre Dame, Ind.: University of Notre Dame Press, 1992), pp. 222-42, 255-64; Francis X. Curran, S.J., "Archbishop Hughes and the Jesuits," *Woodstock Letters* 97 (Winter 1968): 5-56.

18. See Joseph M. White, *The Diocesan Seminary in the United States* (Notre Dame, Ind.: University of Notre Dame Press, 1989), chaps. 1-3.

19. C. Joseph Nuesse, *The Catholic University of America: A Centennial History* (Washington, D.C.: Catholic University of America Press, 1990), esp. pp. 118ff., 171ff.; see also Philip Gleason, "American Catholic Higher Education: A Historical Perspective," in *The Shape of Catholic Higher Education*, ed. Robert Hassenger (Chicago: University of Chicago Press, 1967), pp. 28, 37-39.

20. For matters discussed in this paragraph and the next, see James H. Plough, "Catholic Colleges and the Catholic Educational Association: The Foundation and Early Years of the CEA, 1899-1919" (Ph.D. diss., University of Notre Dame, 1967), passim; John Whitney Evans, *The Newman Movement: Roman Catholics in American Higher Education, 1883-1971* (Notre Dame, Ind.: University of Notre Dame Press, 1980), chap. 3; and Leahy, *Adapting to America,* p. 52.

21. Concerning his troubles with the bishop of Chicago, the founder of Notre Dame wrote of himself in the third person: "Now he knew better than anybody that . . . it would be rash for a religious congregation to attempt to hold a college . . . without the good will of the bishop; but that it would be folly to hope to succeed against his will. In vain would talent and devotedness combine; they would fall against the opposition of the Ordinary." Sorin, *Chronicles of Notre Dame,* p. 255.

22. Gallin, *American Catholic Higher Education: Essential Documents,* pp. 7, 23-24, 43-44, 83, 168-69, 263, 303.

23. Paul A. FitzGerald, *The Governance of Jesuit Colleges in the United States, 1920-1970* (Notre Dame, Ind.: University of Notre Dame Press, 1984), esp. chaps. 7, 12; see also Tetlow, "Jesuits' Mission in Higher Education," pp. 52ff.

24. The NCEA's 1976 "position paper" explicitly acknowledged that "the accreditation process imposes certain limitations on institutional autonomy"; the same point is implicit in its treatment of the legal context within which Catholic colleges must operate. Gallin, *American Catholic Higher Education: Essential Documents,* p. 73, 77-79.

25. These reactions were often linked to a fierce attachment to the traditional classical curriculum. See, for example, Francis P. Donnelly, S.J., "Is the American College Doomed?" *[American] Ecclesiastical Review* 40 (April 1919): 359-65; *Report of the . . . Second Annual Meeting of the National Benedictine Educational Association . . . 1919* (Beatty, Pa.: Archabbey Press, 1919), pp. 23-33.

26. Paul F. Lazarsfeld and Wagner Thielens, Jr., *The Academic Mind: Social Scientists in a Time of Crisis* (Glencoe, Ill.: Free Press, 1958), p. 90. Several Catholic educators did, however, express concern at the methods employed by congressional investigating committees in 1953; see *New York Times,* 9 April 1953, p. 29.

27. Edward Manier and John Houck, eds., *Academic Freedom and the Catholic University* (Notre Dame, Ind.: Fides Publishers, 1967), the first book devoted to the subject, grew out of a symposium held at Notre Dame shortly after the Saint John's episode. For a historical survey of violations of academic freedom in American Catholic institutions, see John Tracy Ellis, "A Tradition of Autonomy?" in *The Catholic University: A Modern Appraisal,* ed. Neil J. McCluskey, S.J. (Notre Dame, Ind.: University of Notre Dame Press, 1970), pp. 206-70.

28. Gallin, *American Catholic Higher Education: Essential Documents,* pp. 7-8, 13-14, 46, 54-55, 75-76, 288, 335-37, 397, 419, 422.

29. Rosemary Rodgers, O.P., *A History of the College Theology Society* (Philadelphia: College Theology Society, 1983). For expressions of concern, see Thomas F. O'Meara, O.P., "Doctoral Programs in Theology at U.S. Catholic Universities," *America* 162 (February 3, 1990), pp. 79ff.; Gerald O'Collins, S.J., "Catholic Theology (1965-90)," *America* 162 (February 3, 1990), pp. 86ff.; Robert J. Wister, "The Teaching of Theology 1950-90: The American Catholic Experience," *America* 162 (February 3, 1990), pp. 88ff.; Matthew L. Lamb, "Will There Be Catholic Theology in the United States?" *America* 163 (May 26, 1990), pp. 523 ff.

30. Sandra Yocum Mize of the University of Dayton is currently at work on a history of the Graduate School of Sacred Theology at Saint Mary's. At Marquette, which was among the more progressive institutions in offering theology, masters-level work was confined to summer school till the end of the 1950s. See Patrick W. Carey, "Theology at Marquette University: A History" (mimeo draft, 1987). At Notre Dame, graduate work in theology was offered only in liturgical studies, and only in summer school, from the late 1940s into the 1960s.

31. See Rosemary T. Rodgers, O.P., "The Changing Concept of College Theology: A Case Study" (Ph.D. diss., Catholic University of America, 1973), esp. chap. 4; Philip Gleason, *Keeping the Faith: American Catholicism Past and Present* (Notre Dame, Ind.: University of Notre Dame Press, 1987), pp. 143ff.

32. Gallin, *American Catholic Higher Education: Essential Documents,* pp. 73-74, 260, 262, 264.

33. These and the following comments on accreditation are based on my ongoing research on the history of Catholic higher education.

34. Gallin, *American Catholic Higher Education: Essential Documents,* pp. 77-79, 261-63.

35. Gallin, *American Catholic Higher Education: Essential Documents,* p. 78. For a discussion of how one of the Catholic schools involved in *Tilton* dealt with the issue, see Joseph Richard Preville, "Fairfield University: The Emergence of a Modern Catholic Institution" (Ph.D. diss., Boston College, 1985), chap. 5.

36. See O'Keefe, "Influence of New York State Aid"; Maureen Manion, "The Impact of State Aid on Sectarian Higher Education: The Case of New York State," *Review of Politics* 48 (Spring 1986): 264-88.

37. See Philip R. Moots and Edward McGlynn Gaffney, Jr., *Church and Campus* (Notre Dame, Ind.: University of Notre Dame Press, 1979); Edward McGlynn Gaffney, Jr., and Philip R. Moots, *Government and the Campus* (Notre Dame, Ind.: University of Notre Dame Press, 1982); Fernand N. Dutile and Edward McGlynn Gaffney, Jr., *State and Campus* (Notre Dame, Ind.: University of Notre Dame Press, 1984).

38. For the Catholic university's cultural role, see Gallin, *American Catholic Higher Education: Essential Documents,* pp. 51-52, 136, 196-201, 337-39, 385-93, 427-28.

39. For elaboration of some of the following points, see Gleason, *Keeping the Faith,* chaps. 7-9; Gleason, "American Catholic Higher Education, 1940-1990: The Ideological Context," in *The Secularization of the Academy,* ed. George M. Marsden and Bradley J. Longfield (New York: Oxford University Press, 1992), pp. 234-58.

40. *National Catholic Educational Association Bulletin* 32 (August 1935): 70-71.

41. For elaboration of this dialectic, which was originally suggested by the example of assimilation in an organization of German Catholic immigrants, see Gleason, *Keeping the Faith,* chap. 3.

42. See, for example, George A. Kelly, ed., *Why Should the Catholic University Survive?* (New York: Saint John's University Press, 1973), and K. D. Whitehead, *Catholic Colleges and Federal Funding* (San Francisco: Ignatius Press, 1988).

43. Gallin, *American Catholic Higher Education: Essential Documents,* pp. 23, 31, 51, 143, 242-46, 289-90, 316-17, 341-42, 400-01, 423-24.

44. Tetlow, "Jesuits' Mission in Higher Education," p. 7; for Henriot and Gallin, see *Current Issues in Catholic Higher Education* 2 (Summer 1981): 2. See also David M. Johnson, ed., *Justice and Peace Education* (Maryknoll, N.Y.: Orbis Books, 1986).

45. Gallin, *American Catholic Higher Education: Essential Documents,* pp. 50, 267-68, 303, 315, 331, 365-67, 420. Only two of these passages (267-68 and 365-67) deal more or less directly with the issue as formulated in the text; the others are more general.

46. Gregory F. Lucey, "The Meaning and Maintenance of Catholicity as a Distinctive Characteristic of American, Catholic Higher Education: A Case Study" (Ph.D. diss., University of Wisconsin-Madison, 1978), pp. 255-56. Tetlow writes: "The truth is that by 1970 most search committees (the fresh expression of faculty self-governance [in Jesuit institutions]) did not even inquire about candidates' religion . . . The mere interest was déclassé." Tetlow, "Jesuits' Mission in Higher Education," p. 33.

COMMENT

DAVID J. O'BRIEN, *College of the Holy Cross*

I am grateful for Philip Gleason's three decades of work on the history of Catholic higher education. This useful paper sets the long- and short-term historical contexts for our discussion. Many of the points Professor Gleason makes here (and elsewhere[1]) are extremely important and unfortunately too little noted. This is a vast subject; he could only sketch its framework in the broadest strokes. To forward the discussion and broaden the context, I would like to offer four supplemental comments, intended less to challenge Gleason's arguments than to offer some alternative perspectives I regard as important.

RECENT, POSITIVE HISTORY

The recent history of Catholic higher education was more positive and constructive than the recent history of most other areas of American Catholic institutional life.

I paraphrase a conversation with a Jesuit university president:

As a young Jesuit I was tremendously impressed by men like John Courtney Murray and Gustave Weigel. I understood their message to us to be excellence: we could best serve the church by developing the intellectual skills to confront effectively the central problems of modern society. When I became president, I saw that the sign at our entrance said "university," not "church," and I set out to do all I could to make this the best possible school. Yes, I looked to the country's best colleges and universities for models of what that meant. I see no reason to apologize for doing so.

This conversation will sound familiar to anyone who has talked to people like Paul Reinert, Theodore M. Hesburgh, or Ann Ida Gannon.[2] The dramatic changes these leaders initiated arose from growth and the needs of specific schools, as Gleason suggests. But they also arose from the deepest aspirations of post-World War II American Catholics. The expansion, growing complexity, and professionalization of the colleges and universities was an almost exact institutional expression of the historic move of European immigrant Catholics to the center of U.S. society and culture. For millions of families, improvement in education, income, and social status was an authentic experience of liberation. There was in that experience little of the passive reaction to events suggested by terms such as *Americanization* and *secularization;* there was much energetic self-help, a good deal of deliberate, purposeful, strategic action, and a great unleashing of talent and energy harnessed to Catholic and American idealism.

The sectarian counterculturalism of Christopher Dawson and a few Catholic intellectuals and the fussy preoccupation with ecclesiastical discipline of nervous church bureaucrats seemed equally unworthy. Both would leave Catholics always strangers in their land and clients, mere externs, in their church. Far better the risks of shared responsibility with lay boards of trustees, the professionalization of academic practice with more diverse and better trained faculty, and acknowledgment of the authority of accrediting agencies, acceptance of some limited accountability in exchange for public assistance rendered for public purposes, and educational reforms appropriate to the perceived economic, social, and political circumstances of lay Catholics in cold-war America.

Professor Gleason says that these changes "necessarily *distanced* 'the church' " from higher education and risked the "secularization" that he claims overtook American Protestant institutions after they made similar reforms. Perhaps such fears account for the fact that elsewhere (save perhaps in Catholic Charities) less self-confident church leaders avoided such risks. In elementary and secondary education, in financial management, in personnel policy, and generally in pastoral practice, the U.S. church usually failed to develop effective structures of shared responsibility, failed to reform its professional practice of pastoral ministry, failed to accept any but internally and clerically generated standards of performance, and hardly tried to develop programs to implement the church's powerful teachings on public matters. It doesn't take Andrew Greeley's statistics to convince us that our church pays a high price for avoiding the risks taken by the religious orders responsible for higher education.

LACK OF THEORY TO MATCH PRACTICE

American Catholic higher education has lacked a theory to match its practice.

Innocent the Hesburghs, Reinerts, and Gannons may have been, but they could not have been more Catholic in the American way. Their problem was that the American way of being Catholic, at least after 1900, had little theory for its practice. Despite the modest interest in Catholic action in the 1950s, the countercultural Catholicism of papal encyclicals and the required philosophy and religion courses served neither to enlist many Catholics in mission nor to challenge prevailing secular practice except in sexual matters. Instead, in popularized form, Catholic claims helped support the denominational imperatives structured by religious pluralism: clarifying religious boundaries, enhancing exclusive religious claims, motivating commitment to and support for Catholic institutions, and legitimating clerical control of ecclesiastical life. The universities could generate Catholic philosophy and Catholic art, but they could not speak convincingly to the challenges of twentieth-century life. As a result, not only did the church have little positive impact on public life, but also the laity lacked theological and spiritual resources to endow its political, economic, and intellectual experience with Christian meaning.

The academic revolutionaries wanted to do better than that. They dreamed of a more intelligent and responsible church, measured by prevailing standards of intelligence and responsibility, and a laity that would find in their new-found power in society opportunities to make a better world. Faced with the challenge of a Christopher Dawson or a Dorothy Day (or, here, Michael Buckley, S.J.) to be really Catholic or of a John Cogley to be really a university, institutional leaders responded (and still respond) with a crude if gutsy Americanism: let's be both. They took a lot for granted. It turned out to be a lot trickier to combine discipleship and citizenship than anyone had suspected. As my Jesuit friend knew, it was a very different matter to be a Catholic in the church and a Catholic in the university (or in the marketplace and city hall, for that matter). But he and many like him decided to try, and they took the risk of turning their schools over to lay people, some of them authentic outsiders.

And as the schools took hesitant steps outside the subculture, where more and more Catholics lived, so did many theologians, opting to do theology from new perspectives, some distance from what had long been thought of as church. Whether it was theology or the university, the dialogue with contemporary culture, like the turn to shared responsibility, required a host of other changes, more risks. Other Catholics made other choices; many still have trouble with those Americanist decisions.[3]

One source of our present uncertainty is the decline of that crude Americanism. Most of us think of our recent history as American Catholics in terms of Americanization. When that process was linked to one or another form of Americanism, it provided both an explanation of change and a vision of the future that could motivate commitment and sacrifice. The decline of Americanism leaves Americanization, sometimes incorrectly equated with secularization, as a negative term, implying the loss of Catholic identity or Christian commitment. The next step is the current debate between Catholic restorationists, with their sectarian and subcultural strategies, and a muddle through pragmatism often associated with a soft evangelical piety. Each side, on campus and off, resigns itself to a pluralism that leaves religion a matter of personal choice and voluntary community with little purchase on work, politics, or public discourse, on vocation or citizenship. And this is as true in church as on campus. One exasperated lay academic, faced with yet another charge by a bishop that Catholic educators were not "turning out loyal and committed Catholics," snapped, "Neither are you!"

Perhaps the comprehensive Catholicism of *Ex corde Ecclesiae,* filtered through the marvelous theological vision of Michael Buckley in his paper for this conference, can provide a theory to inspire our schools; surely something like it provides the normative basis for Philip Gleason's surprisingly harsh judgments of our recent experience. But as soon as we enter that integrating Catholic discourse, hard questions arise.

For example, where on our campuses can an undergraduate student go who wishes to integrate faith and learning? To the core curriculum? To the honors program or to a special Catholic studies program? Perhaps, on Jesuit campuses, to a faith-and-justice program? Knowing many students of deep faith, great love for the church, and boundless curiosity, my own reflection on this question makes me feel a bit ashamed.

Perhaps that Catholic vision as described by Buckley, echoing the more positive sections of the papal text, has given rise on our campuses to creative proposals to bring faith and church to the center of learning in the heretofore all-but-independent medical and law and business schools. Perhaps we already know how to do that and only lack the will. Or perhaps we are ready to attack the beast of discipline-based learning and departmental power in its den by bringing Catholic self-understanding to the research and teaching in our graduate programs so that, among other things, our universities will turn out scholars and teachers ready to take part in interdisciplinary learning and teaching.

With that last suggestion, you know I am reaching for utopia. But in the absence of programs like these, of creative and constructive projects aimed at reintroducing religion into our intellectual life and into our curriculum and our training, hiring, and supporting of scholars and teachers who share that vision, the product of our discussion of *Ex corde Ecclesiae* will simply be one more addition to our already too numerous "cultures of complaint."[4]

HISTORY IS ABOUT RESPONSIBILITY

All of us made choices; all of us are responsible. History is about such responsibility.

If there is one lesson of historical study, I think it is that the church, like any other organization, is profoundly influenced not only by broad social forces, but also by the deliberate actions of those who decide to attempt to influence it. Ultramontanism and Vatican I, Americanism, aggiornamento, and the academic revolution discussed above all happened in part because of decisions that specific people made. Since Land O'Lakes, American Catholic academic leaders have organized effectively to defend their interests against Roman intervention. But, most of the time, those leaders respond to the actions of ecclesiastical authorities with the same shrug of resigned helplessness characteristic of most American Catholics: witness their response to Roman concerns about gay rights and prochoice campus groups. This professed powerlessness reflects an odd refusal to claim a share of responsibility for the life and work of the institutional church, with which, for better or worse, the destiny of Catholic higher education is inextricably intertwined.

Political analysis of recent history would suggest some other items for consideration:

1. The importance of the bishops' and presidents' committee in the uniquely American arrangement of institutional autonomy. Similarly, we should consider the loose, collaborative ecclesiological practice that produces what Gleason sees as the chronic Vatican dissatisfaction with inexplicit expression and inadequate provision for maintenance of Catholic identity.

2. The general weakness of theologians in church politics and their failure to develop any significant allies within the church bureaucracy or the Catholic population.

3. The all-but-total absence of organized ecclesiastical action by anyone else connected with higher education: trustees, students, lay administrators and professional staffs, or faculty, aside from a relatively small group of conservatives who appear to have some disproportionate influence.

As a result, it is not hard to understand why issues such as the ones on the table for this conference, when they are not simply ignored, are usually discussed on campus in terms of the need for episcopal and Vatican restraint, not institutional responsibility; in terms of the personalities of the bishops rather than the absence of structures for the much celebrated but seldom evident dialogue and cooperation; in terms of abstract processes like secularization rather than creative programs dealing with religion and the intellectual life, Catholic scholarship, or the connections between faith, knowledge, and power.

THE CHURCH'S HISTORIC LOCATION

After "Americanism," discussion of recent U.S. Catholic history suffers from a lack of compelling arguments about the church's historic location; so does discussion of Catholic higher education.

In its earliest stage, Catholic higher education in the United States was designed to help Catholics survive, in part by recruiting and training priests and sisters. In its second stage, it assisted Catholics to move up the social and economic ladder; people like Hesburgh, Gannon, and Reinert pushing outsiders inside. In the first stage people struggled to create and sustain colleges and universities. Later they worked hard to make them very good colleges and universities. The model for the first stage was the priest helping his people build a church and root themselves in America and its local communities. During the second stage we continued to celebrate our priests and sisters, but there were some new models: the talented, tough, ambitious veterans of World War II becoming doctors and lawyers and businessmen, carving out for themselves and their people a place at the center of American life: Democrat Bruce Babbitt and Republican John Sears, my classmates at Notre Dame, Edward Bennett Williams, a symbol for Holy Cross.

Now what is the next stage? Surely there is much more we could do, and in fact much we are doing, to inspire and educate ministers for the church, even the unreformed church that seems not to know what to do with them. And surely too there are many outsiders still in need of assistance to move inside. But I suspect that Catholic colleges and universities, and the American church, will find neither subcultural maintenance nor social mobility in themselves adequate to inspire the personal and financial sacrifices, the creative programs, or the courageous leadership these schools so desperately need.

But perhaps another possibility lies buried in our own experiences on Catholic campuses and in the church's teachings on social responsibility which Professor Gleason unfortunately trivializes in his paper.[5] The models of the next generation? I think of a few: a nurse building a hospice for AIDS patients in San Francisco. A doctor with the World Health Organization in east Africa. In Baltimore a community organizer developing affordable housing and another creating a new way to support high-school students through the perils of urban poverty and violence. A graduate student studying ethics and arms control in hopes of improving the quality of public discourse, then working awhile in social services until his wife gets her law degree. Another young couple with several children who decide that she will work at a job she loves while he works at home with the children and provides leadership in ministry and religious education in their parish. A Catholic Worker couple opening a new hospice in Hartford. A Hartford insurance executive helping other lay people discover opportunities to make the search for human dignity part of their everyday experience at work. And three young Fordham graduates, community organizers and youth outreach workers, driving across the United States to join two successive political campaigns of another Fordham graduate, a one-time Jesuit seminarian committed to his Latino people in San Diego.

Once we celebrated those tough priests and tougher sisters, and we still must attend to the need for talented, educated leadership for our church. Then we celebrated those successful business and professional people, and we still need to help people gain the knowledge and skills and access they need to make a life for themselves and share responsibility for the common life. But today we celebrate especially, in our speeches on and off campus, those women and men for whom faithful discipleship and competent and responsible citizenship are personal commitments. Perhaps they point the way for us. As Jesuit General Peter Hans Kolvenbach put it, "our schools cannot succeed in their formative purposes unless society itself becomes an object and horizon of their apostolic outreach." I think that view is echoed again and again in the writings of the Holy Father.

The beginning of the next phase of Catholic higher education may require more, not less, attention to the apostolic rather than the institutional dimensions of our identity. Catholics bring rich resources to contemporary culture: a concern for the culture of pluralism that we have made our own, a willingness to talk about important matters in real forums with diverse communities, and a commitment to a faith that is intellectually serious despite the a-intellectual instincts in American religious culture. To ask what the Jesuits call the faith-and-justice questions and the pope calls the dialogue between faith and culture, to ask those questions and frame some answers in the midst of contemporary history and not in a self-constructed church—the effort to do so alone makes our continuing effort to clarify the Catholic mission of Catholic colleges and universities worthwhile.

CONCLUSION

The challenge posed by *Ex corde Ecclesiae* is to avoid actions that will jeopardize the very existence of U.S. Catholic colleges and universities and search for ways to turn Catholic identity from a series of problems into a set of possibilities. It is proper to ask bishops and the Vatican for restraint and to seek to deal with differences through the processes well developed by the bishops' and presidents' committee and associated initiatives. It is also important that the schools themselves, and Catholic trustees, administrators, and faculty take their positive responsibilities more seriously. Faculty recruitment and development, curricular innovation, and more enthusiastic cooperation with local and national church programs could enrich both the church and the schools. These institutions are a valuable legacy from past generations for the service of church and society. What is most needed is courageous and wise leadership committed to providing that service.

NOTES

1. For many years the best brief survey of the history of Catholic higher education was Gleason's "American Catholic Higher Education: An Historical Perspective" in *The Shape of Catholic Higher Education,* ed. Robert Hassenger (Chicago: University of Chicago Press, 1967). His recent essays are leading to a comprehensive history of Catholic higher education. See in particular "From an Indefinite Homogeneity: The Beginning of Catholic Higher Education in the United States" (Paper delivered at the Cushwa Center for the Study of American Catholicism, University of Notre Dame, March 15, 1976); "In Search of Unity: American Catholic Thought 1920-1950," *Catholic Historical Review* 65 (April 1979) and "American Catholic Higher Education, 1940-1990: The Ideological Context," in George M. Marsden and Bradley J. Longfield, eds., *The Secularization of the Academy* (New York: Oxford University Press, 1992).

2. Through the courtesy of Alice Gallin, O.S.U., I was privileged, along with Professor Gleason, to participate in just such a conversation with these three leaders in September 1992.

3. It is a measure of how great the collapse of liberal Catholicism has been that the following remark by Professor Gleason will likely be taken as an unbiased and objective assessment:

> Certainly the main tendency since Vatican II—in Catholic higher education as elsewhere in the Catholic world—has been toward embracing the world in a positive way, deprecating the peril of secularization, and treating dismissively the "prophets of gloom" who warn against it. But the danger of total absorption is there if what is distinctive to Catholicism has been so much weakened by self-criticism and repudiation of the "outdated" that it is rendered exiguous.

Perhaps such attitudes existed briefly in the immediate postconciliar years. So-called secular theology is hard to find these days, as is ignorance of the problems posed by the segmentation of culture and the marginalization of religion. But the requirements of pluralism remain: dialogue, articulating common ground, expressing differences carefully. Similarly, the disciplines imposed by shared humanity require finding ways to speak the truths of faith from the inside of the world's many cultures.

4. Robert Hughes, *Culture of Complaint: The Fraying of America* (New York: Oxford University Press, 1993).

5. "The peace-and-justice theme ... associated with liberation theology and general intellectual leftism ... almost certain to decline ... as a result of the collapse of formerly communist regimes and the overall discrediting of revolutionary socialism." In any case, Gleason writes, faculty regard "activism" as "too far removed from the properly academic."

COMMENT

REV. J. BRYAN HEHIR, *Harvard Divinity School*

Philip Gleason is uniquely qualified to address this symposium on the Catholic identity of higher education in the United States. He has long been recognized as a wise interpreter of the role of the Catholic church in the United States. He has also been a "participant-observer" in the discussion of the nature and role of Catholic higher education. His paper gives us a sense of how the issues we are gathered to discuss have been defined and debated by our predecessors in Catholic colleges and universities. As always, he has given me a broader and deeper sense of the issues he is addressing.

My response will focus primarily on the structure of his argument rather than the substantive conclusions he draws from it. For the most part the response argues for amending the framework he has used; on one issue I do have a substantive difference.

The basic interpretive framework of the Gleason paper looks at the internal life of universities and then at the external cultural and social forces in American life that influenced Catholic policy on higher education. My first amendment is to suggest a tripartite framework, with Vatican II at the intersection of internal and external factors. The reason for enhancing the status of the Vatican Council is the impact it had on both the internal and external forces that Gleason analyzes. His assessment of the internal actors in the higher education debate involves religious communities, lay boards of trustees, and bishops.

But the theology of Vatican II had a profound influence not only on how all three groups understood their relationship to the university, but also on how they defined their vocational roles as a whole. This is most evidently seen in the substantial changes undertaken in religious life after the Council, but Vatican II was also a major influence in inviting lay men and women to assume the kind of high-profile role in the life of the church that the lay boards have played since the 1970s. Indeed Vatican II recast the very ideas of church, authority in the church, and the content of lay-religious relationships so that the terms of the discussion in the 1940s and 1950s were not those of the postconciliar period.

In terms of external influences upon Catholic colleges and universities, the conciliar theology had profound influence on how the church-world relationship was defined and pursued. The conciliar text *Gaudium et spes* (1965) initiated a process of engagement with civil society that called the church and all its institutions to new and increasingly significant responsibilities in the social order. My suggestion, therefore, is that we probe in more detail how the Council changed the terms of the already existing discussion of Catholic higher education. The change is a matter of degree on some key themes, but a difference of degree on such topics as conception of vocation, understanding of authority, and social responsibility can yield a qualitative difference in the shape of an argument.

A second move, which really follows from an enhanced weight for the Council, would be to give the role of theology greater saliency in understanding how the church-university dialogue unfolded after Vatican II. The point here is not the precise weight of theological studies in the curriculum, but the wider influence that theology exercised on the life of the church because of the role played by theologians at Vatican II. The conciliar experience was a moment of episcopal-theological collaboration with little precedent in the twentieth century. The very success of the conciliar period threw into sharp relief the changed atmosphere of the 1970s and 1980s. In these years collaboration declined and points of conflict multiplied, particularly after the publication of *Humanae vitae* (1968). Disputes about the limits and scope of episcopal teaching authority, the rights and obligations of theologians, and the role of authoritative teaching in conscience formation formed the background for specific struggles about doctrinal and moral issues.

All this had direct effects in Catholic universities. To some degree there is an inherent polarity (as well as an inherent complementarity) built into the relationship of the teaching office of the episcopal magisterium and the teaching role of theologians who also, in their own fashion, are authorities. This polarity is a structural reality in the Catholic teaching ministry. But the conflicts of the postconciliar period—substantive conflicts about principles and issues— were then entwined with the structural polarity.

Since most theologians were found in universities after the Council, an added dimension of complexity existed in the church-university relationship. A different postconciliar history could have greatly enriched the reflection on the role of Catholic universities; the actual events tended to make the discussion more difficult. In any case, this theological component of the picture would fill out Professor Gleason's already rich narrative.

I wish to turn now from the structure of Professor Gleason's paper to four questions of substance.

First, I support strongly his stress on the central role of the faculty in any discussion of the Catholic character of a university. In the postconciliar era, the faculties of Catholic colleges and universities have grown in size and diversity, making the discussion of Catholic character a more complex topic. The fact of diversity, in my view, is not a liability; the presumption should be that it is an enrichment of the larger life of the university. What is necessary, however, is that a critical mass of Catholic faculty members be maintained within the faculty (and within departments). Such a core group is necessary if the understanding of and care for the Catholic character of the institution is to be maintained in each institution. Obviously, the simple fact of being Catholic is not sufficient to guarantee that a given faculty member will be a productive participant in these discussions. By critical mass, I mean a core group of persons who have shown explicit interest in addressing the Catholic identity of their institution.

If this argument about a core group is valid, it would seem that the administration of the university, presumably working through departments, has to attend to the long-term question of how such a representative group is to be maintained within the faculty.

A second issue, not addressed by Professor Gleason, is curriculum. It holds, in my view, an equally important place with the question of faculty. If the Catholic character of a university is to be retained, there must be a visible systematic way in which Catholic intellectual life is carried forward as a dimension of the broader inquiry of the university. The curriculum provides a setting and a structure, particularly at the undergraduate level, to bring students into contact, in a systematic fashion, with Catholicism as a structure of ideas. A variety of factors and forces over the last thirty years have reduced the possibility of using the curriculum as a method of relating Catholic intellectual life with the core curriculum. Proposals for curriculum reform are always contentions, and designing a curriculum to provide more space and time for Catholic intellectual themes would be particularly delicate in the 1990s. Both the faculty's role and the content of the curriculum are at the heart of identity issues in a Catholic college or university.

Third, my only point of substantive disagreement with Professor Gleason relates to his discussion of the role of justice-and-peace themes in a Catholic university.

While it is undoubtedly the case that issues of justice and peace involve an "activist" conception of Christian faith, I would contend that justice-and-peace issues are solidly rooted in the Catholic intellectual tradition and should be presented that way in Catholic colleges and universities. In brief, in the university setting "justice and peace" should be intellectually grounded; indeed the university is precisely the institution that can both transmit the intellectual tradition of "social Catholicism" and refine its meaning and application in relationship to the domestic and international issues of a new century. In the wider world of American academic life, there is today substantial interest in the ethical dimensions of domestic and foreign policy. It is a moment of opportunity for a tradition that has cultivated these themes when they were not well addressed in other institutions of higher learning. It would be a tragic mistake for Catholics to reduce the social tradition to "activism" in our universities precisely when we can easily be part of the broader conversation between ethics and the empirical disciplines today.

Finally, a fourth substantive issue is the opportunity that Catholic universities have to make an institutional statement of Catholic identity. This can be done by the events, programs, symposia, etc., that such universities sponsor. These are more individuated actions, singular events that a university can host, gathering scholars concerned with the Catholic intellectual tradition from many places. Such events provide an opportunity to project a conception of Catholic intellectual life in the broader academic world. Along with the more internal issues of faculty involvement and curriculum, such institutional actions can be woven into a systematic effort to advance Catholic intellectual life and to join its progress to the future of Catholic higher education in the United States.

DISCUSSION

Discussion focused initially on the important influence of the Second Vatican Council on the recent history of American Catholic higher education. Subsequently, attention turned to developments since Vatican II.

Vatican II should be "contextualized" in the American situation. Vatican II legitimatized greater Americanization: It helped American Catholic education along the path it was already headed. The old neo-scholastic synthesis had lost its vitality. Vatican II removed lingering obstacles to the adoption of American norms in higher education. The problem was that in the 1960s traditional American norms "flew to pieces." Accommodation and acceptance and assimilation of American standards were thrown into question by the turmoil of the 1960s, when all authority was called into question. It is not easy to sort out Vatican II from basic cultural changes that took place in America in the 1960s.

Vatican II marked another important watershed: If the earlier history of American Catholic higher education involved integration of the curriculum through philosophy, this task was shifted to theology precisely at the time when traditions of theology lost "integrative certainty" in terms of both method and content. The integrating vision does not exist. The theological resources have become more tenuous. This is a period of creative readjustment.

A number of Catholic colleges used to promote a core of common knowledge through a standard required curriculum. Philosophy and theology were not necessarily the integrating forces. This role was sometimes played by common courses in English and history that provided a curricular focus or relationship among these courses.

Some of the moves Roman Catholic higher education made to adapt and change were a form of the acculturation process. This should not be scorned as "secularization," but rather a change in the nature of Catholic culture expressed by the universities. What is secularization? It is not at all clear how we ought to think about secularization. Philip Gleason's paper suggests that it has happened and that it's bad. David O'Brien has suggested that it hasn't happened and that it's not such a bad thing in any case. Others have suggested that it is simply a rapprochement with American culture. A case can be made that John Courtney Murray had something to do with secularizing the world culture of Catholicism.

Can we write or think intelligently about the change in higher education without understanding more about elementary and secondary Catholic education, which is undergoing enormous changes? Although it is true that Catholics bring a remarkable degree of ignorance about Catholicism to their higher education experience, this same problem was appalling to higher education authorities in the 1930s and 1940s, who at that time actually gave tests on knowledge about Catholicism. Nevertheless, there probably has been a real decline in basic literacy about Catholicism among Catholics attending Catholic institutions of higher education.

If secular accreditation can be said to undermine the Catholicism of American Catholic universities, isn't it clear that *Ex corde Ecclesiae* represents an effort to impose an ecclesiastical accreditation? Secular accreditation had a very positive role in Catholic higher education, most people would agree. These were rules drawn up by civil authorities outside the university that had to be followed; if they weren't followed, a school would not have any students.

The Sister Formation Movement in the 1950s imparted new requirements for teacher certification that combined both spiritual and professional criteria.

To some extent, Vatican II validated a legitimate autonomy for the secular. John Courtney Murray made this argument, an important argument, but a limited one. His was a validation of pluralism in society as a whole. The university acknowledges the validity of the secular in the wider society, but this is a different matter than secularizing religion.

Another way of expressing the role of Vatican II is that it sought to change the crude Americanism: that the role of the church is to reinforce ethnic loyalties and the family-church nexus. Traditionally there was little spiritual significance given to work, politics, and anything other than the family.

Although John Courtney Murray's work in the 1950s and 1960s legitimated secularization, he did not mean bifurcation of the religious and secular spheres or bifurcation of religion and the university. Murray said explicitly that there was need for a new synthesis after the bifurcation—a need for a higher unity.

The U.S. Catholic universities have been affected by professionalization, not necessarily secularization. Now there is a need to move beyond professionalism to talk about what might be the next step—what might be a synthesis. Part of the problem has been the way in which traditional academic culture itself has fallen apart. And post-Vatican II developments have witnessed the coming apart of the collaborative relationships between academic and hierarchical theologians forged during the time of Vatican II.

Throughout discussion several speakers explored ways to provide a "vision of integration" for an institution's Catholic identity.

Peace and justice may not be a suitable focus. Sometimes these topics are simply a form of "politicized ethics." To the contrary, peace-and-justice issues are not just a form of "energetic volunteerism" but raise profound issues of the relationship between citizenship and vocation, faith and family life, and fundamental problems of the connection between knowledge and power: How are we to live an integrated life? Students who spend a semester in South or Central America come back with penetrating questions and are often alienated either over what they find about the role of the church in these countries or the lack of the American church's similar involvement in its cultural and political world. A profound kind of education but indeed risky.

Besides peace and justice, are there other potentially good themes for developing a Catholic identity? There are a variety of experiments in Catholic colleges with integrated liberal arts programs, but typically these do not involve much focus on Catholic studies or Catholic perspectives. The possibilities of broadly planned curricular reform are subject to two serious barriers: (1) the extraordinary difficulty of faculty discussions in this area; anyone who has participated in years of faculty discussion over the last decades can only be cynical about the possibilities; (2) the practical problem that staffing significant curricular reform almost always leads to extensive use of adjunct faculty who are not integrated into the full-time teaching staff.

Peter-Hans Kolvenbach has argued that the rationale for research lies beyond the academy. The same problem of synthesis is a challenge to secular knowledge. The university is not the home of truths but the home of activity that becomes truth when it is integrated in the world outside. This synthesis is less a vision of truth than a means of using the tools of understanding: Decision making becomes a crucial activity. Visions of justice and peace transcend the university and address movements beyond the university.

Social justice themes raise significant questions about the relationship between the university and the world and between the church and the world. The Third World may have much to teach U.S. universities.

Core curricular programs, either peace-and-justice or Catholic studies, have an important place in the curriculum. There may be significant learning to be gained from the Third World's different sense of the church in society and a different sense of the meaning of these curricular questions.

Rev. Joseph A. Komonchak, *The Catholic University of America*

The Catholic University in the Church

I take my title from a crucial section of *Ex corde Ecclesiae:* "The Catholic University in the Church." Note that it says "*in* the Church," not "*and* the Church." If it said the latter, it could suggest the idea that the university and the church are exterior to one another. The title instead inserts the university within the church, so that, if the question still arises as to relations between the two—since the Catholic university is not the whole church—the relation is now understood from the start to be one between an institutional dimension and a vast and complex reality that at once greatly transcends this particular dimension and defines the dynamic context and movement within which the university must be understood.

It is also of some importance to clarify one term from the beginning: the meaning and referent of the word *church* in my title. In the integral sense recovered by the Second Vatican Council, it refers to the whole assembly of Christian believers (*congregatio fidelium*) gathered into a communion of faith, hope, and love, served and governed by the apostolic ministry of pope and bishops, and sent by Christ to be his redemptive sign and instrument in the world. I stress this because of a not uncommon tendency to define the relation between university and church as the relation between university and hierarchy, but while that is a dimension of the total question, it is not primary but depends in fact for its solution on the question of the relationship between a Catholic university and the total reality of the communion of faith.

This definition of the church includes both identity and mission. The church is the people distinguished from all other human communities by a faith, hope, and love that derive from and center around Jesus Christ. Its mission derives immediately from this identity, for even by its very existence the church, as the social and historical sign of Christ's redemptive work, exists in order, as its instrument, to keep alive the memory of Jesus of Nazareth, to communicate his offer of salvation, and to reflect his light and to offer his power for the shaping of human history, both individual and collective. As Jesus Christ is himself confessed by the church as Redeemer, so the community of his disciples exists for a redemptive purpose in human history.

In my title, the word *Catholic* qualifies the word university. It is tempting to assign it a merely sociological meaning (Catholic as opposed to Protestant, Jewish, or secular) or a sectarian meaning (as in the jibe that a Catholic university is a contradiction in terms or in the comment attributed to a Jesuit educator: that of the two adjectives used of his institution, *Jesuit* and *Catholic,* he thought Jesuit to be the more comprehensive!). But, of course, *Catholic* is first of all a theological term, so much so that in an Augustine it could be used as a noun, the *Catholica,* and as a synonym for the church. It refers to a distinguishing characteristic and imperative responsibility of the church: that as the community of faith it has as one of its chief tasks the integration of all of humanity, with all its varied gifts, into unity under Christ and in his Holy Spirit.[1] A university is Catholic, then, when it lives and realizes its role, precisely as a university, within a church with this distinctive identity and this integrating mission.

I begin with these clarifications because, for various reasons, some of them the church's own fault, the discussion of the very possibility of a Catholic university and the identification of its nature and mission seem often to be distorted from the start. Consider, for example, the jibe just mentioned: that a Catholic university is a contradiction in terms. Its assumptions may be manifold. One of them may be that *Catholic* means hierarchically controlled, with the assumption that such control violates the academic freedom and institutional autonomy considered essential to a university. Here, unfortunately, there is sufficient evidence of the abuse of hierarchical authority to give some plausibility to the assumption, although one should not neglect the fact that dogmatic assumptions about freedom and autonomy sometimes drive the criticism.

Another assumption may be that *Catholic* simply means sectarian, and its plausibility rests upon the contraction of the *Catholica* that resulted from the schism between the Eastern and Western churches but especially from the defensiveness and even introversion that so often marked Catholic responses to the Reformation, the Enlightenment, and liberalism.[2]

But another, more basic assumption may often underlie the jibe: that, if I may assign paradigmatic meaning to two historical figures, Tertullian was in fact right and Justin wrong when it came to judging the compatibility between Jerusalem and Athens, between faith and reason. Tertullian, at least in certain of his writings, was a sectarian, and it is not entirely surprising that he ended his life among the Montanists and that the Donatists were in many ways his heirs. Justin was a Catholic, comprehensive and confident in his vision, and his heirs were the great Fathers of both East and West, and a Boethius, an Anselm, an Aquinas, a Newman, none of whose efforts is conceivable in the heritage of Tertullian. The great church, the *catholica,* chose to follow Justin.

But it is crucial to note that while the immediate issue in choosing between the two lines was what meaning to assign to the adjective *Catholic*—Tertullian's sectarian meaning or Justin's comprehensive and integrative meaning—the real issue may be the most basic one of all: whether faith itself can be reasonable or represents an irrational choice. And this issue should not be ignored when confronting the claim that a Catholic university is a contradiction in terms, because in Tertullian's line it clearly is, while in Justin's it clearly is not. That issue—which of them is correct on the relations between faith and reason?— is not settled in the end on historical or sociological grounds but by personal judgment and decision. If faith is absurd, Jerusalem has nothing to do with Athens, the church with the academy, theology with science. The question of the possibility of a Catholic university is the question of the very possibility of an enterprise like that embodied in Aquinas's *Summa contra Gentes* and his *Summa Theologica.* If such an effort is possible, then a Catholic university is possible; if it is not possible, then neither is a Catholic university. This foundational question should not be ignored, since it is possible to define, or assume, not only what *Catholic* means, as an institutionalization of "faith," but also what a university means, as an institutionalization of "reason," so that the issue is settled in advance.

"THE CHURCH" AND CATHOLICITY IN "EX CORDE ECCLESIAE"

With all this said at the start, let me get down to my task by stating from the start my view that *Ex corde Ecclesiae* reflects, first, the sort of ecclesiology I summarized above and, second, a comprehensive and integrating and not a sectarian understanding both of the noun *church* and of the adjective *Catholic.* First, then, I have found no statement in this document in which "the Church" clearly means only the hierarchy. Obviously, the role of the hierarchy is everywhere presumed and at times stressed, but "the Church" of this document is the whole community of the faithful, owing its existence to Jesus Christ and engaged in the task of bringing his light and power to redeem human history. I emphasize this because, in spite of efforts to retrieve the word *church* from its identification with the hierarchy, it is still not at all rare for people somewhat unconsciously to assume that identification when they read such statements as, to quote a few of those made in *Ex corde Ecclesiae,* that a Catholic university enables, assists, serves, and helps the church or that it "has a relationship to the Church that is essential to its institutional identity," which requires of the members of its community "a personal fidelity to the Church"

(n. 27), etc. The immediate reference of these statements is not the hierarchy, or something called the institutional church, but simply the church: the whole vast body of people that once arose out of the event of Christ and lives still to bring him to the world for its redemption.

Second, the presupposition of the whole text of *Ex corde Ecclesiae* is a nonsectarian view of Christianity and of the church. Among the most frequently occurring words in the whole document are *dialogue* and *encounter,* and the most frequently mentioned partners in this conversation are the sciences and, especially, culture or cultures. The underlying ecclesiology is mostly implicit, given that the pope's attention concentrates on the Catholic university, but in what he says about the university, as an institution within the church, one can glimpse a vision of a church whose identity is clear in its foundations and outwardly focused in its mission. What the church and the university have to offer the world is "a true Christian anthropology, founded on the person of Christ, which will bring the dynamism of the creation and redemption to bear on reality and on the correct solution to the problems of life" (n. 33). Its scholars "will be engaged in a constant effort to determine the relative place and meaning of each of the various disciplines within the context of a vision of the human person and the world that is enlightened by the Gospel and therefore by a faith in Christ, the *Logos,* as the center of creation and of human history" (n. 16). Note the coincidence here of the distinctive identity and of the universal, integrating mission: the identity centers around Christ, but since he is the *Logos,* the principle of the intelligibility of the world and of human history, this is a center that must radiate outward to all that is human. The pope quotes an earlier comment of his own: "A faith that places itself on the margin of what is human, of what is therefore culture, would be a faith unfaithful to the fullness of what the Word of God manifests and reveals, a decapitated faith, worse still, a faith in the process of self-annihilation" (n. 44).

The epistemological presupposition here is the one mentioned earlier, for the Catholic university's "privileged task is 'to unite existentially by intellectual effort two orders of reality that too frequently tend to be placed in opposition as though they were antithetical: the search for truth, and the certainty of already knowing the fount of truth' " (n. 1). It is supposed to be a "sign of the fecundity of the Christian mind in every culture" and to found the "hope for a new flowering of Christian culture in the rich and varied context of our changing times" (n. 2).

The issue at stake is no minor one, since "the dialogue of the Church with the cultures of our times is the vital area where 'the future of the Church and the world is being played out as we conclude the 20th century' " (n. 3). The Catholic university is supposed "to assure in an institutional manner a Christian presence in the university world confronting the great problems of society and culture" (n. 13). In it the church encounters "the development of the sciences and . . . the cultures of our age"; it is the institution in which the church finds "cultural treasures both old and new" (n. 10). It seeks to produce students who are "outstanding in learning, ready to shoulder society's heavier burdens and to witness the faith to the world" (n. 9). It is "to help the Church to respond to the problems and needs of this age" (n. 30), to be "an instrument of cultural progress for individuals as well as for society" (n. 32), to promote social justice and development (n. 34), which is why it must be "particularly attentive to the poorest and to those who suffer economic, social, cultural or religious injustice" (n. 40).

This correspondence between distinct identity and concrete, integrating mission is summed up in the final paragraph on the university and evangelization. The very definition of evangelization points the way: "The primary mission of the Church is to preach the Gospel in such a way that the relationship between faith and life is established in each individual and in the sociocultural context in which individuals live and act and communicate with one another" (n. 48). Evangelization means not only spreading the gospel everywhere, but also "affecting and, as it were, upsetting, through the power of the Gospel, humanity's criteria of judgment, determining values, points of interest, lines of thought, sources of inspiration and models of life, which are in contrast with the Word of God and the plan of salvation" (n. 48, quoting Paul VI). In this context, the university is "a living institutional witness to Christ and his message" (n. 49), and its primary, distinctive activities (research, education, professional training, dialogue with culture, and theology) have an evangelizing dimension. "Within a Catholic university the evangelical mission of the Church and the mission of research and teaching become interrelated and coordinated" (n. 41).

In all this it is clear that the papal document does not purchase a distinct identity, either of the church or of a Catholic university, at the price of a mission in the world. It is precisely because of this identity, and of its catholic, integrating character, that the church and the university have something to bring to the world. What distinguishes the church and the Catholic university is what relates them to the larger society and culture. *Ex corde Ecclesiae* illustrates how far the Catholic church has come from that Novatianism that Newman saw all around him under Pius IX, when, he said, "we are shrinking into ourselves, narrowing the lines of communion, trembling at freedom of thought, and using the language of dismay and despair at the prospect before us, instead of, with the high spirit of the warrior, going out conquering and to conquer."[3]

A last point to make about the ecclesiology of the document and its implications for a Catholic university. *Ex corde Ecclesiae* almost always uses the term *church* in the singular, which may be an indication of a primarily universalistic focus that is not unusual in papal documents. But *Ex corde Ecclesiae* does say that the Catholic university's immediate relationship to the church is to the *local church* (n. 27), which requires that "In its service to society, a Catholic university will relate especially to the academic, cultural and scientific world of the region in which it is located" (n. 37). Few as these references are, they perhaps suggest that the general statements that predominate in the text need to be read as heuristic indications, meant to guide the Catholic university in its service within a church that does not exist and does not carry out its redemptive mission except in and through the local churches.

Concretely, this means that one should expect that the specific character of a Catholic university, as a participant in the church's redemptive service in history, will vary from region to region, being determined not only by general principles but by the distinct challenges and opportunities that define historical, social, and cultural situations. It is these that constitute the specific histories that need redemption, and they will, one hopes, generate different goals, orientations, curricula, and structures for Catholic universities.

If I may try to sum up what I have said so far: the Catholic university is one of the institutions through which the church attempts to fulfill the redemptive mission in human history that results immediately from its identity as the community of believers. The church's nature grounds its mission, and its mission actualizes its nature. This mission relates the church, in its inmost and distinctive nature, to the vast project by which human beings construct their individual and collective history. It is this great project that constitutes the great drama within which the church plays its distinctive, redemptive role. The church's self-constitution is not some separate and alienating act but precisely the continued presence in and to the world of the world-originating and world-defining *Logos* that became flesh in Jesus Christ. Its presence in the world determines the probability that people will take into account, in the deliberations and decisions that will make the world what it will become, the truth and grace of which he was the bearer and the incarnation. This is the church, in its nature and in its mission, within which the Catholic university must be located and defined.

A UNIVERSITY

What remains, of course, is the one word in my title of which I have so far said nothing: *university*. Everything I have said so far might be said of any other institution or movement within the church. But what we are discussing is the specific role within that large task of a Catholic *university*. The papal text borrows its definition of this distinct institution: a university is

> an academic community which, in a rigourous and critical fashion, assists in the protection and advancement of human dignity and of a cultural heritage through research, teaching and various services offered to the local, national and international communities. It possesses that institutional autonomy necessary to perform its functions effectively and guaran-

tees its members academic freedom, so long as the rights of the individual person and of the community are preserved within the confines of the truth and the common good. (n. 12)

That is about all that the document offers by way of a general description or definition of a university. The text goes on immediately to its primary focus, the realization of this ideal within the church. Leaving aside whether the description is adequate, we might focus on what it means for such an institution to serve as one of the ways in which the church carries out its redemptive function in history.

One of the ways of answering this question is to look for the differences *Ex corde Ecclesiae* expects to find in a *Catholic* university. Once again, it borrows four "essential characteristics" from an earlier description: the Christian inspiration of individuals and of the university community; continuous reflection in the light of faith on the growing body of human knowledge, to which it also contributes; fidelity to the Christian message; an institutional commitment to the church and to the whole human family (n. 13). It is a presupposition of the whole text that no one of these nor all of them together detracts from the university-character of the institution but rather inspires and guides its realization of it.

But what does this Catholic character mean more concretely? In a footnote (19) Newman's authority is invoked for the strong statement that a Catholic university should promote the integration of all knowledge into a higher synthesis that includes the all-illumining light of Christ (n. 16; see also nn. 20 and 35).[4] It should be a living demonstration of the harmony of faith and reason (n. 17). It should be particularly concerned with "the ethical and moral implications both of its methods and of its discoveries" (n. 18). It should be a place where theology both illumines other disciplines and is illumined by them (n. 19). I think this internal integrating character needs special attention, both because it so closely corresponds to the properly theological definition of catholicity and because of the challenge to it represented by the tremendous specialization of disciplines and methods characteristic of universities today.[5]

The Catholic identity of a university also has implications for the kinds of things to which it devotes its research and teaching. These go far beyond the mere presence of theology among its faculties and reflect the pope's broad views of the church's own mission in the world. Many of these implications are described in the section on the Catholic university's service to society. As an "instrument of cultural progress," it should include among its research topics such serious contemporary problems as "the dignity of human life, the promotion of justice for all, the quality of personal and family life, the protection of nature, the search for peace and political stability, a more just sharing in the world's resources, and a new economic and political order" (n. 32). Particular attention should be given to an evaluation of "the predominant values and norms of modern society and culture" and to the promotion of "those ethical and religious principles which give full meaning to human life" (n. 33). The Catholic university should serve social justice and the development of peoples (n. 34).

We have thus two sets of characteristics that ought to distinguish a Catholic university. One set is more formal, deriving from its central Christian inspiration, the other is more material, specifying the kinds of things in which such inspiration ought to evoke interest. Both sets of characteristics provide useful questions and criteria with regard to the inspiring vision, structure, faculties, curriculum, and specific research-interests of any genuinely Catholic university. The examination of conscience they might suggest should itself be "catholic": here too the distinctive inspiration defines integrating redemptive commitments.

THE UNIVERSITY AND THE HIERARCHY

I come now to the question of the relationship between a Catholic university and the hierarchy. It has been left till now not only because this question is by no means the primary focus of the document but especially because an answer to it presupposes answers to prior questions about the nature and mission of both the church and the Catholic university. It might even be said that this narrower question does not even arise in full seriousness unless a university understands itself within the larger notion set out above: as an institution that is primarily defined, not simply by generic standards that apply to any university, but also by an institutional commitment to offer what only a university can offer to a church that seeks to be the sign and instrument of Christ's redemption of human history. Only then do we have the two terms that define the general relation—that between a redemptive church and a genuine university—within which this more specific question arises.

In a general review of what *Ex corde Ecclesiae* has to say about relations with the hierarchy, the first thing to note is that a Catholic university arises as a differentiated institution within the whole ecclesial communion. The initiative for establishing a university may come from the Holy See, an episcopal conference, a bishop, a religious order, or lay people. Within the church "it possesses that institutional autonomy necessary to perform its functions effectively" (n. 12),[6] a view reflected in the general norms when they say that "The responsibility for maintaining and strengthening the Catholic identity of the university rests primarily with the university itself" (art. 4, sec. 1). While the document acknowledges that it may be that bishops "do not enter directly into the internal governance of the university," neither are they, as heads of the local church, to be thought of simply as "external agents but as participants in the life of the Catholic University." The relationship between university and bishops should be one of communion, whereby bishops promote, assist, and protect Catholic universities, and there are "close personal and pastoral relationships . . . characterized by mutual trust, close and consistent cooperation and continuing dialogue" (n. 28).

Second, a Catholic university "guarantees its members academic freedom, so long as the rights of the individual person and of the community are preserved within the confines of the truth and the common good" (n. 12; repeated in art. 2, sec. 5). The text acknowledges that "each academic discipline retains its own integrity and has its own methods" and states its confidence that, when properly carried out, it "can never truly conflict with faith" (n. 17). That is why "The Church, accepting 'the legitimate autonomy of human culture and especially of the sciences,' recognizes the academic freedom of scholars in each discipline in accordance with its own principles and proper methods, and within the confines of the truth and the common good" (n. 29). This means, in turn, that "In ways appropriate to the different academic disciplines, all Catholic teachers are to be faithful to, and all other teachers are to respect, Catholic doctrine and morals in their research and teaching" (art. 4, sec. 3).

Third, *Ex corde Ecclesiae* gives special attention to theology in the Catholic university. It requires every Catholic university to have a faculty or at least a chair of theology (n. 19). It acknowledges that theology "has proper principles and methods which define it as a branch of knowledge" and that "Theologians enjoy this same [academic] freedom so long as they are faithful to these principles and methods." "At the same time, since theology seeks an understanding of revealed truth, whose authoritative interpretation is entrusted to the bishops of the Church, it is intrinsic to the principles and methods of their research and teaching in their academic discipline that theologians respect the authority of the bishops, and assent to Catholic doctrine according to the degree of authority with which it is taught." This is why "dialogue between bishops and theologians is essential" (n. 29; see art. 4, sec. 4).

Finally, the text says that, in addition to being required to be faithful to the magisterium, Catholic theologians also "fulfill a mandate received from the Church" (art. 4, sec. 3), a mandate which, it seems, is more than a general role assigned, since a footnote (50) quotes from the Code of Canon Law: "It is necessary that those who teach theological disciplines in any institute of higher studies have a mandate from the competent ecclesiastical authority" (c. 812).

Some comments are in order. First, the presupposition is that a Catholic university undertakes its distinctive task within the communion of the church, which includes a proper acknowledgment of the role of bishops and pope as leaders and teachers of the church. In turn, this requires of the latter an acknowledgment of what is required for a Catholic university to be a proper university, able to make a university's contribution to the general ecclesial mission, namely institutional autonomy and academic freedom.

A second presupposition is that communion in the church and an acknowledgment of church authority are not incompatible with either institutional autonomy or academic freedom. Institutional autonomy is a specific implication of the general rights of individuals and of associations within the church: in other words, not all things originate with the hierarchy nor are they all immediate actions of the hierarchy. Underlying the acknowledgment of academic freedom are the presuppositions that faith and reason cannot be incompatible and that Catholic theological method includes an acknowledgment of the teaching office in the church.

My further reflections on the question of relations between Catholic university and Catholic hierarchy will draw upon some statements and some experiences of John Henry Newman. In doing so, I will not restrict myself to his classic work *The Idea of a University,* written while he himself was trying to midwife a Catholic university into existence, but I will also draw on later comments that reflect not only on that particular experience, but also on Newman's overall experience as a Catholic thinker.[7] These experiences led Newman not only to reconsider the practical apostolic effectiveness of separate Catholic university-education in the circumstances and church of his time, but also to extend his remarkable defense of academic freedom in *The Idea of a University* into the realm of theology itself.

Newman's classic statement on academic freedom within a Catholic university is found in the chapter on "Christianity and Scientific Investigation."[8] His argument pivots around two "cardinal maxims" and the "practical conclusion" he drew from them. The first maxim is that "truth cannot be contrary to truth." This fundamental Catholic principle is well represented in *Ex corde Ecclesiae,* as I tried to illustrate above. But the real problems that a Catholic university must face arise less from this maxim than from the other that Newman immediately adds: that "truth often *seems* contrary to truth." He would later offer the general principle that in such cases the Catholic could be confident that the alleged contradiction "will eventually turn out, first, *not* to be proved, or, secondly, not *contradictory,* or thirdly not contradictory to any thing *really revealed,* but to something which has been confused with revelation."[9] This position was also expressed at the First Vatican Council: "the specious appearance of such contradiction arises either when the dogmas are not understood and presented according to the mind of the Church or when opinions are considered conclusions of reason" (DS 3016). In other words, the difficulty of apparent contradiction can arise from both sides: from a misunderstanding of church teaching or from an elevation of opinion to certain conclusion. Pope John Paul II's remarks at the conclusion of the study he commissioned on the Galileo case indicate clearly enough his agreement with this second truism, and there is no reason to doubt that it is assumed also in *Ex corde Ecclesiae.*

But Newman added an immediate "practical conclusion" from these two maxims: that "we must be patient with such appearances, and not be hasty to pronounce them to be really of a more formidable character."[10] The institutional implications of this need for patience, for avoiding hastiness in judgment, are less well represented in *Ex corde Ecclesiae;* there is, it seems, only the recommendation of friendly relations between university and bishop and of "dialogue" between theologians and bishops.

The result is a certain juridical or institutional imbalance. To preserve the integrity of faith there is the requirement that Catholic theologians have a mandate from ecclesiastical authority, but to preserve the exigencies of reason, there is only the affirmation, in principle, of institutional autonomy and of academic freedom; no institutional safeguards of these are indicated. The rights of the Holy See and of bishops are protected but not the rights of scholars. The result is that *Ex corde Ecclesiae* proposes no means for addressing the problems that arise from the second of Newman's maxims, "that truth often *seems* contrary to truth," from the fact that it may be a misunderstanding of church teaching that causes the appearance of conflict, or from the need for patience and to avoid hastiness in judgment until the appearances are dissipated.

Now one does not have to agree that contemporary secular customs of institutional autonomy or of academic freedom represent a perfect and *de iure divino* realization of the nature of a university to be able to find this structural imbalance regrettable. One may find them unworthy precisely of a *Catholic* university, that is, of one that understands and commits itself to assist and enable the church in the ways Pope John Paul II has described. The task of dialogue with contemporary culture and with the sciences for the sake of participating in the great decisions that will determine the future history of both church and world can be stated fairly easily as a goal. But this task is effectively undertaken only when translated into the hard work of research, scholarship, critical reflection, and theological investigation. If these were easy tasks, there would be no need for universities; if the full mission they are supposed to serve were easy, the church would not found or encourage Catholic universities. What is at stake in the integrity of a Catholic university-enterprise is the very ability of the church, at our stage of historical development and opportunity, to participate in the universal project of human self-realization. And this means that the question of academic freedom—by which I mean a scholar's immunity from any other coercion or even pressure than that of the truth—is not just a question of a scholar's individual rights but of the church's own ability and effectiveness to participate in mankind's contemporary project of self-realization.

A Catholic theologian contributes to this task from within the tradition of belief and the community of faith. This communion is intrinsic to his work, or else it is something other than Catholic theology that he is about. It also determines certain parameters of his investigations and defines certain methodological exigencies, among them a properly differentiated respect for the church's teaching office.

But that said, it remains that the theologian's contribution is precisely a scientific or scholarly one, and this kind of contribution has its own exigencies, which also need to be acknowledged, respected, and defended. Newman referred to this general exigency when he said that "great minds need elbow-room,"[11] and if in *The Idea of a University*, he nuanced this by adding, "not indeed in the realm of faith, but of thought," he was later to use the same metaphor to explain his reluctance to publish his own work *in theology*:

> ... as well might a bird *fly* without wings, as I write a book without the *chance*, the *certainty* of saying something or other (not, God forbid! against the Faith) but against the views of a particular school in the Church, which is dominant. I cannot accept as of faith, what is not of faith; who can? I cannot, as I said before, work without elbow room. I cannot fight under the lash, as the Persian slaves. To be the slave of Christ and of His Vicar, is perfect freedom; to be the slave of man is as bad in the mind as in the body. Never, as I know, was it so with the Church, as it is now, that the acting authorities as [at] Rome ... have acted on the individual thinker without buffers. Mere error in theological opinion should be met with argument, not authority, at least by argument first.[12]

Newman's expostulation is worth a moment's reflection. The work on which he was then engaged would finally appear, years later, as *The Grammar of Assent*. The church was in the meantime deprived of the assistance of this classic, not because it offended the faith, but because Newman knew that it ran counter to a particular and dominant Roman school, which confused the faith with what was not the faith, a confusion that would also restrict its influence during the antimodernist reaction. The absence of buffers between the individual thinker and final Roman authority represented something new in the church. It reflected what Newman thought a general situation:

> There was true private judgment in the primitive and medieval schools— there are no schools today, no private judgment (in the *religious* sense of the phrase), no freedom, that is, of opinion. That is, no exercise of the intellect. No, the system goes on by the tradition of the intellect of former times.[13]

But also new was the exalted and immediate role assigned to Roman authority:

Why was it that the Medieval Schools were so vigorous? because they were allowed free and fair play—because the disputants were not made to feel the bit in their mouths at every word they spoke, but could move their limbs freely and expatiate at will. Then, when they were wrong, a stronger and truer intellect set them down—and, as time went on, if the dispute got perilous, and a controversialist obstinate, then at length Rome interfered—at length, not at first—Truth is wrought out by many minds, working together freely. As far as I can make out, this has ever been the rule of the Church till now when the first French Revolution having destroyed the Schools of Europe, a sort of centralization has been established at headquarters—and the individual thinker in France, England, or Germany is brought into immediate collision with the most sacred authorities of the Divine Polity.[14]

Even from these comments it is clear that Newman was now, as he had not clearly done in *The Idea,* including theology in his defense of the scholar's "elbow room." Here the classic statement, as rhetorically powerful as the earlier one, occurs in the pages of the *Apologia* in which he defends the Catholic intellect against the charge that papal infallibility must make its exercise impossible.[15] Here it is precisely dogmatic authority and theological freedom that are placed in dialectical relationship, each indispensable to the other. He offered historical arguments, first, that "it is individuals, and not the Holy See, that have taken the initiative and given the lead to the Catholic mind, in theological inquiry." The same was true of the ecumenical councils:

Authority in its most imposing exhibition, grave bishops, laden with the traditions and rivalries of particular nations or places, have been guided in their decisions by the commanding genius of individuals, sometimes young and of inferior rank. Not that uninspired intellect overruled the superhuman gift which was committed to the Council, which would be a self-contradictory assertion, but that in that process of inquiry and deliberation, which ended in an infallible enunciation, individual reason was paramount.

Newman then adduced the habitual slowness of Roman authority to interfere in medieval disputes, which left room for theological discussion and local intervention: "Meanwhile, the question has been ventilated and turned over and over again, and viewed on every side of it, and authority is called upon to pronounce a decision, which has already been arrived at by reason."

But this historical example reflected a wisdom that is of general validity:

It is manifest how a mode of proceeding, such as this, tends not only to the liberty, but to the courage, of the individual theologian or controversialist. Many a man has ideas, which he hopes are true, and useful for his day, but he is not confident about them, and wishes to have them discussed. He is willing, or rather would be thankful, to give them up, if they can be proved to be erroneous or dangerous, and by means of controversy, he obtains his end. He is answered, and he yields; or on the contrary he finds that he is considered safe. He would not dare to do this, if he knew an authority, which was supreme and final, was watching every word he said, and made signs of assent or dissent to each sentence, as he uttered it. Then indeed he would be fighting, as the Persian soldiers, under the lash, and the freedom of his intellect might be said to be beaten out of him.[16]

I have invoked Newman here, not only for his statements of principle, but because of the example furnished in his own life and work of the crippling effect on a scholar *and* on the church of an unbalanced reliance on the principle of jurisdictional authority. First, on the level of principle: the church makes progress in the understanding of its own tradition and in its effective communication of it to successive generations through the dialectic of authority and freedom Newman described in this chapter of the *Apologia.* Church authority, even in its supreme instances, relies upon the work of individuals, and these individuals need not only courage but freedom. They need the freedom to express their opinions, and they need the correction and confirmation that can only be provided by free discussion, on the basis, first, of argument: "Truth is wrought out by many minds, working together freely."

Newman's is not an argument for academic freedom on the basis of a liberal theory of individual rights. It rests upon a balanced theory of the relation between faith and reason, upon an unequaled appreciation of the subtleties and difficulties of that relation, and upon an ecclesiology that knows that freedom is as important as authority if the church is to be able adequately to understand and effectively to communicate the faith to an unbelieving or skeptical culture. It is the church, and not just the individual scholar, that needs academic freedom.

But Newman's own history serves also to ensure that our discussion of this question does not stay at the level of abstractions such as "the magisterium," "theology," "faith," "reason," etc. Newman bowed to few people, before or since, in his recognition of the role of authority. As the citations themselves indicate, he did not think authority contradicted freedom or made it impossible. But he was also able to distinguish between the principles of authority and freedom and their concrete realization in the individuals who occupied places of leadership in the institution that embody those principles. He did not face the magisterium in general but Pope Pius IX, whom he thought quite wrong on certain matters; he accepted the authority of ecumenical councils but he not only criticized an "arrogant and insolent faction" for trying to control

Vatican I,[17] he thought that its definition of papal sovereignty and infallibility needed to be balanced:

> The late definition does not so much need to be undone, as to be completed. It needs *safeguards* to the Pope's possible acts—explanations of the matter and extent of his power. I know that a violent reckless party, had it its will, would at this moment define that the Pope's powers need no safeguards, no explanations—but there is a limit to the triumph of the tyrannical.[18]

He acknowledged the unique authority of the Holy See, but what he discovered was that the "acting authorities" in Rome were a dominant Roman party that in fact represented only one school in the church but identified its views with "the faith." And if he was acute enough to recognize this about the unique authority of Rome, he certainly harbored no illusions about ecclesiastical authorities in lesser posts.

This is what I mean by speaking of the example of Newman's life as a help to keeping the discussion concrete. By their provision that theologians at Catholic universities have a mandate to teach, the new Code of Canon Law and *Ex corde Ecclesiae* take into account the possibility that an individual theologian may violate the communion with the faith that is required of a Catholic theologian. This requirement represents a juridical response to a potential danger to the faith and an effort to defend the rights of the faithful and the good of the church. It is nicely concrete. But no such concreteness in idea or in practice is visible in the provisions of either document when it comes to the exercise of authority in the church.

But just as there is no such thing as "theology," but only theologians, so also there is no such thing as "the magisterium," but only a pope and bishops. Just as theologians can betray their role by abuse of their freedom, so pope and bishops can betray their roles by abuse of their authority. Just as theological abuses can harm the faithful and the good of the church, so can abuses of authority infringe the rights of theologians and harm the good of the church. But to prevent this second set of dangers, no less visible in the history of the church than the former, no provisions are made in *Ex corde Ecclesiae*. As Vatican I's definitions of papal prerogatives contained no safeguards against abuse, this text ignores juridical safeguards against abuse of episcopal authority. In the case of a theologian's potential abuses, the church's interests are served by direct juridical provisions; in the case of potential episcopal abuse, the church must, apparently, simply trust in unaided Providence.

A last point on this issue: the requirement of a mandate to teach represents a jurisdictional response to a potential problem. It is a typically modern response, dependent perhaps more than many of its defenders would be willing to acknowledge on certain modern ideas of political sovereignty, those in particular that have some difficulty in admitting that there can be any social body within the state that does not derive its existence and authority from governmental concession. The church has always resisted this idea of the state, endorsing instead the principle of subsidiarity and defending the rights of the family and of civil and cultural associations. But, paradoxically, in the last century a certain ecclesiology has borrowed powerfully from that modern political theory, articulating papal primacy in terms of a like sovereignty and tempted to see all other bodies in the church as existing by concession of papal authority. Tendencies in this direction were, one hopes not only temporarily, thwarted by Vatican II's teaching on the episcopacy. But a tendency to do something similar with educational institutions in the church and particularly with regard to the role of theologians has revived, and it is this tendency that many people fear is at work in the effort to define the Catholic theologian as one who teaches "in the name of the church" and to translate that notion into the requirement of a mandate from ecclesiastical authority, with implications that threaten the institutional autonomy of the Catholic university itself.

The danger is that this effort will reduce ecclesial communion to hierarchical subordination and that it will once again place greater emphasis on the pope's or bishop's jurisdictional authority than on his magisterial authority. It is, after all, a lot easier to refuse or to withdraw a canonical mandate from a troublesome theologian than to offer an effective magisterial reply to his errors. As things are, and certainly as provided for in *Ex corde Ecclesiae,* no reasons need be given for the former and there is no right of appeal. The bishop may act as a pure administrator. To teach, and to teach effectively, is a more complex matter. It would require the bishop to examine the theologian's writings, to make a personal judgment about the theologian's orthodoxy, to identify what the bishop thinks are errors and why he thinks them so, and to make a case for the truth he feels bound to defend. This, of course, would mean to enter into a conversation, a dialogue, to listen, and to reply, at least initially, with arguments and not authority. If administrative solutions are much cleaner and faster, they will give the impression that it is not only critics who, as Newman put it, "think that the Church has no other method of putting down error than the arm of force, or the prohibition of inquiry."[19]

Once again, it is important to recognize that what is at stake is not only the rights of individuals within the church but the good of the church itself. In many of the disputes that have marked the conflicts between magisterium and theologians in the last two centuries, it was the church's participation in the great dialogue with modern culture and science that was at stake. In some cases, one might judge today that the magisterium was correct in its position, if not always in its method. But there are many other cases in which the magisterium was as incorrect on the issues as it was unjust in its methods. It is enough to think of a catalog of the names of some of the Catholic thinkers who at one time or another fell under Roman suspicion and suffered various degrees of ecclesial disability: Montalembert, Newman, Rosmini, Lagrange, Duchesne, Blondel, Rousselot, Batiffol, Bardy, Bonsirven, Maritain, Teilhard, Chenu, Congar, de Lubac, Bouillard, Rahner, Murray. There was not only personal suffering and even tragedy in many of these cases, which is unjust enough; was not harm also done to the church itself, to its own life and to its effectiveness in meeting its historic challenge? But who was there and what canonical provisions were there for protecting the church and its mission from abuse by authority?

I return to where I began: to an insistence that the issues we are discussing concern the church itself and its evangelical and redemptive mission. The terms of our discussion are not hierarchy and Catholic university and not even church *and* Catholic university, but the Catholic university *in* the church, where this preposition *in* points not to a place where it happens to exist but to the living body and movement in which the Catholic university participates *both* by a commitment of faith that relates it vitally to the whole historical project *and* by the academic integrity that defines its distinct and indispensable contribution. No doubt, in the real world if not on the level of ideals, there are tensions between the adjective *Catholic* and the noun *university,* tensions also between the leaders of the church and administrators and faculties of universities, but perhaps it has been of some help to name them for what they are and to identify what is at stake: the ability of the whole church to serve the redemptive mission of Christ in human history.

APPENDIX: A PERHAPS USEFUL ANALOGY

Perhaps Margaret O'Brien Steinfels will permit me a comparison that has frequently come to my mind of late: between a Catholic university and a lay Catholic journal of opinion, *Commonweal.*[20] As a journal of opinion, the latter engages a large problematic, the public conversation by which, at least in part, a democratic society clarifies issues, sets agendas, and makes its choices. Participation in that public conversation does have to follow certain criteria, some of them conventional, some of them more substantive. It helps, for example, if one is intelligent, knows how to argue, and can write. After that, I suppose that the arena is rather wide open, and criteria for what counts as a rational argument are going to vary widely, which would in fact seem to be the reason why there are so many journals of opinion. I do note one important difference from the university here: there are, as far as I know, no accrediting agencies (the academic equivalent of the Congregation for the Doctrine of the Faith) able to censure a journal and to recommend that people not subscribe or write for it.

Commonweal was founded to bring a distinctive Catholic contribution to the public conversation: "The idea, broadly stated, was this: How can Catholic thought, the Catholic outlook on life and the Catholic philosophy of living, as distinct from what might be called the Catholic inlook and individual religious experience, be conveyed to the mind of the whole American people?"[21] That nice distinction between "inlook" and "outlook" should be noted, and I suspect that Michael Williams was more keenly aware of it than many a Catholic college or university at the time. I note again that it was the identity that grounded the mission, the mission that realized the identity.

Commonweal has called itself Catholic because of this founding and defining orientation. This commitment determines many things about the journal. The topics it chooses to discuss are very broad, catholic if you will, but it includes many that one would not expect other journals to consider. One does expect, however, that a certain perspective—let us simply call it a perspective of faith—will be brought to bear upon the topics, if not in every article or editorial, at least in general. A great deal of freedom is also allowed to authors, letter-writers, and reviewers. It thus is a forum within which people argue out what it means to be a Catholic and what difference being a Catholic should make in the world. It is a diversity within a commitment.

Margaret O'Brien Steinfels, the current editor of *Commonweal,* spoke of these implications in an address to presidents of Catholic colleges and universities:

> *Commonweal* has been a bridge for a two-way conversation between faith and life; my job is to continue that conversation. We are a particular tradition operating in the framework of the Catholic one. Though non-Catholics write in our pages, in a straightforward and unembarrassed way we have to be clear about our own identity in commissioning manuscripts, reviews, opinion pieces, and sometimes in rejecting them. We have to be that in our own writing and editing. Each of you has such a tradition to draw on from your own history as well as from our common tradition. If we have worked carefully to delineate our Catholic identity, then there are some ways that we will find ourselves at odds with our culture, while in others we will be deeply in tune with it.

In the same talk, she herself pressed still other points of comparison: "I point to my own work because I imagine in some ways it is like your own process of interviewing and selecting faculty, of reforming curricula, of admitting students, of putting together lecture programs." This makes explicit the parallel I have only implied between the kinds of interests *Commonweal* promotes by its choice of topics and the sorts of curricula one might expect a Catholic university to sponsor. It also suggests an analogy when it comes to personnel decisions. Could *Commonweal* remain a lay *Catholic* journal of opinion without a core group of committed lay Catholics? Can a university be expected to remain Catholic without a largely Catholic faculty?

Finally, there is the question of relations with the hierarchy. *Commonweal* has, as far as I know, never sought official recognition, nor have its editors ever been thought to need a "mandate" from ecclesiastical authority. It represents one of those Catholic associations that, Vatican II and the new Code of Canon Law now assure us, all the faithful have a right to found and direct for the good of the church and for its work in the world. The editors have crossed swords with priests, bishops, even popes every now and then (I remember when I was in high school being told by one of my parish priests that *Commonweal* was anticlerical), but they have never denied that the great Catholic enterprise in which their journal wishes to participate is the work of a church led by a hierarchy. In turn, so far as I know, no bishop has sought to shut the journal down or to declare it non-Catholic—a restraint inspired, one trusts, by something more than fear of the usual reaction when books used to be banned in Boston.

This institutional autonomy and journalistic freedom suggest a last comparison, which might be considered by church authorities. *Commonweal*'s circulation (around eighteen thousand), while only an infinitesimal part of the total Catholic population in this country, is larger than the population of any Catholic college or university. Its influence on its readers may be as great as that of the colleges or universities on their students. Might not bishops consider that the wiser policy is to adopt the same attitude toward the colleges and universities that call themselves Catholic as they do toward independent Catholic journals? To press my analogy to a last point: would they like to see Catholic colleges and universities more closely resemble a typical diocesan newspaper than they do *Commonweal*?

NOTES

1. See *Lumen gentium*, n. 13.

2. I take it to be one of the chief contributions of such scholars as Henri de Lubac and Yves Congar in the last decades before Vatican II to restore to Catholic consciousness a sense of the confident and comprehensive breadth and depth of Catholicism before these contractions took place; this is especially apparent in de Lubac's *Catholicism*.

3. *Letters and Diaries of John Henry Newman* XXII (London: Nelson, 1972), pp. 314-15.

4. Newman's position was that a university is not supposed to be "a bazaar, or pantechnicon, in which wares of all kinds are heaped together for sale in stalls independent of each other." John Henry Newman, *The Idea of a University*, ed. I. T. Ker (Oxford: Clarendon, 1976), p. 421.

5. Hence the pope's insistence on the importance of interdisciplinary studies (n. 20). It might be interesting and revealing to study whether these are any more common at Catholic universities than at others.

6. See also general norms, art. 2, sec. 5: "A Catholic university possesses the autonomy necessary to develop its distinctive identity and pursue its proper mission."

7. The best work on Newman's Irish university is still Fergal McGrath, *Newman's University: Idea and Reality* (London: Longman's, Green and Co., 1951). For the later development, see John Coulson, "Newman's Idea of an Educated Laity—The Two Versions," in *Theology and the University: An Ecumenical Investigation,* ed. John Coulson (Baltimore: Helicon Press, 1964), pp. 47-65. For the general context, see Joseph A. Komonchak, "Newman's Infallible Instincts: The Argument for Elbowroom," *Commonweal* 117 (August 10, 1990): 445-48.

8. Newman, *Idea of a University*, pp. 368-86. It should be noted that Newman's defense of freedom of investigation here is expressly limited to disciplines other than theology; but, as I will argue below, fuller experience led him to expand its relevance, within limits, also to theology.

9. Newman, *Idea of a University,* p. 376.

10. Newman, *Idea of a University,* p. 372. For an illustration of Newman's serene acceptance of this necessity, consider his reply to a man troubled by recent claims about the antiquity of the human race: "Even though that antiquity proved to be as great as certain men of science maintain, and proved even in the same clearness as the motion of the earth is proved . . . still the discovery would as little interfere with the truths of revelation, with the dogmas of the Church, or with the inspiration of the sacred writers, as the scientific doctrine of the motion of the earth interferes with those supernatural informants. If we were able to throw ourselves back three centuries, we should understand something of the great unsettlement of mind which the latter doctrine occasioned at that era. The Dominican Fathers made Galileo recant it. Educated people in Italy thought it simply inconsistent with Christianity. It went against both the letter and the spirit of Holy Scripture. And yet in this day no religious man has any difficulty in receiving it. In like manner the doctrine of the great antiquity of the human race is either true or not true; if it is not true, scientific men will not be able to prove it; if it is true, it will take its place in general knowledge, just as Galileo's doctrine has been received by all now, and the Bible will turn out not to be the worse for what appeared at first sight so formidable; though at this minute we may not be able to see *how* this will come to pass." *Letters and Diaries of John Henry Newman* XXI (London: Nelson, 1970), p. 491.

11. Newman, *Idea of a University,* p. 383.

12. Newman, *Letters and Diaries* XXI, pp. 48-49; compare: "What influence would I have with Protestants and Infidels, if a pack of Catholic critics opened at my back fiercely, saying that this remark was illogical, that unheard of, a third realistic, a fourth idealistic, a fifth sceptical, and a sixth temerarious, or shocking to pious ears?" *Letters and Diaries* XXIV (Oxford: Oxford University Press, 1973), pp. 316-17.

13. Newman, *Letters and Diaries* XX (London: Nelson, 1970), p. 447.

14. Ibid., p. 426.

15. John Henry Newman, *Apologia pro Vita Sua,* ed. M. J. Svaglic (Oxford: Clarendon, 1967), pp. 217-41. Newman wrote these pages, apparently at the urging of Lord Acton, as a response to the threat to theological freedom represented by Pope Pius IX's indictment of the Munich Congress of 1863.

16. Ibid., pp. 237-39.

17. Newman, *Letters and Diaries* XXV (Oxford: Oxford University Press, 1973), p. 19.

18. He added: "Let us be patient, let us have faith, and a new Pope, and a re-assembled Council may trim the boat." Ibid., p. 310.

19. Newman, *Idea of a University*, pp. 375-76.

20. A letter to the editor in the issue of *Commonweal* that arrived twenty minutes ago makes the same point, when it speaks of the need for "creative leadership within the American Catholic community to forge at least a few institutions that would do for higher education what *Commonweal* does for the American religious and political dialogue: that is, be both clearly Catholic and intellectually respectable." *Commonweal* 120 (April 9, 1993): 2.

21. Michael Williams, as quoted in Rodger Van Allen, *The Commonweal and American Catholicism* (Philadelphia: Fortress, 1974), p. 5.

COMMENT

Rev. John P. Langan, S.J., *Georgetown University*

CATHOLICS, NEAR CATHOLICS, COMETS, AND CAMPARI

Father Komonchak's fine paper, "The Catholic University in the Church," helps us to appreciate some positive aspects of *Ex corde Ecclesiae*. Among these are: (1) the way in which the church is understood as the "whole assembly of Christian believers" and is not equated with the hierarchy—an understanding that has been recovered for us by Vatican II; (2) the close linkage between the church's identity and its mission, so that mission to and dialogue with the world are not relegated to some peripheral realm of metaphysical accidents, secondary objectives, and optional practices; (3) the integrating and nonsectarian view of Christianity and of the church, which is manifest in a desire for dialogue with the sciences, for engagement with culture, and for a commitment to the promotion of justice that requires an openness to the needs and the voices of the poor. At the same time, while he notes that the document in several places acknowledges the institutional autonomy of the university and the academic freedom of the faculty, he is concerned that it fails to indicate institutional safeguards for these key values and to provide protection against possible abuses of authority. These concerns do not, if I read him correctly, manifest a desire to structure the university-church relationship along adversarial lines; for such an interpretation would be at odds with the fundamental concept of the Catholic university in the church, which provides Father Komonchak with both the central theme and the title of his paper. Nor do they reflect a spirit of anxious mistrust and academic self-protection; rather, they reflect a prudent reading of ecclesiastical history (particularly in the nineteenth and early twentieth centuries) and a canny assessment of the possibilities for painful conflict when the leaders of one institution exercise oversight over the activities of a kindred but not identical institution, an institution with its own inherent finality and distinctive interests and concerns.

The absence of institutional safeguards and of protections against abuses of authority is a consequence of two facts. One is that this document does not originate within a liberal culture, which takes a concern for such things as an appropriate, indeed a centrally important, element in any serious discussion of the scope and identity of major social institutions. The other is that this document does have its origins in the renewal of Catholicism that found its decisive moment in Vatican II. One of the major themes of this renewal was a sustained effort to ensure that the major institutions in the church and the life of the church itself were not understood in predominantly juridical terms but rather in terms of animating charisms and ideals and virtues. This, I think we can affirm, has been a necessary and valuable development, even though it has been accompanied by some intellectual confusion and some practical deviations. But a situation in which high ideals are frequently invoked and juridical safeguards are not clearly established can easily become a situation in which both utopian rhetoric and passionate conflict flourish among the righteous.

Here it is helpful to consider the vision of the university community or what I am tempted to call *The Peaceable Kingdom* (Isa. 11:1-9), which is sketched in *Ex corde Ecclesiae:*

> A Catholic university pursues its objectives through its formation of an authentic human community animated by the spirit of Christ. The source of its unity springs from a common dedication to the truth, a common vision of the dignity of the human person and ultimately the person and message of Christ, which gives the institution its distinctive character. As a result of this inspiration, the community is animated by a spirit of freedom and charity; it is characterized by mutual respect, sincere dialogue, and protection of the rights of individuals. It assists each of its members to achieve wholeness as human persons; in turn, everyone in the community helps in promoting unity, and each one, according to his or her role and capacity, contributes toward decisions which affect the community and also toward maintaining and strengthening the distinctive Catholic character of the institution. (n. 21)

Now it is hard to find much to quarrel with in this particular commendation of the true, the good, and the beautiful. It does state an important and valuable ideal for a religious-social-educational community. It is an ideal that for a few happy moments may indeed be approximated by an exceptionally blessed and prosperous institution.

But it also serves to remind the rest of us of ways in which we fall short of the full realization of the academic and religious hopes with which most of us began our careers. For if we look around us at the institutions within which we labor, we find that often there are clashes among schools and departments, sectarian wars within disciplines, and continuing patterns of mutual suspicion between faculty and administration. The religious character of the university threatens to become formalistic and alienating; and policies that affirm or extend it come to be seen as administrative fiats or concessions to particular factions. I would not want to say that this somber picture is the whole or the defining reality of any Catholic university with which I am familiar; but I would maintain that it is based on occurrences that have happened in many, if not most, of the Catholic universities in this country.

Of course it is true that no large organization lives precisely according to the norms that its leadership formulates for it, and it is also true that not much could have been said about the internal problems and tensions of Catholic universities that would have been universally applicable and constructive. It is also likely that such comments would have to touch on certain professional deformations of the academic character and on careerist and individualistic tendencies among students and would also have had to acknowledge the church's increasing difficulty in evangelizing the economically advanced countries. This would clearly have resulted in a document that would sound more realistic and more conflictual. Such a document would also have struck an ominous note and might have stirred in many the fear that high authorities were planning drastic measures to deal with a troubled situation. So on balance we may all be better off with the idealizing and conflict-minimizing document that Rome has given us.

But in our own thinking about these matters we need to acknowledge that there are very important elements in the current composition of Catholic universities in this country that make it unlikely that the ideal university community sketched (n. 21) will be widely accepted as a goal seriously worth desiring and striving for. Some of these elements are present in many areas of our society, for instance, the distrust of the language and the style of *Gemeinschaft* forms of association; the cultural preference for a more understated, more pragmatic way of stating goals; the widespread anxiety about appearing to be exclusive on grounds other than economic; the powerful desire to shape one's life as one sees fit oneself without dependence on elders, a local community, or some grander authority. But beyond recognizing these widespread elements, we also need to acknowledge that in some key respects the most we can hope to achieve is a university that is half-Catholic or half a community. I do not mean this in some numerical or quantitative sense that one might measure in the faculty or in the student body. Nor do I mean it in a disparaging sense, much as one might point to an adulterated or contaminated product. Rather, I intend it as a challenge to us to recognize both the perils and the possibilities of our actual situation and as a step toward building a better understanding of that situation. Our current situation may be transitional to something quite different and even more secular; but it may in fact prove to have a vitality and a durability that, being rooted in very important American values and experiences, may surprise both secularists and religious prophets of doom. The occurrence of this phenomenon should also alert us to a very important aspect of ministering to and leading contemporary American Catholicism.

What I am concerned with may be illuminated by two different metaphors, one of which I will elaborate now and one of which I will save for the conclusion of my remarks. I suggest that we think of a Catholic university as something like a comet, moving around the sun of the church not in the steady, slightly elliptical orbits followed by the planets but in more highly elliptical orbits, only intermittently visible and not readily predictable. Comets are, as you know, somewhat loose collections of matter, often sprawling over vast distances. For long portions of their careers, they move away from the sun, but they do return at periodic intervals. Their contacts with planets and other bodies in the solar system are too complex and too infrequent to yield simple regularities.

I think that you can readily guess the intent of this comparison. What we are dealing with in the contemporary Catholic university in the United States is an institution that is not in fact subject to a steady and consistent control from the center, which is actually moved by a number of other forces as well as by its relationship to the church, and which is composed of members who are not all that tightly bound together and who may in fact be captured by (or exported to) other institutions, some of which are part of the church system and some of which are not.

What we have in the contemporary Catholic university is a mixture of people working on a common enterprise but working from quite different religious and ideological perspectives. This mixture is probably somewhat different from that found in public universities, in private universities with no religious affiliation, and in private universities that are linked with other religious traditions, but the differences are less pronounced than they once were. The proportion of strongly committed Catholics may well be higher in the upper reaches of the administration and in theology departments than among the junior faculty or in some professional schools. The precise religious identity of many of their colleagues is likely to be unknown to many of the faculty; the presence or absence of a religious commitment is regarded by many either as a matter of supreme indifference or as a deeply personal and private question. Now the existence of religious pluralism within Catholic universities is well known, and the apostolic constitution in several places explicitly acknowledges the need to protect the rights of individuals (n. 21), and it affirms the religious liberty of non-Catholics (n. 27). We should also note that it sets such affirmations within the moral bounds set by certain fundamental values, as, for instance, where we are told that the Catholic university "possesses that institutional autonomy necessary to perform its functions effectively and guarantees its members academic freedom, so long as the rights of the individual person and of the community are preserved within the confines of the truth and the common good" (n. 12). The insistence on the broader moral framework constituted by truth and the common good is a move characteristic of the Catholic approach to human rights; for at one and the same time it opposes overly individualistic conceptions of rights and leaves unspecified just how truth and the common good are to be determined and evaluated in the concrete. If we shift our attention from rights to duties, we can see that the document later distinguishes three levels of obligation with regard to the Catholic character of the university: (1) institutional fidelity of the university to the Christian message; (2) personal fidelity to the church on the part of the Catholic members of the university "with all that this implies"; (3) respect on the part of the non-Catholic members of the university (n. 27). But the document fails to convey any strong sense of the divisions to be surmounted if the Catholic university is really to function as a religious intellectual-social community.

Let me point briefly to four of these difficulties. First, it seems to me that the church needs to develop a more nuanced and more positive account of the spiritual and intellectual situation of those Catholics who are in various ways and different degrees estranged from significant parts of its teaching and its life. Whether we think about these people as nonpracticing Catholics, lapsed Catholics, dissenting Catholics, liberal Catholics, modernist or postmodernist Catholics, or, as my title suggests, near Catholics, we have to recognize that there are lots of these folks in and around Catholic universities. They may want their children baptized but would prefer that this be done by a female minister. They can be strongly critical of a pastor who changes the music of a liturgy they no longer attend. They will regret that the world no longer supports the family values that the church commends, even while they make it clear that the teaching of the church on economic justice is an irritating irrelevance. They will often manifest the passionate inconsistency that marks the disillusioned critic who was once an enthusiastic lover. This, of course, makes it difficult to generalize about these people who can be found on both the left and the right. Their situation is often a source of pain to themselves and of embarrassment to friends and to the church. But it needs to be taken seriously as one continuing element in the life of the Catholic university.

Obviously, the situation cannot be resolved by the church's offering to withdraw from any positions that are unacceptable to "enlightened" members of the university. Such a policy would be unfaithful to the gospel and demeaning to the church itself. But the church needs to develop a strategy of being present to these people in modes of dialogue, criticism, support, challenge, and partial coalition. It is especially within the university that the church has to employ such an approach. In effect, what this means is that the process of dialogue and collaboration between the church and the world that was sketched in such generous and hopeful terms in *Gaudium et spes* has to serve as part of the model for how the church deals with this portion of the flock.

Second, there is a need to recognize that the line between the religious and the moral cannot be drawn in a simple, permanent, and noncontroversial way. The fundamental reason for this is that the line gets drawn in different ways, depending on whether we are looking to the logical characteristics of types of propositions, to the psychological attitudes and social perceptions of members and nonmembers of religious groups, or to the history of ideas and institutions. Even when the church is eager to respect the religious beliefs of non-Catholics and when all parties agree about the necessity of following moral principles with integrity and respecting one another's right to do so, painful conflicts are still likely to arise. This is particularly true because the locus of political conflict within our society has shifted from broad economic issues to the culture wars, which range from the control of images to the promotion of a form of representational justice that aims specifically at including previously excluded groups. Thus we confront conflicts in our culture in which the church's condemnation of abortion, though founded on a natural-law prohibition of killing, is often denounced as the imposition of religious beliefs on those who do not share them, while at the same time the church's refusal to ordain women is treated as a violation of moral principle before which purely religious considerations should yield. The point I want to make here is not that religion and morality cannot be distinguished, but that in a controversial situation we cannot proceed on the assumption that the distinction has the same meaning for all the key participants. The church and other parties in these controversies need to reflect on the different evaluations and reactions that follow from different ways of making the distinction.

Third, current trends in U.S. law and culture encourage pluralism manifested by individuals working within institutions and discourage it when it is manifested by institutions themselves. This, I think, particularly affects institutions that want to preserve a distinctive ethos while not cutting themselves off from the mainstream of American society. The task of those institutions that want to deepen and renew the values of their distinctive traditions even while they are enriched by the diversity and pluralism of American society as a whole is not an easy one—both because the law presses them either to be sectarian in their personnel policies or to accept a prohibition against religious discrimination except when religion can be shown to be a bone fide occupational qualification and because most institutions and groups often have changing and conflicting desires about how to strike the balance between distinctiveness and diversity. Sometimes they will want to fit in with the mainstream; sometimes they will want to affirm countercultural values; sometimes they will present themselves as quintessentially American; sometimes as profoundly Catholic.

Fourth, we should reflect carefully on the tension between much of the moderate leadership of American Catholic higher education that directs institutions that are committed to the values of the Catholic tradition and the proponents of "traditional values" in the "culture wars" that currently rage from local school boards to the National Endowment for the Arts and from elite university campuses to abortion clinics. Many of the conservatives, neo-conservatives, and Christian evangelicals who are denouncing the mass media, the artistic avant-garde, and the performance of public education are also promoting a political agenda that strikes most moderates as reactionary and repellent. This juxtaposition does not establish logical inconsistency nor does it preclude the possibility of limited coalitions for specific purposes. But it does mean that there are likely to be mutually embarrassing agreements and disagreements, accusations of insincerity and inconsistency, and confusion among both friends and foes. Thus some opponents of renewing the Catholic character of the university will misinterpret this as a commitment to a compre-hensive cultural, political, and economic conservatism or as a denial of cherished rights and liberties. Both sympathizers and critics run the risk of reducing the commitment to Catholic identity to a stand on a set of very controversial moral and religious issues.

Clearly, these observations about the Catholic university in the church in a highly pluralistic and contentious society do not amount to a theory of anything. Rather, they are intended as reminders of some serious difficulties that stand in the way of renewing and deepening the Catholic character of our institutions. In the absence of a theory, I may perhaps be permitted a concluding image. It seems to me that maintaining a Catholic university is something like making a good Campari and soda. This is an admirable drink, lively and not too sweet, and very refreshing in the middle of a Roman summer afternoon. Neither the tartness of undiluted Campari nor the blandness of soda water is nearly as interesting or agreeable as the drink. The mixture allows for a certain flexibility with regard to proportions, and it embodies a more complex idea. This more complex idea, the recipe for the mixture, has to include the soda, which is not to be thought of as a concession to human weakness or to economic necessity but is in fact an integral part of the mixture. Recipes that call for its drastic diminution or elimination are not formulas for Campari and soda but for something else (which may have its own merits).

It seems to me that in the contemporary American Catholic university we are aiming at something like the mixture that is Campari and soda, that we are shaping an educational community inclusive of both Catholics and non-Catholics, a community that aspires to be comprehensively learned, generously sharing the process and the results of its inquiries, wisely forming new members of the scholarly and professional communities, responsibly maintaining an ethos shaped by democratic values and religious commitments. This composite or mixture of disparate elements will not always be easy to maintain, but it is the realization of an ideal that is both humanely attractive and profoundly worthwhile.

COMMENT

REV. GEORGE H. TAVARD, A.A., *Marquette University*

Reading the beginning of Father Komonchak's paper, I am reminded of two small incidents. Some years ago having used the word *catholicity* in conversation with a minister of the United Church of Christ, I was shocked by his question: "When you say 'catholicity,' do you mean 'censorship'?" Whatever my surprise at the time, this question could have expressed the feelings of many academics before the advent of Pope John XXIII. Undoubtedly, mentalities have changed, and the apostolic constitution *Ex corde Ecclesiae* does not fill the word *Catholic* with the content, censorship. It does not even intend censorship when it explains that "Catholic theologians . . . fulfill a mandate received from the Church" (art. 4, sec. 3) and that they should be faithful to Catholic doctrine.

The other incident was of another kind. When I was professor of religious studies at Pennsylvania State University, I was delegated by my colleagues, along with another professor, to meet with a group of local ministers who had questions for us. A Presbyterian minister asked, "By what authority do you teach the gospel at the university?" In terms of what we taught, of the object of courses, I could have answered that in a state university we do not teach the gospel. But I responded to the question of authority. I said, "Whatever we teach, we teach by the authority of scholarship . . . " When I read a church document about universities, I therefore ask myself first, what is the mandate in question and to what extent does the text uphold the authority of scholarship?

My remarks will be set between these two incidents, which may be taken as symbolic of a double concern. On the one hand, there is religious authority; one finds it in the gospel, in the Scriptures, in the tradition, in the church's episcopal hierarchy. On the other hand, there is the authority of scholarship, both in universities in general and in Catholic universities. The former demands that Catholicity, the quality of being Catholic, extend, like faith itself, to the

63

whole scope of the human intellect. The second implies that catholicity in the realm of the intellect is not achieved by directives of the hierarchy but by the research and teaching of scholars.

Within this broad framework I will limit my remarks to three points, namely, the authority of scholarship, the nature of a university, and academic freedom.

THE AUTHORITY OF SCHOLARSHIP

Father Komonchak's appraisal of the apostolic constitution *Ex corde Ecclesiae* welcomes the open perspective of the text when it is seen in the context of two opposite orientations. Facing the pagan culture of their times, Saint Justin of Rome and Tertullian adopted opposite stances on the relations between faith and reason, the one positive (reason prepares for faith), the other negative (faith is beyond reason and does not need it). The church eventually opted for Justin against Tertullian. The present document stands squarely in the line of Justin and the rationality of faith.

I would be less assertive as to the effectiveness of the choice that was made in the first centuries. For elements of irrationality have turned up time and again in the history of the church, as in the proceedings of the Inquisition against witches and heretics or in the struggles of Gregory XVI and Pius IX against the rise of the modern world—that are properly evoked in Father Komonchak's paper—or, more broadly, in the general tardiness of the church's officials to read the signs of the times and to adjust behavior and methods to the needs and mood of each period.

While I also am grateful for the openness of *Ex corde Ecclesiae* to Catholic universities as places of teaching and research, I would begin by being more critical of the document. I regard the apostolic constitution as being both excessively generous and highly unrealistic. It is too generous when it uses the word *theologians* to designate professors, though I am not sure it has in mind Catholic professors of theology or professors of Catholic theology. Neither all Catholic professors of theology nor all professors of Catholic theology are in fact theologians. In the present context of American institutions of higher learning, including Catholic institutions, it is unrealistic to assume that all who teach Catholic theology are themselves Catholic. Yet this is, I gather, the assumption of *Ex corde Ecclesiae,* as it is that of canon 812 of the Code of Canon Law, quoted in Father Komonchak's paper. In the real world of academia Catholics differ less and less from other committed Christians. There exists a communion of learning and scholarship that ignores denominations and church separations and that properly carries legitimate authority in its own order.

In its origin the word *magisterium* designated not the teaching responsibility of bishops but the teaching capacity of experts in their area of knowledge.

Pope John XXIII recognized this when he called a number of theologians to Vatican Council II. The term *magisterium* being practically reserved to bishops, these conciliar theologians were not called *magistri* but *periti*. However, it is not only in councils that *periti* have a task and responsibility of their own, which derives from a different gift of the Spirit. It is in the church at large and chiefly in the university as the place where scholars gather and work. In this sense, the university shares the authority and the responsibility of scholarship.

THE NATURE OF A UNIVERSITY

Father Komonchak rightly emphasizes the formula—the title of his paper— "The Catholic University in the Church." But there is a hidden irony in the expression. If we still spoke good Latin, the conjunction of the two words, *Catholic* and *university,* would be tautological. For *university* translates *universitas studiorum,* the universality and totality of studies, and *catholic* already qualifies that which is really or potentially "universal." An institution where everything can be taught and studied is by its very nature catholic, at least with a small c. And this is true whether or not it has been authorized by a bishop to call itself Catholic with a capital c. Catholicity as universality is of the essence of a university. It is not the adjective, I would contend, but the words *within the church* that denote the ecclesial and, in that sense, Catholic character of an academic institution.

But what does it mean to be "within the church"? The church cannot be, for institutions of higher learning, their exclusive locus. Catholic universities are also in the world of a given country, as is noted in *Ex corde Ecclesiae* (n. 32). And, along with Protestant, state, secular, and possibly other universities, they are in academia, which is itself a world within a world. This is exactly what the document calls "a university world" (n. 13). In this world Catholic universities indeed testify to the persistence of intellectual pursuits in the church. But they also risk losing their standing if they identify too closely with the canonical and magisterial dimensions of church life, if, that is, they admit that a higher authority than scholarship is able to determine the methods and the conclusions of an academic discipline. In the first place, the contention (n. 18) that all human endeavors, including academic pursuits, must have a moral end does not by itself justify episcopal supervision of academic disciplines and their teaching. In the second place, I do not share the belief that "the complete answer" to the "increasingly broader questions" that are treated in interdisciplinary studies "can only come from above through faith" (n. 20). I hear in these lines a Catholic echo of Paul Tillich's correlation, "Philosophy asks the questions, and theology gives the answers." This, however, opens difficult problems of epistemology on which I would not expect an apostolic constitution to take sides.

Father Komonchak examines this question at length from the standpoint of academic freedom. He rightly points to the absence, in the constitution, of proper procedures to protect scholars from unwarranted or incompetent interventions of the hierarchy. He gives the example of John Henry Newman's judgment on the function of theology as the organizing architectonic principle of knowledge in a Catholic university. Yet there should be a previous question. As Newman himself painfully discovered, there existed several Catholic theologies in his time. Dominant in the schools of Rome, a type of neo-scholastic theology, still in its formative stage, was struggling to bridge the discontinuity that was imposed on Catholic culture by the French Revolution. Not unnaturally it was implicitly taken for granted, in the offices of the Roman curia, as the proper model for all theology. Indeed it marked an advance on the traditionalism that had come to the fore in France in the first decades of the century. But in its understanding of modern culture, it lagged behind the school of Tübingen and behind Newman's patristically based theological reflection.

History shows that once the patristic period was over, the Catholic world in general and the primacy of the bishop of Rome in particular have not been well served by advocacy of one theology over against others. The great councils of the West in fact have never opted exclusively for one school of thought. But in the daily routine of Roman dicasteries, the predominance of a set pattern considered to be traditional traces the line of least effort. Thus Newman had to count with the theology of tradition that was in favor in Rome. And Henri de Lubac had to contend with Garrigou-Lagrange's reading of Saint Thomas.

Today there are, for good or ill, many theologies. Tomorrow there will be many more, if at least the ascent of Latin American, Asian, and—perhaps later—African thinking is to bear fruit in the academic world. It is the function of Catholic universities today to prepare students for the pluralistic world of tomorrow, whichever theology may, for good or bad reasons, be preferred in the Roman curia. From this point of view, the modern university, whatever its religious background and principles, is a place where students are offered choices, and where they choose their own philosophy and way of life in the respect of their human and legal freedom. I therefore see a hidden danger in the way *Ex corde Ecclesiae* (nn. 32-33) places such questions primarily on an ethical or moral level where the church's bishops are used to speak with authority. I would be more hopeful of results if such questions were placed at the level of the development of personality in the context of the interpersonal relations that are constitutive of society. Behavior and its principles exist for the sake of human persons. Human persons do not exist for the sake of law.

ACADEMIC FREEDOM

This brings me to the specific point of academic freedom. Here, I must say that I would recognize, perhaps more than Father Komonchak does, the positive contribution of *Ex corde Ecclesiae*. Although I am not certain it was intended to be read as I read it, I find the following definition of academic freedom quite remarkable: "The Church . . . recognizes the academic freedom of scholars in each discipline in accordance with its own principles and proper methods . . . " (n. 29). Taken literally, and I see no reason to take them otherwise, these lines imply that one is equipped to judge matters of academic freedom only within each discipline. Only those who share the principles, and who practice the methods, of an academic or intellectual discipline are qualified to delimit the scope of their academic freedom. As this implies, each area of scholarship is self-regulating and therefore, in regard to the limits of academic freedom, a scholar can be judged only by his peers. This, I would argue, rules out bishops as proper judges in matters of academic freedom.

Indeed Father Komonchak is correct in noting an imbalance in *Ex corde Ecclesiae*. In both its reflections and its regulations, the document seeks to preserve the rights of the hierarchy. And since it—quoting Father Komonchak—"ignores juridical safeguards against abuse of episcopal authority," it seems to neglect the rights of professors and of universities should a conflict arise. But I am more skeptical than he seems to be as to the virtues of set regulations in such an area. Because laws are applied and interpreted by lawyers, they are no guarantee of the rights they are designed to protect. They can be manipulated, misapplied, and ignored. An apostolic constitution has done its proper work when it has stated principles. It should not become an appendix to the Code of Canon Law, even if it includes a set of general norms and transitional norms. In *Ex corde Ecclesiae* I take the enunciated norms to be no more, but no less, than a declaration of intent.

In case of conflict one would do well to reflect on principles that were expounded by Karol Wojtyla the philosopher in the last section of his book *The Acting Person*. As the author explained, human action and, all the more so, Christian action are never the acts of an isolated person. Action implies "intersubjectivity" and "participation." Participation in society and, by the same token, in the church, requires two interlocking attitudes.

> The attitude of "solidarity" cannot be dissociated from that of "opposition," for each is necessary to the understanding of the other . . . The attitude of solidarity means respect for all parts that are the share of every member of the community. To take over a part of the duties and obligations that are not mine is intrinsically contrary to participation and to the essence of the community.[1]

And again,

> The one who voices his opposition to the general or particular rules of the community does not thereby reject his membership; he does not

withdraw his readiness to act and to work for the common good . . .
[The attitude of opposition] expresses the strong need to participate in
the common existing with other men and even more so in the common
acting. There can be no doubt that this kind of opposition is essentially
constructive: it is a condition of the correct structure of communities
and of the correct functioning of their inner system.[2]

I do not know if the writers of *Ex corde Ecclesiae* were familiar with the
volume I have quoted, or even to what extent the pontificate of John Paul II
is in continuity with the philosophy of Karol Wojtyla. But I should remark
that the principle of responsible autonomy for Catholic universities and their
professors is clearly contained in this book, specifically in its analysis of the
person who acts in communion with the other members of society. If conflicts
between the church's *periti-peritae* and its *magistri* are handled in this spirit,
then canonical regulations are superfluous. Catholic universities and their professors need not fear to engage in the critical aspects of their providential tasks
of research and teaching.

Let me conclude with another quotation, this time from Karol Wojtyla
the poet:

> *Truth doesn't drip oil into wounds to stop the burning pain*
> *or sit you on a donkey to be led through the streets;*
> *truth must be hurtful and hide.*
> *Structures contract in the brain: raised in man*
> *a building leans; we want to straighten*
> *not its pediment but the ground resisting far beneath*
> *as waves resist boats. . .*
> *. . . we range over astounded streets*
> *where the donkey is led.*
> *(Is there less and less truth in the streets—or more?)*
> *We look ahead calmly: we are beyond dread.*[3]

NOTES

1. Karol Wojtyla, *The Acting Person,* trans. Andrzej Potocki (Boston: Reidel Publishing Company, 1979), p. 285.

2. Ibid., p. 286.

3. Karol Wojtyla, "Gospel," from a poem sequence "The Church," in *Easter Vigil
and Other Poems,* trans. Jerzy Peterkiewicz (New York: Random House, 1979), p. 61.

DISCUSSION

Discussion initially focused on the document's ecclesiological context, its relative emphases on "centralization" and "autonomy," and the possible impact of the forthcoming ordinances.

It is important to understand that *Ex corde Ecclesiae* arises at a time when there is increasing alienation between the academic community and authorities within the church, at a time when what commands obedience is less the moral authority of the pronouncement than sheer power. This is an enormously serious issue and is the real context of this document. The document's unresolved perspective on the nature of academic freedom in *Ex corde Ecclesiae* is found in article 2, section 5, of the general norms, which recognizes freedom in research and teaching "so long as the rights of the individual and of the community are preserved within the confines of the truth and the common good." Who is to judge these issues? How is the university to defend its own members from negative judgments?

To the question of whether the *Ex corde Ecclesiae* is too authoritarian, no real answer can be given since the document, by its very terms, calls for regulations. The problem is that the process of developing regulations raises questions about whether the regulations are, in fact, similar to the goals of the original formulation of *Ex corde Ecclesiae,* which were much focused on juridical control of the universities.

Isn't the problem that the people of God (the church) don't approve the ordinances implementing *Ex corde Ecclesiae?* Who in fact does approve the ordinances? What really is the dialogue in the evolution of this document? If theology is the center of the dialogue, who defines which theologians are at the center? The Roman idea of theology or other ideas such as liberation theology? In this whole process, the universities do not have the initiative to determine the means of resolving the problems. It is not the people of God who define the resolutions of issues but the Roman curia.   *69*

The origin of the thinking behind the document is that universities in Eastern Europe believe deeply that granting authority to the Vatican is the only way to defend their autonomy. This document was originally devised for Catholic universities behind the former Iron Curtain, but the structures are imposed on the whole church. This is an important clue for interpreting the document, which should not be taken as literally as it seems to be taken in the American church. To the extent that this document and *Sapientia Christiana* were premised on the need for centralization in the Vatican to protect against the encroachments of the state, this protection is not necessary in the United States. The whole notion of secular accreditation in the United States is almost incomprehensible to the Vatican.

Although the Eastern European background may be interesting in understanding the origins of the document, it would be a real mistake not to understand that the document is aimed directly at universities in the United States. This document is simply one more symbol of strong centralization in the American church. There needs to be some kind of corrective force, which may come from academic institutions.

On the contrary, the primary feature of *Ex corde Ecclesiae* is *not* centralization, as has been claimed. Perhaps it represents some overbureaucratization, but isn't the real question of the document whether the dynamism of faith is actually meeting the dynamism of the university? Is there a university where that is actually happening?

The ordinances of the bishops under the terms of *Ex corde Ecclesiae* must be reviewed by Rome. So the dynamics of this document are, in fact, open to centralization.

Ex corde Ecclesiae may militate against the response of universities to this challenge. Linking answers to hierarchical control will inevitably mean less room for spontaneity, adaption, and creativity within the local culture of the university.

Most Catholic universities have thought long and hard about these questions and are unsure how to answer them. They do not need more obstacles like *Ex corde Ecclesiae*. But 98 percent of the text of *Ex corde Ecclesiae* is *not* about the control by the hierarchy. The document has much helpful language about autonomy. There is absolutely no need to be paranoid about the document.

This document, in fact, does represent a major modification in approach: a juridical approach to the question of the Catholic nature of higher education.

Discussion returned to a topic introduced in the first session—the nature and possibility of "integration" within the Catholic university. Participants explored the challenges inherent in such an undertaking, particularly the obstacles to achieving consensus about an institution's Catholic identity.

The document represents a kind of "platonic" concept of the university, an ideal in which real universities participate only in some degree. The question remains how one finds some measure of integration between the dynamics of Christianity and the traditional dynamics of the modern university.

In all the discussion of integration, let us not forget the fact that there are a host of forces in the contemporary university arrayed against it. For example, literary theory seriously questions the role of human reason.

Are there certain topics that particularly lend themselves to integration? The integration of knowledge cannot be accomplished by theology. The integration of knowledge is really done by personalities, not by fields such as theology or philosophy, history or English.

There is an important distinction between undergraduate and graduate education in this regard. Undergraduate education is much more susceptible to activities of integration than the specialized world of graduate education. The question is not whether there is some grand integration but what is actually happening in the programs of Catholic universities. For example, if a Catholic university has a business school, shouldn't we expect that at least some questions are asked in that school's program that one wouldn't find at other business schools? One would like to think that there are some perspectives of faith that would get into the conversation at a Catholic university. That surely is more important than some grand theory of the integration of faith and knowledge.

One of the advantages of U.S. education, in contrast to European, is the many possibilities of pursing integration at the undergraduate level. But it is important not to consider integration an unrestricted good. We should be careful to avoid maximalist forms of integration. The way of making a strong Catholic university is not to import so much Catholicism that you misconceive the social reality of the contemporary university. It does no good to throw some kind of idealized veil over the politics of the situation.

Most people in the universities have no complacency about the Catholic nature of their institutions. The problem is how best to realize this goal of a stronger identity. One approach would be to privilege certain questions within Catholic institutions, whereas no answers would be so privileged.

Where is the dynamic of Catholicism in the university actually going on? The answer must be the faculty. The problem is that for most of the best faculty, Catholicism is not an important issue. Rather, their research interests, determined by their particular guild, are paramount. If faculty are the central issue, that directly implies hiring practices or ways in which the administration of the university can make these questions attractive to the existing faculty.

Faculty at Catholic universities are beginning to become polarized about the Catholic character of the institution for the first time. The high degree of passive assent, traditional in the faculty, has eroded. Even the indifferent are becoming less tolerant of the officially declared Catholic character of the institution.

In thinking about the importance of the Catholic culture of the university, we cannot overlook the importance of curriculum. For example, are interdisciplinary courses more common at Catholic universities than elsewhere?

The absence of discussion about liturgy, worship, and prayer as one important dimension of the community is particularly striking in this conversation. It has a relationship to research and teaching.

Liturgy and public worship have not arisen in conversation because most Catholic universities feel they are relatively strong in this area. But this strength is no substitute for intellectual engagement. This document is supposed to be challenging the universities to a larger vision. The Catholic presence in the Catholic university has a "fractured character." While it is true that the liturgical dimension is strong in American Catholic universities, many faculty resent attending acts of worship.

Much of the balance of discussion probed the problematic issue of the Catholic university being "in" both the church and society.

How cohesive can a Catholic university be in view of the "fractured" nature of the Catholic community and Catholic institutions? (We need greater specificity about the ten or twenty different varieties of "fractured" Catholics— what they are saying, what their problems are. And what is the role of non-Catholics in Catholic universities?) What does it mean to be "in" the church? Do people have any clear notion of what that means for a university? Do they have any sense of what institutional actions for promoting theology would be necessary? It is important to worry less about what Rome meant in *Ex corde Ecclesiae* than to understand what it is we in the university mean by being "in" the church.

The Komonchak paper helped us to understand the idea of the Catholic university "in" the church. But the university exists not only "in" the church, but also "in" society. Most of us live lives not so defined by Catholicism that we go first to the church to determine what kind of art we wish to enjoy or how we approach difficult problems of medical policy or a host of other issues. For example, it is not helpful to say that a medical school of an American university is "in" the church. It is not a useful way to think about a medical school or a hospital since so much of what it does has little direct relation to church policies, procedures, or understandings. Rather, it would make more sense to talk about a set of relationships or instrumentalities in building the community of the church.

The university is the arena where culture and the church meet, where there is real give and take. This exciting relationship is concentrated at a good university. It is a great opportunity for the church, a great place for the encounter.

We must change the intellectual quality of American Catholic culture, which arguably is in decline. This is an enormous responsibility. And we must all be more imaginative about this task.

The notion of the university as "in" the church is a source of great frustration. Outside the university lay people run into all kinds of walls and obstacles within the church. One of the problems of the American university is our peculiar detachment from reform of the local church. There is a sense that we think we can do nothing about affecting the church.

Ex corde Ecclesiae speaks of the local church, which is expected to be an active participant in framing the conversation. Although the document itself does not express great centralization, this may be latent in it. Whereas Pius XII headed a centralized church with a centralized theology, today the situation is a centralized church with a decentralizing theology.

While the first session on the American background of *Ex corde Ecclesiae* reviewed some old arguments that have to do with the future of American higher education, the current session on the Catholic university "in" the church talks about ideas that will carry through the entire symposium. This includes ideas about structure and the style of being Catholic. How, for example, can a Catholic university be a "nonsectarian Catholic university" that resists sectarian appeals from both the left and the right within the Catholic church?

One of the new features in accreditation by secular authorities is the diversity required of every department. This is a form of enforced homogeneity, which militates against an internal dynamic of a university based on distinctiveness.

We have touched upon diversity as a legal requirement in American higher education. Certainly diversity, both inside and outside the church, is a more radical question after Vatican II.

How much integration is appropriate or possible? What kind of authority counts? Intellectual authority? Moral authority? Ecclesial authority? If *Ex corde Ecclesiae* and *Sapientia Christiana* and canon 812 were necessary as a result of needs in Eastern Europe, how are they to be applied to the very different setting in the United States?

Rev. Michael J. Buckley, S.J., *Boston College*

The Catholic University and the Promise Inherent in Its Identity

The problem of self-identity is not just a problem for the young. It is a problem all the time. Perhaps the problem. It should haunt old age, and when it no longer does it should tell you that you are dead.

—Norman Maclean
Young Men and Fire[1]

THE QUESTION AND ITS URGENCY

On the noon of September 16, 1992, Boston College, led by its president, was at prayer. The Mass of the Holy Spirit, celebrated on the steps of the O'Neill Library, was not a time for the president to address the faculty nor for administrators to make welcome incoming students nor for instructors to inaugurate their classes in semester requirements and contents. This had all been done—at faculty convocation, over many meetings, and in initial classes. Now this complex of president and administrators and students and doctoral candidates and faculty—this university—turned formally and explicitly as a university to address God. The prayers and readings that floated on the air of that brilliant autumn afternoon spoke repeatedly of the influence that is the heart of academic inquiry and learning, the Spirit of Truth; and the Scriptures gave focus to the petitions threading their way through the liturgy: that the Spirit of Truth would descend upon this university over the coming year, that this Spirit would mark its teaching, guide its inquiry and research, and permeate its collective life as a *collegium,* that this university as a Catholic university would realize the promise of the gospel: the Spirit of Truth who will guide us to all truth (see John 16:13).

That the Mass of the Holy Spirit was being celebrated indicated a Catholic university, conscious of its past and faithful to its identity, possessed of a conviction that the religious and the academic belong in concert, that their union is to be celebrated in beauty and worship; that classes remained in session, that sundry students made their way indifferently through the congregation to reach the library, and that the university community attended only in the middle hundreds, bespoke a detached disinterest and problems unresolved but pervasive in Catholic universities throughout the nation.

I found myself wondering during the liturgy: What is this upon which we invoke the unspeakable mystery of God? What are "we" who are at prayer? The question did not seem a distraction. It seemed pressing, a question upon which we might well have meditated as we worshiped as a university. For many voices state with increasing urgency that the Catholic university will disappear; that it is already disappearing as a specific reality in American higher education; that the Catholic university will repeat the secularizing history of so many of the very great universities in the United States; that this evanescence of its religious character is inevitable, disclosing gradually the unfaced irrelevance of the religious to the intellectual; that as the university becomes more authentic, more academically distinguished, its Catholic character will proportionately dissipate and disappear. Only last February in a widely remarked article, David R. Carlin wrote that the Catholic identity of Catholic colleges and universities has since the 1960s "grown increasingly tenuous . . . Catholic colleges seem to be traveling the same road many Protestant colleges journeyed in the nineteenth and early twentieth centuries—a road leading to complete secularization, to complete loss of religious identity."[2]

Many of the greatest universities in the United States and Europe have already written such a history of religious atrophy. One can wander about their campuses and remark the chapels and statues, the maxims on the gates or the portraits on the walls, and confront symbols that speak of a former religious intensity now long since dead. There one can paraphrase something of the cultural diagnosis of Friedrich Nietzsche: What are these universities now if not the tombs of God—monuments to the death of God within academic culture?[3] It would be unwarranted to imagine that we are not liable to the same influences, naive to believe that we cannot repeat their history. Catholic universities have already repeated much in the history of their secularized academic peers.

One may recall the address of Robert Maynard Hutchins, the then president of the University of Chicago, to Catholic educators in 1937: "I find it necessary to level against you a scandalous accusation . . . You have imitated the worst features of secular education . . . What I say is that Catholic education is not Catholic enough." This despite the fact that

> the Catholic Church has the longest intellectual tradition of any institution in the contemporary world, the only uninterrupted tradition and the only explicit tradition; that is, it is the only institution which is conscious of its tradition. What I say is that this tradition must not be merely an idea, but must be practiced.

Despite the countervalence of the church's enormous rich tradition, Hutchins found the Catholic imitation of the worst in secular education in athleticism, collegiatism, vocationalism, and antiintellectualism, in all of which, he said, "I believe Catholic education is as bad as, maybe worse than, secular education."[4] Now some fifty-five years after that judgment, one can wonder whether this imitation will reach out further, whether it will or has gradually extended itself into the Catholic identity of these institutions as well.

For the Catholic university is not a stable fact, not simply a here-and-now-and-always reality, not complete in itself. The nature and possibilities of anything human can be disclosed only if its temporality is taken seriously. So the university must necessarily understand itself in its traditions and its promise, in all the variant realizations that historical circumstances will evoke, but it also must recognize the possibilities of its own death. "Human creations," wrote Sigmund Freud, "are easily destroyed."[5] Both the liabilities of any human project and contemporary readings of the Catholic university, then, should make us peculiarly sensitive to the threat irretrievably native to such a life-form: the Catholic university can be destroyed; it can destroy itself in a dissolution that proceeds gradually and as imperceptibly as drops of water noiselessly permeate a sponge.[6]

If this is true, then, one can only read the mission statements of some Catholic universities with a sense of regret. The very vagueness of their language and the indeterminacy of their general commitments leave one with the sense that the decline in some institutions may be already advanced, that the conjunction between a vibrant Catholicism or a Catholic culture and these universities appears increasingly faint, that the vision may be fading. Presumably the mission statement is the document in which the university expresses its self-understanding, its character and its dreams—to be confirmed or attenuated through subsequent resource allocations and hiring. The apostolic constitution *Ex corde Ecclesiae* is not alone in its expectation that there, or in some similar document, "every Catholic university is to make known its Catholic identity" (art. 2, sec. 3).

Let me confine myself to three mission statements that come out of Catholic colleges and universities, each of them Jesuit. They frame general statements about education within the Jesuit or Judeo-Christian or Catholic tradition and identify the university as Jesuit or Catholic. They allude to the "service of faith and the promotion of justice," the generic focus given to all Jesuit apostolic commitments by the order's Thirty-Second General Congregation.[7] However, there is not much beyond this level of generality. When one has left deference and set phrases behind, they do not indicate how this Catholic tradition tells significantly and uniquely upon the educational core of these institutions. "Faith and justice" does not concretely play out as much more than a general ideal for all apostolic work; certainly it is not specified as an ideal precisely for higher education or for an academic integration of gospel and culture. The faith of Christianity—what constitutes the content and richness of the creed and inspired two thousand years of Catholic reflection and life—seems reduced to a general social ethic or morality. It is not what is contained in these documents that suggests decline. On the contrary, they make many fine and important commitments. The problem is what is left out or reduced to bland generalities.

Contextualized by that tradition and wishing that the students develop their "full range of human qualities: intellectual, personal, social, moral, and spiritual," University X will afford students "the opportunity to have meaningful contact with art, music, history, philosophy, literature, and the religions of the world." This is the only mention of "religion" in a statement devoid of reference to the self-disclosure of God or to Christ or to the Catholic church and in which the term *church* appears only to indicate the history of "service to church and state" that has characterized Jesuit colleges since the founding of Georgetown. I submit that Occidental or Smith could and would be willing to say almost as much, i.e., to speak respectfully of their religious traditions, to espouse "spiritual" development and to include with their commitment to the liberal arts the study of "the religions of the world."

The goals do not advance much beyond this faint picture. The only implication for the Jesuit tradition in education is that this institution "aims to emphasize the importance of moral and spiritual values; to offer religious studies on an academic, ecumenical, professional basis; and to provide opportunities for religious worship and activities." Once again, it is hard to see any real difference between this and the goals set by any number of serious liberal arts colleges, once committed to a particular religious tradition.

In the prologue to its statement of identity, University Y also acknowledges the tradition out of which it comes, a religious heritage that comprises "compassionate service of persons in need, commitment to quality education, the service of faith and the promotion of justice." When one comes to the mission statement itself and how these charisms tell upon the academic community, one finds stated that "the University takes its mission from its educational traditions which emphasize concern for the dignity of the person and for the common good of the world community. This education seeks to integrate intellectual, spiritual, moral and social development." Later in the document, "religious" will be added to this list, and the university said "to provide a value-based holistic education of exceptional quality."

Whatever its rich tradition, this mission statement has a vision so indefinite in anything specifically Christian that a good secular university could almost locate itself comfortably within its rubrics. Granted its impressive emphasis upon social leadership and responsibilities, the statement does not advance much beyond American civil religion and a committed social ethic. One looks in vain for anything that needs or demands—as inescapably appropriate—the name of God, of Christ, of church, and of theology or indeed for anything uniquely Christian or Catholic in the paragraphs that speak of the core curriculum. They do not appear. What I found here, I found in others. The Catholic,

Christian character was shaded off into a vacuity that offers neither specification nor direction to the education given by the institution.

One could take University Z as a final example, an institution whose

> primary objectives are to develop the creative intellectual potential of its students and to foster in them ethical and religious values and a sense of social responsibility. Jesuit Education, which began in 1547, is committed today to the service of faith, of which the promotion of justice is an absolute requirement. [University Z] is Catholic in both tradition and spirit. It celebrates the God-given dignity of every human person.

This university is satisfied to give the generic orientation of the Society of Jesus and to offer as the only academic specification of the Catholic tradition and spirit the celebration "of the God-given dignity of every human person" and the welcome given to diversity. Beyond this, nothing is offered in the paragraphs that follow about the vision that Catholicism carries and about any unique character that such a Catholic, Jesuit commitment effects within the institution. Nothing specifically religious or theological figures in the descriptions of the liberal arts and professional schools, nothing about the interchange between culture and gospel or about how the genius of Catholicism tells upon the kind of student that the university hopes to produce. It would be hard to imagine any cultivated pagan who could not embrace the actual educational ideals that are concretely enumerated.

If I were to guess the reason for the blandness in these documents, my suspicion is that it emerges as the liability of a general advance. Over these years, the Catholic university has progressively added more and more faculty from traditions other than its own. This seems to me significant progress. It is essential to the very nature of a university to have represented the variant forms of human culture within the university. But then when one attempts to write a common statement of mission or purpose for the institution and to pass this through the faculty, the diversity within the faculty inhibits anything much beyond religious banalities. No faculty member should be excluded or made to feel second class; none should be imposed upon. Further, Catholics can remember the narrowness of parochial rubrics that denominated the Catholic character of preconciliar higher education. What emerges is the lowest common denominator, offending no one and subsuming the Catholic commitments of the university under general phrases about tradition and slogans that have become almost politically correct.

This may also result from the need to garner funds from state and federal agencies or from foundations or benefactors suspicious of religion. But here the history of the nineteenth century may be repeating itself:

> Philanthropic foundations also figured in the secularization of higher education. The Carnegie Foundation before World War I specifically

excluded church-related schools from receiving grants, holding that such institutions by definition put limits on intellectual freedom and could not meet the test of a true college or university. In 1905, it offered to fund pensions for faculty, but restricted eligibility to nonsectarian higher education. Anxious for financial support, Bowdoin, Wesleyan, Rochester, Drake, Coe, Hanover, Occidental, and other schools cut their already tenuous denominational ties. In the century following the Civil War, several hundred colleges, once strongly Protestant, became officially non-sectarian.[8]

Other examples could be selected from the identity statements of Catholic universities, but let these three suffice. I say this not to embarrass academic institutions that have served the church well and continue to do so today. I do not disparage these universities in any way. But it is precisely when such institutions have allowed the Catholic character of their education to be subsumed by contextual references to a religious heritage, by general phrases that bespeak this tradition but remain unspecified for American higher education, and by moralisms that any enlightened figure would applaud, then one who admires them and hopes for great things from them cannot but suspect some decline at least in collective vision. This seems to me an enormously serious situation.

SOME RESPONSES

In response to the threat or anticipation of such a decline, outstanding Catholic educators have attempted to articulate for our own time the meaning of such a distinct academic institution as the American Catholic university. Some have described the Catholic university as one in which there is a strong Catholic presence, and others have defined it through the activities of campus ministry and the presence of religious and Catholic lay faculty and a requirement in religious studies or in theology.

Let me take only one example. In his annual report for the academic year 1980-1981, the late Timothy Healy, an important, much loved and admired Jesuit educator, framed the issue in this manner: "How does the Church live within a university? How do the two institutions interact on common ground? Indeed how do they share in the minds and hearts of faculty and students? In more local terms, what is it that makes and keeps Georgetown Catholic?"

In response, Father Healy suggested a vision in which the church and the university are cast as two distinct, interacting institutions: "The Church also lives here [in a Catholic university] in two distinct ways: first, it leads *its own life* on our grounds; secondly, the Church *joins in, shares and influences the life and the work of the university* itself."[9] In explaining the latter, Father Healy maintained that at Georgetown "education remains principally a secular business, and the university is a secular entity with a clear secular job to do. The Church can deeply influence how that secular job is done."[10] Presumably the Catholic university is a secular reality modified by the presence and the influence of the sacred—without ceasing to be its secular self.

EXTRINSICISM

For whatever truth each of these possesses, such understandings seem to me seriously inadequate. At best, they present a vision of the Catholic university in which the religious and the academic, however interrelating and intersecting, are fundamentally extrinsic to one another: in no way does either bring the other to its own intrinsic or inherent completion nor do they form a cultural unity. Such an understanding of the Catholic university reads like theologically dated theories of "pure nature" and "the supernatural." Father Healy's "two distinct ways" in which the church is to share in an institution could describe the presence of the church within any major secular society, as the church "joins in, shares, and influences the life and work" of the city of San Francisco, the deliberations of the federal government, and the University of Massachusetts, the essentially secular somewhat directed and shaped by the religious.

To understand the genius and the unique academic promise of the Catholic university, however, one cannot make the relationship between knowledge and faith, nature and supernature, the "secular" and the "sacred" extrinsic to each other, two distinct entities related to each other additionally or influentially. The failure of so many *apologiae* for the Catholic university may well issue from a heritage of the neo-scholastic misunderstanding and miscasting of the relationship between nature and grace.

For one must not think that this extrinsicism is a modern compromise, a contemporary concession to secular respectability. From 1894-1952, the annual catalog of Boston College carried a four-page statement of the educational system of this Catholic institution, informing its readers that

> education is understood by the Fathers of the Society in its completest sense, as the full and harmonious development of all those faculties that are distinctive of man . . . Learning is an instrument of education, not its end. The end is culture, and mental and moral development.

There follows a detailed exposition of the academic training of the student, defended in terms of the training of faculties.

Religion, let alone theology, is not mentioned until the last paragraphs:

> Lastly, the system does not share the illusion of those who seem to imagine that education, understood as an enriching and stimulating of

the intellectual faculties, has a morally elevating influence in human life. While conceding the effects of education in energizing and refining imagination, taste, understanding and powers of observation, it has always held that knowledge and intellectual development of themselves have no moral efficacy. *Religion* only can purify the heart, and guide and strengthen the will.

The Jesuit system of education, then, aims at developing, side by side, the moral and intellectual faculties of the student and sending forth to the world men of sound judgment, of acute and rounded intellect, of upright and manly conscience. And since men are not made better citizens by the mere accumulation of knowledge, without a guiding and controlling force, the principal faculties to be developed are the moral faculties.[11]

The catalog is quite clear. The secular subjects develop the intellect in habits and knowledge; the teaching of religion develops the student morally. By the most amazing of paradoxes, this is not too distant from the secularist's distinction: science deals with facts; religion deals with values. What is even more remarkable is that this statement "was embodied in whole or in part in the catalogs of a number of other Jesuit colleges from coast to coast."[12] The reduction of religion to morality has a long history.

Is that simply because the prose of the catalog failed to do justice to the Catholic character of the college? Yes and no. The Catholic colleges of those years—many, a combination of what is now the four-year high school and three years of college—were custodial institutions: Catholic because their components were Catholic—students, faculty, administrators—with courses that excluded alien influences and libraries and textbooks ecclesiastically censored. These institutions were to safeguard the faith and morals of their students and to defend Catholic truth against contemporary error. Much of the "Catholic character" of these institutions came out of this custodial focus and penetrated the discipline, the round of studies, the conversations, and the expectations of the campus. The Catholic culture of these institutions sustained much of their Catholic character, e.g., the daily Mass, First Friday devotions, and monthly confession.

But that being said, the catalog was more a mirror than a distortion. Theology was not taught; religion was; and philosophy was taken as the culmination of the curriculum. These courses in religion were catechetical and apologetic and not infrequently taught by the more inept members of the faculty. What is important to notice even during these years is the separation of serious studies and professional education from an inherent relationship with theological reflection. Religion was for propositional orthodoxy and Christian morality. In no way did it organically come out of the other disciplines, bringing the dynamism of the mind to its native completion in the self-revelation of

God. One can legitimately explore not so much how Catholic such an institution was, but how much of a Catholic *university*.[13]

It is, then, critically important to note—perhaps especially in our present inquiry into the identity of the Catholic university—that the contemporary problematic does not present a single vector, that of inevitable or threatened decline. Like most historical phenomena, the situation emerges far more pluriform and complicated than such an oversimplification would express. For example, the Catholic character of the universities has been strengthened significantly by the attention given to theology. Catholic theology, either as a graduate or undergraduate discipline, has become a much more serious, academic presence on the campus. As a result of this change in curriculum, there can be found in the United States something unprecedented in the history of the church: thousands of young women and men studying theology in their early adult years with the intellectual care that higher education offers. In addition, theology itself is becoming no longer a clerical preserve, but a lay discipline as well. This bespeaks a radical change in the nature of these institutions and an enormous contribution to the contemporary church. Another such positive vector is the growing commitment to social justice and the number of students who give some time after graduation to religious volunteer groups.[14]

Such positive indicators do not settle the question about the possible decline in religious identity, and academic courses do not supply for the intellectual formation that only a vital Catholic culture can give, but they may well contribute to the hope that the issue can be addressed effectively. One must admit that, in the lack of a structured relationship among the disciplines within the curriculum, these disciplines and theology still embody an extrinsicism. Theology is one more course among others.

THE INHERENT INTEGRITY OF THE ACADEMIC AND THE RELIGIOUS

The fundamental proposition of the Catholic university is that the religious and the academic are intrinsically related. Any movement toward meaning and truth is inchoatively religious. This obviously does not suggest that quantum mechanics or geography is religion or theology; it does mean that the dynamism inherent in all inquiry and knowledge—if not inhibited—is toward ultimacy, toward a completion in which an issue or its resolution finds place in a universe that makes final sense, i.e., in the self-disclosure of God—the truth of the finite. At the same time, the tendencies of faith are inescapably toward the academic. This obviously does not suggest that all serious religion is scholarship; it does mean that the dynamism inherent in faith—if not inhibited—is toward its own understanding, toward its own self-possession in knowledge. In their full development, the religious intrinsically involves the academic, and the academic intrinsically involves the religious—granted that this development is *de facto* always imperfectly realized at best or even seriously frustrated.

To grasp the character or promise of the Catholic university, one must understand this unique institution as an organic fulfillment of the two drives for knowledge out of which it issues: the drive of inquiry toward an ultimacy or that comprehensive meaning that is the object of religion; the drive of Christian faith, i.e., of living within the self-giving of God in Christ and in the Spirit, toward the appropriation of this comprehensive experience in understanding. The inherent integrity of faith-experience moving toward intelligence and of finite intelligence moving toward completion, this mutual entailment is what a Catholic university must affirm and embody, however halting and imperfect its attempts.

It is no accident that historically the university issued out of the church—not the hierarchy alone, but the people of God, the community that is the sacrament of human salvation. The present pope has stated that "such an ecclesial origin of the university cannot have been fortuitous. Rather it expresses something more profound. But why does the church need the university? . . . The reason for this need should be sought in the very mission of the church. In fact, the faith that the church announces is to be a *fides quaerens intellectum,* a faith that demands to penetrate human intelligence, to be thought out by the intellect of the human person."[15] The Catholic university is that academic community of higher education that issues out of the church and in which the church—in the words of the Second Vatican Council—"strives to relate all human culture to the announcement of salvation."[16]

The Catholic university is to obtain this intrinsic relationship of culture and gospel in the ways in which it is a university: in research and instruction and the conversations that give a peculiar mark to its spirit; in service and symbols and collective life and the richness of an ecumenical Catholic culture; in the intellectual growth of its students and faculty and in the sharing of the diverse traditions out of which they come; in the passion for a just society that must characterize its graduates and that will in turn measure the religious and humane quality of their education. For the promised Spirit of Truth is to guide us into all truth—not only to know the truth, but to do the truth in lives driven by compassion and the desire to serve.

The university is Catholic in its deliberate determination to render the church and the broader world this unique service: to be an intellectual community where in utter academic freedom the variant lines of Catholic tradition and thought can intersect with the most complex challenges, contradictions, and reinforcements of contemporary thought or "secular culture" and move toward a reflective unity—whether in the habits of the students or in the direction of the research or in the community life of the academic community—between world culture and the self-revelation of God.[17] It is not that these simply intersect, but that one is seen as bringing the other to its own completion: the self-disclosure of God effected through revelation is completed in knowledge; the human dynamic to understand is completed in the self-disclosure of God. The Catholic university exists to further the development of both serious faith and all the forms of knowledge. No other institution within human culture can render this unique and critically important contribution to the church and to the contemporary world.

This unique finality gives or should give a particular cast to the internal academic structure of the university, both in the priority of questions its research will entertain and in its evaluation of the knowledge that is most worth having as well as in the common life that it fosters as its own culture. Such an order of questions for inquiry and of knowledge for instruction gives each institution of higher learning its formal identity and integrating spirit. In a Catholic university, this organic integrity of the several disciplines and sciences should be embodied in a theological wisdom in which all of the sciences and arts, professions, and forms of human achievement are integrated both in the structure of the curriculum and in the habits of mind that such an education should elicit.

It is not that the university is an institution in which the church—almost as a foreign body—is present and has an influence. It is rather that the university is a single community, one constituted by the drive toward the unity of the gospel with all human culture, one formed by its consecration to "the Spirit of Truth." In the fine expression of the apostolic constitution: "A Catholic university pursues its objectives through its formation of an authentic human community animated by the spirit of Christ" (n. 21). That is why this community must include within itself all that passes for knowledge, all human traditions and cultures as well as the academic freedom that makes open discussion possible. Without the active presence of all of these various traditions, it would be impossible to promote this relationship of the gospel "to all human culture."[18] The fullness of the academic is essential if Christianity is to achieve its reflective depth and union with all that is human; and the seriously religious is essential if the pursuit of knowledge is to attend to its own reach toward ultimacy and final meaning.

IDENTITY

When one talks about identity, one does it often in "substantial" terms, granting that a university is not a substance or a person, but defining it as if it were— as if there were a substantial reality that continues to grow or decline. So, for example, canon law can speak of public and private juridical persons. But however useful such fictions are in law, it is not the case that the university is a substance and in actual fact it can be misleading to speak of it as if it were a substance. It is a network of relationships, built upon the activities that these relationships entail and that are in turn supported by them. In Aristotelian metaphysics, the university is a relation built upon the giving and receiving, the actions and the undergoings of human experience. This means that the university has the character that its activities give it, and these themselves must be recognized as historical, as temporal, as variant in different cultures and as dynamically ordered to a future.

This bears upon the discussions of identity: what a Catholic university is. Sometimes that definition is made descriptively: one finds out what is called a Catholic university and then describes its operations. Sometimes that definition is made prescriptively: one searches the documents and then deduces from them what is a "real" Catholic university. Both of these have their values, but each has its limitations. The descriptive model can excise vision and challenge; the prescriptive model can describe a university that never was and never will be. A further possibility lies with taking the dynamic, developing components of such a university as a point of departure and seeing in the term of their inherent development and organic relationship the nature of the Catholic university. One can understand what anything dynamic is through its completion, i.e., through its native promise—even though so much of this remains to be realized. Let me take this last method to summarize much of the argument of this paper.

The components of the Catholic university can be subsumed under faith and human culture, however multiple the realization of either. But faith, I have argued, tends organically and inherently toward the academic and the academic in the same intrinsic manner tends toward an ultimacy through which knowledge reaches its completion, i.e., the self-disclosure of God. This inherent unity bespeaks the promise of the Catholic university: to allow the dynamism native to each to reach its completion in the other. Rather than truncate the dynamism of knowing through interdicting the religious dimension of life or isolating the religious from the academic, the Catholic university has the resources and the charge to integrate them by allowing each its full development.

Something of this occurs in the Catholic universities of the United States. I would suggest that they realize their own unique identity to the degree that this integration is their achievement. No other institution in the church can promote the full development and embody the inherent dynamic unity between the academic and the religious. This may constitute the major challenge for the contemporary Catholic universities: to become gradually what they are, to realize their identity, to allow what is prescriptive discourse to become valid description. In this identity is their promise; in this promise is their identity.

EX CORDE ECCLESIAE

Now I turn to *Ex corde Ecclesiae* on this issue of identity. I find such a call in the apostolic constitution. Its emphatic identification of the issue of identity as that of the organic integration of faith and knowledge is not found so much in the document itself and its norms as with the papal introduction.[19] These first eleven paragraphs take up precisely the point I think crucial, the inherent and dynamic integration of the academic and the religious. The pope phrases the unity as that of a "universal humanism," which conjoins reflectively all "aspects of the truth in their essential connection with the supreme Truth, who is God" (n. 4). The components that are brought to their natural unity are variously described as "faith and reason" (n. 5) or "the richness of revelation and of nature" (n. 5) or "the Gospel" and "the fields of knowledge" (n. 6) or the church with science and world cultures (n. 10). The pope envisages in the university "the united endeavor of intelligence and faith that will enable people to come to the full measure of their humanity, created in the image and likeness of God, renewed even more marvelously after sin, in Christ, and called to shine forth in the light of the Spirit" (n. 5).

Such a united endeavor issues out of an "encounter . . . between the unfathomable richness of the salvific message of the Gospel and the variety and immensity of the fields of knowledge" (n. 6). The "encounter" with a clear determination of its components brings the discussion of the specificity of the Catholic university into a focus that seems absent from a number of mission statements of the American Catholic universities. The papal introduction does not speak explicitly of the native dynamism of the intellect for the ultimacies of the religious or of the religious for its self-possession in knowledge, but it suggests this organic unity of desire with its understanding of the Catholic university as "distinguished by its free search for the whole truth about nature, man, and God" (n. 4). And it strengthens this mutual orientation with its appeal to Augustine and Anselm: *"Intellege ut credas; crede ut intellegas"* (n. 5).

The initial section of the apostolic constitution takes up the Catholic university as described by the final document of the Second International Congress of Delegates of Catholic Universities, and here the theory seems to me less satisfactory. The list of four characteristics is neither clear nor is its adequacy self-evident (n. 13); and the university is distinguished into the community of scholars conceptually distinct from "an academic institution in which Catholicism is vitally present and operative" (n. 14). But in this section also the unitive functions of the university are given an important emphasis: the integration of the disciplines with the aid of philosophy and theology; the dialogic integration between faith and reason, both bearing witness to the unity of truth; the unity of the ethical and scientific; and the intergrative function of theology (nn. 16-19).

What is critical to note is that these forms of the unity between the academic and the religious are placed within the elaboration of the identity of the Catholic university. What the norms will later legislate must be seen as instrumental to this finality, as subservient to it, and they are to be judged accordingly. The apostolic constitution allows such judgments, permitting flexibility in their incorporation into the statutes of Catholic universities through the phrase "as much as possible" (art. 1, sec. 3).

What are the implications, then, of the apostolic constitution *Ex corde Ecclesiae,* for the American Catholic universities? It is calling for a much stronger, much more concrete affirmation or articulation of the Catholic character of these universities and calling for it as an organic unity between the gospel and culture. In this, it seems to me, *Ex corde Ecclesiae* performs a valuable, needed service. The apostolic constitution can be read as an opportune summons of the church for these universities to possess a deeper, more articulate sense of what they are before the Catholic, Christian character evanesces into directionless vagueness and finally disappears. Such calls at such a time seem needed. William P. Leahy concludes his recent study of Catholic higher education with this judgment: "Catholic postsecondary schools suffer from a lack of vision; and as Proverbs 29:18 proclaims, 'Where there is no vision, the people perish.' "[20]

The American Catholic universities will not likely receive a more authoritative summons to renew their vision, to become what they are, however appropriate or inappropriate one finds particular statements or norms by which this identity is to be fostered. (These latter this paper will not consider so that the importance of this general summons is not crowded out by a series of tactical considerations.)

But will such a voice and such a summons be heard? The dangerously growing alienation from the Holy See within the United States may well make this more difficult than it should be. Many in the Catholic academy have been alienated by what they see as an excessive centralization in the church and— more particularly in the fields of education—by the impositions of mandates, professions of faith, and oaths of fidelity and by repeated reports of the unwarranted use of the present powers of the Holy See to inhibit academic appointments or promotions or public recognition through honorary degrees.

This is admittedly a very serious situation, but to cite it as grounds for denying the central summons of *Ex corde Ecclesiae* a sympathetic hearing would be tragic. This voice and this summons to a more definitive understanding of the Catholic university deserve to be heard.

NOTES

1. This statement was found in Maclean's files after his death along with other notes that he had written for a preface. See "Publisher's Note," *Young Men and Fire* (Chicago: University of Chicago Press, 1992), p. vii.

2. David R. Carlin, Jr., "From Ghetto to Hilltop: Our Colleges, Our Selves," *Commonweal* 120 (February 12, 1993): 7.

3. See Friedrich Nietzsche, *Die Fröhliche Wissenschaft,* iii.125.

4. Robert M. Hutchins, "The Integrating Principle of Catholic Higher Education," Address delivered at the Midwest Regional Unit of the College and University Depart-

ment of the National Catholic Educational Association, 7 April 1937, *College Newsletter, Midwest Regional Unity, NCEA* (May 1937), pp. 1, 4. In describing collegiatism, Hutchins speaks of "the production of well-tubbed young Americans. They don't have much in the heads, but are acceptable as decoration of at least one political party and make good additions to a house-party."

5. Sigmund Freud, *The Future of an Illusion,* trans. James Strachey (New York: W. W. Norton, 1961), p. 6.

6. Ignatius of Loyola used this metaphor—"como gota de agua que entra en una esponja"—to denote the gradual, almost unnoticeable progress of either disintegration or of development. See "Rules for Discernment of Spirits," II.7, in *The Spiritual Exercises,* trans. and ed. Joseph Rickaby (London: Burns, Oates, Ltd., 1915), p. 117.

7. See "Jesuits Today," decree 2 of the Thirty-Second General Congregation of the Society of Jesus, nn. 1-3; "Our Mission Today," decree 4 of the Thirty-Second General Congregation, pass., etc., as in *Documents of the 31st and 32nd General Congregations of the Society of Jesus, An English Translation,* prepared by the Jesuit Conference, ed. John W. Padberg, S.J. (St. Louis: Institute of Jesuit Sources, 1977).

8. William P. Leahy, S.J., *Adapting to America: Catholics, Jesuits, and Higher Education in the Twentieth Century* (Washington, D.C.: Georgetown University Press, 1991), p. 16.

9. Timothy Healy, S.J., "Belief and Teaching," *Georgetown Magazine* (January-February 1982), p. 3; italics added.

10. Ibid., pp. 4-5. One of the five ways the church can shape the university is through the presence of theology, but the value of theology seems mostly therapeutic: Academic theology challenges absolute science, absolute art, absolute athletics, etc., and denies the completeness of any other kinds and subsets of learning. See pp. 6-7.

11. Charles F. Donovan, S.J., "Father Timothy Brosnahan, National Spokesman for Jesuit Liberal Education, Boston College President, 1894-1898" (unpublished manuscript), pp. 5-7. For the appearance and duration of this statement, see p. 1.

12. Charles F. Donovan, S.J., David R. Dunigan, S.J., Paul A. FitzGerald, S.J., *History of Boston College from the Beginnings to 1990* (Chestnut Hill, Mass.: University Press of Boston College, 1990), p. 99.

13. See Michael J. Buckley, S.J., "The Catholic University as Pluralistic Forum," *Thought* 46 (June 1971): 202-205.

14. For the need to include within the liberal or humanistic education of the student a "disciplined sensitivity to human life in its very ordinary or even wretched forms," as a foundational stage toward a sense of human solidarity, see Michael J. Buckley, S.J., "The University and the Concern for Social Justice: The Search for a New Humanism," *Thought* 57 (June 1982): 229-33.

15. John Paul II, "The Church Needs the University," 8 March 1982, *L'Osservatore Romano,* English edition (May 3, 1982), p. 6.

16. *Gravissimum educationis,* n. 8. The actual Latin of this text that gives the finality of all Catholic education reads: "universam culturam humanam ad nuntium salutis prostremo ordinare." Joseph Alberigo et al., ed., *Conciliorum oecumenicorum decreta,* editio 3 (Bologna: Instituto per le scienze religose, 1973), p. 964.

17. This is a slightly reworked statement from Buckley, "The Catholic University as Pluralistic Forum," p. 208. This statement is also contained in "Jesuit, Catholic

Higher Education: Some Tentative Theses," *Review for Religious* 42 (May-June 1983), p. 343 as well as in a report on the nature of a Catholic university, given to the members of the Academic and Faculty Affairs Committee of the Board of Trustees of Notre Dame University on 2 May 1991. For the conjunction of this with some of the areas in which this purpose is obtained, see the first draft of the Mission Statement of the University of Notre Dame as printed in *The Observer* (Monday, September 7, 1992), pp. 6-7.

18. See Buckley, "Jesuit, Catholic Higher Education," pp. 343-44.

19. This paper will not touch upon the canonical declarations and norms of *Ex corde Ecclesiae.* For a fine analysis of these, see James H. Provost, "The Canonical Aspects of Catholic Identity in the Light of *Ex corde Ecclesiae,*" *Studia Canonica* 25 (1991): 155-91.

20. Leahy, *Adapting to America,* p. 156.

COMMENT

REV. DAVID HOLLENBACH, S.J., *Boston College*

INTELLECTUAL AND SOCIAL SOLIDARITY

Michael Buckley's paper is a timely challenge to a deeper kind of reflection on the promise and identity of the Catholic university than has been common in recent decades. Since the Second Vatican Council, Catholic universities in the United States have been undergoing rapid changes that mirror the shifting place of Catholics in American society and culture. The Catholic community has moved from being a sort of religious and cultural enclave, largely insulated from the society around it, to having full and free participation in the mainstream of its pluralistic environment. This changed location of the church was brought about in part by the Council's renunciation of former claims by the church to a privileged role in political society and by the Council's acknowledgment of the reality of pluralism and of a legitimate autonomy of culture and the sciences from hegemonic control by the church.[1] In a similar way, Catholic universities have sought to demonstrate that the principles of academic freedom and wholehearted respect for methods of rigorous academic inquiry mean that they are true universities, not branch offices of the Holy See or the local diocesan chancery office. Both American Catholics in general and Catholic universities in particular have rejected that mode of pre-Vatican II Catholic thought and practice known as integralism—a view that in society and the academy all wisdom can be deduced from religious or theological premises.

Father Buckley's paper presupposes these developments in the self-understanding of American Catholic universities. It has been observed, however, that the movement of Catholics into the mainstream of American social and political life threatens to dilute the distinctive contributions their faith and tradition can make to that life. In the same way, Buckley is worried that recent trends

90

threaten to alienate faith and reason from each other in a way that is damaging to *both* the religious *and* the academic dimensions of the Catholic university. He rightly argues that a Catholic understanding of the relation of faith and reason implies that the religious and academic are intrinsically related to each other: "The self-disclosure of God effected through revelation is completed in knowledge; the human dynamic to understand is completed in the self-disclosure of God." The Council's rejection of integralist arguments that only through church-state unity can the church bring the light of the gospel to bear on social and political life did not mean that the gospel should be privatized or marginalized from public life. Far from it. Again in the same way, Buckley's full acceptance of the integrity of the academic and its legitimate autonomy from stifling ecclesiastical control in no way means the bifurcation of the academic and religious dimensions of a Catholic university's identity.

Buckley's argument on the relation of the academic and the religious parallels John Courtney Murray's reflections on the mission of the church in secular society in light of the Second Vatican Council's acknowledgment of the reality of pluralism and its affirmation of the right to religious freedom. Murray said that the Council recognized that

> A work of differentiation between the sacral and the secular has been effected within history. But differentiation is not the highest stage in human growth. The movement toward it, now that it has come to term, must be followed by a further movement toward a new synthesis, within which the differentiation will at once subsist, integral and unconfused, and also be transcended in a higher unity.[2]

Achieving such a higher unity of the religious and academic, a unity in which the full integrity of each is maintained, is the great challenge facing Catholic universities today. On this central point I am in full agreement with Buckley. I also agree with him that there is enough evidence to warrant at least a fear that the challenge is not being adequately met.

Buckley states that the intrinsic linkage of the religious and the academic is a historical, temporal process in which "faith . . . tends organically and inherently toward the academic and the academic in the same intrinsic manner tends toward an ultimacy through which knowledge reaches its completion, i.e., the self-disclosure of God." This way of stating the issue contains resonant echoes of Thomas Aquinas's robust confidence in the complementarity of faith and reason, grace and nature. I fully affirm this complementarity as the ultimate word that needs to be spoken about the connection of the religious and the academic. At the same time, I think realism demands that we not forget Augustine's somewhat less sanguine emphasis: we are dealing not only with the ultimate complementarity of nature and grace, but also with the struggles between sin and grace in all of human history, including the history that unfolds in both the university and the church.

This means that there can be conflicts, sometimes very deep ones, that impede the achievement of an integration of the religious and the academic. On the academic side, the diversity of disciplinary methods and the deepening awareness of the cultural pluralism of our world discourage efforts to achieve an integration of the multiple forms of knowledge. Intellectual specialization can easily close academic disciplines, including theology, to insights that arise beyond the boundaries of their fields of inquiry. This situation has led a number of contemporary thinkers to conclude that all we can aspire to in intellectual life are fragments of meaning. Further, these fragments are sometimes regarded as purely human constructs rather than vistas onto what is real or true. Thus our historical period is witnessing the return of an intellectual tendency that has appeared before with the Sophists in ancient Greece and with the nominalists of the late Middle Ages and early modern period—a tendency that denies the capacity of the human mind to grasp the truth of reality, whether this reality be mundane or divine. As with the Sophists and nominalists in the past, this can lead to the reduction of intellectual undertakings to matters of power and will. Where suspicion grows of any claim to know the whole or the ultimate, even through a glass darkly, it generates a deep bias against taking religious or theological matters seriously within the academic context.

While I affirm with Buckley that the religious and the academic are intrinsically linked at the deepest level, a number of the surface phenomena of academic culture today can be real obstacles to the articulation of this connection. In addition, lingering tendencies toward ecclesiastical or theological domination reinforce this suspicion in Catholic universities. Therefore the effort to pursue the mutual completion of the academic and the religious through each other is likely to be characterized by a measure of conflict. The harmony of faith and reason is not something that can be simply presumed; we must also be prepared to struggle to attain it.

The spirit that is required for this endeavor might be called intellectual solidarity—a willingness to take other persons and other intellectual methods seriously enough to engage them in conversation and debate about what makes life worth living. Such a spirit is partially the same but entirely different from an appeal to tolerance. Tolerance is a strategy of noninterference with the beliefs and intellectual styles that are different from one's own. The spirit of intellectual solidarity is similar to tolerance in that it recognizes and respects these differences. It does not seek to eliminate pluralism through coercion. But it differs radically from pure tolerance by seeking positive engagement with other persons and modes of thinking through both listening and speaking. It is rooted in a hope that understanding might replace incomprehension and that perhaps even agreement could result. When conversation and argument between the tradition of Catholic belief and all the diverse forms of contemporary thought and culture take place with all the rigor of serious academic inquiry, the Catholic university comes into being.

In what must appear as something of a paradox, the virtues that are needed to pursue such a conversation successfully are simultaneously courage and humility. Those who seek to discover the intrinsic links between faith and culture will need courage because on occasion, perhaps even frequently, this effort will be resisted by strong currents in academic life today. These currents are present in the American Catholic university, so courage will be needed within it. Such courage is also needed because the challenge of linking faith and culture is a more arduous intellectual undertaking today than ever before, precisely because of the complexity and diversity of contemporary academic disciplines and because of the deep pluralism of global culture. Only a protracted and sustained process of inquiry will make the effort to link faith and culture even partially successful. For this, intellectual as well as moral fortitude will be needed.

At the same time, this dialogue requires humility. Specialists in all the academic disciplines, including theology, need to recognize the limits of their modes of thought and must be ready to encounter and learn from ways of thinking that are different. This intellectual humility is very different from the skepticism about our ability to assess the adequacy or truth of the claims of religious faith that is widely present in American universities and culture at large. It also counters those Promethean and Nietzschean currents in the academy that maintain that all knowledge is a human construct and a projection of human will and power. Though the presence of these currents in the university is often exaggerated, it would be a mistake to underestimate their influence. In my judgment they can threaten the academic project itself and undercut any attempt to uncover the connections between the religious and the academic.

Both courage and humility will also be needed if the Catholic university is to rise to the challenge of integrating the commitment to the *social solidarity* that has moved to the center of the Catholic tradition's self-understanding during the years since the Second Vatican Council. Buckley notes that several Jesuit universities include references in their mission statements to a kind of education that promotes a faith that issues forth in active efforts to achieve a more just world. Such a commitment is not, as some have suggested, a way of politicizing the university or turning it into a school for activists.

Both Buckley and I are in agreement that there is a profoundly intellectual task involved here that deserves the full attention of the Catholic university as both university and Catholic. The intellectual solidarity that is required if religion and the academic are to be brought into a higher unity must be accompanied by a social solidarity that links the Catholic university to the struggles of a world marred by high levels of poverty among American children, by lack of health insurance for large numbers of Americans, by the attempts at genocide in Bosnia, by the explosive potential for race war in South Africa, to name only a few of the most obvious recent events in the long history of human beings' sinful propensity to treat one another in inhuman ways. As Buckley has noted elsewhere, the origins of the Catholic university in the Middle Ages and its development by the Jesuits and other religious communities at the dawn of the modern period were manifestations of the conviction that a Christian humanism is both possible and required by the dynamic of Christian faith itself. The challenge of Christian humanism remains central to the task of achieving the identity of Catholic universities. But today that humanism must be a social humanism, a humanism that recognizes that it must address not only heights to which human culture can rise but also the depths of suffering into which societies can descend.[3] There are strong currents in American life today that insulate both professors and students from experience of and academic reflection on these sufferings. A university that aspires to be Catholic must do more than include nods to the importance of social solidarity in its mission statement. It must translate this importance into teaching and research priorities and integrate the commitment to these priorities into its day-to-day activities in classroom and library. To do so will take both the courage and the humility that the privileged learn only when they encounter the reality of poverty and other forms of suffering.

On the academic scene today these are a few of the obstacles I see to the realization of the identity and promise of the Catholic university. I have not sketched them to induce discouragement or to suggest that Buckley's vision is utopian. Rather my intent is to encourage us to focus not only on the ultimate objective of achieving a greater integration of the religious and the academic, but also on some of the more immediate challenges we must face in the effort to do so. In light of these challenges, it might be possible to develop priorities in the research and teaching of the Catholic university today that will bring it closer to realizing the promise that is its identity.

NOTES

1. *Dignitatis humanae,* passim, and *Gaudium et spes,* nn. 53, 59, in *The Documents of Vatican II,* ed. Walter M. Abbott and Joseph Gallagher (New York: America Press, 1966).

2. John Courtney Murray, "The Declaration on Religious Freedom: Its Deeper Significance," *America,* 23 April 1966, p. 593.

3. See Michael J. Buckley, "The University and the Concern for Justice: The Search for a New Humanism," *Thought* 57 (1982): 219-33; and "Christian Humanism and Human Misery: A Challenge to the Jesuit University," in *Faith, Discovery, Service: Perspectives on Jesuit Education,* ed. Michael J. Buckley et al. (Milwaukee: Marquette University Press, 1992), pp. 77-105.

COMMENT

RABBI DAVID NOVAK, *University of Virginia*

Although certainly honored to have been invited by my alma mater Georgetown University to participate in this significant symposium, I am still quite puzzled why I have been invited to offer my opinions in a discussion of Catholic identity, specifically one involving the relationship between this Catholic university and the Roman Catholic church as its *mater et magistra*—at least heretofore. It would seem at first glance anyway that the inclusion of a non-Catholic scholar, a Jewish theologian like myself no less, in what is in essence an intra-Catholic occasion for soul searching, could very likely complicate rather than simplify your important discussions here and now. Well aware of this sort of difficulty, we Jews are usually quite precise in separating our internal discussions about our "identity" (which are legion) from our external discussions with the members of other communities and especially with the adherents of other faiths (which are still few and far between). Thus it would be most unlikely that in a comparable discussion of the Jewish identity of a Jewish institution by Jews, a non-Jewish scholar, a Catholic theologian no less, would be invited to participate. And if, by chance, such a Catholic theologian were indeed invited to participate in such a Jewish discussion, he or she would probably be as puzzled by that invitation as I am puzzled by yours.

Nevertheless, although I cannot answer the question of why the leaders of Georgetown University have invited me to be here with you today, I do know why I accepted the invitation—indeed, with enthusiasm. And reading Father Buckley's insightful paper has further convinced me that accepting this invitation is good for me because it enabled me to ponder the significance of my own relationship with this university. And, I hope, my comments will be good for your own discussions, too. Basically, I have come here today to publicly reaffirm the reason I came to Georgetown as a graduate student in   *95* philosophy in 1966, the same year I was ordained a rabbi and began my rabbinical career. Neither factor, my being a rabbi nor Georgetown being a Catholic university, was accidental in this relationship.

I came to Georgetown to study philosophy because, at least in 1966, Catholic philosophers were just about the only academics philosophically interested (as distinct from being historically interested) in the perennial philosophical question of natural law, the question that lies at the heart of all ethical, political, and legal philosophy. And that interest has surely not been accidental to their being Catholic philosophers. Then as now natural law has been my own most abiding philosophical interest, and it is an interest that has guided a great deal of my theological reflection on the Jewish tradition. So, long before *Ex corde Ecclesiae* was written, I was fully able to comply with its requirement (which is hardly surprising) that "All teachers and all administrators [and, certainly, *all students]* . . . respect, that identity," namely, "the Catholic identity of the institution and its implications" (art. 4, sec. 2). And in section 4 it is explicitly recognized that there are "university teachers and administrators" and "students" who are non-Catholic.

My purpose is relating all of this has not been to bore you with details from my own autobiography. I have certainly not been invited here to speak confessionally. Instead, I relate all of this because I think that if this (indeed any) Catholic university is to retain and develop its Catholic identity, then it must regain a sense of its philosophical vocation, that philosophical vocation that attracted me, who in the words of *Ex corde Ecclesiae* "belong[s] to" one of the "other religions" (art. 4, sec. 4). Thus my own connection to Georgetown is nothing more than a case in point. Furthermore, I explicitly distinguish here between "Catholic philosophy" and "Catholic theology," although it cannot be denied that they are both historically and conceptually related.

Let me now clarify what I mean by quoting directly from Father Buckley's paper. That will be my text, and the rest of this "comment" will be a reflection thereon. Father Buckley writes,

> Any movement toward meaning and truth is inchoatively religious. This obviously does not suggest that quantum mechanics or geography is religion or theology; it does mean that the dynamism inherent in all inquiry and knowledge—if not inhibited—is toward ultimacy . . . At the same time, the tendencies of faith are inescapably toward the academic. This obviously does not suggest that all serious religion is scholarship; it does mean that the dynamism inherent in faith—if not inhibited— is toward its own understanding, toward its own self-possession in knowledge. In their full development, the religious intrinsically involves the academic, and the academic intrinsically involves the religious.

First of all, it is evident that Father Buckley sees the interaction of the "religious" and the "academic" to be "relational" rather than "substantial";

that is, neither is fully contained in the other; instead, each is independent *of* yet interactive *with* the other. (Later, under the heading "Identity," Father Buckley makes this distinction between substance and relationship explicit.) Each, then, can be seen, following the Augustinian conceptuality favored by both the Pope in *Ex corde Ecclesiae* (n. 5: *"Intellige ut credas; crede ut intelligas"*) and Father Buckley, as *seeking* the other. Thus we have both *fides quaerens intellectum* and *intellectus quaerens fidem*. What does it mean to see both faith and knowledge seeking (*quaerere*) each other, to see faith and knowledge as both subject and object of the act of seeking? What would be the case if we had only one kind of seeking as opposed to two?

I submit that if a Catholic university is interested in only one of the forms of spiritual seeking, it ceases to be a university—at least in a contemporarily justifiable sense—and in effect becomes something else. Being both a "university" and "Catholic" (the respective roots of which in Latin—*universitas*—and in Greek—*kata holos*—are equivalent in meaning) involves a dialectic between these two forms of spiritual seeking, between these two universes.

On the one hand, if a Catholic university is only interested in *fides quaerens intellectum,* it would be more authentic to redefine itself as a theological seminary, namely, a place where those concerned with the explication of *their* faith should go to pursue that already accepted religious goal. To quote one of the ancient rabbis, "an ignoramus cannot be pious,"[1] which is no doubt an assertion the heirs of a scholastic tradition like yours can well appreciate and endorse. However, by contemporary standards a *sine qua non* of any university is that, whatever its source of identity might be, it is not a place the primary goal of which is the explication of religious faith. For if that were the case, no non-Catholic could be a student in and *of* a Catholic university with good faith—as I was very much a Jewish student here at Catholic Georgetown a generation ago.

On the other hand, if a Catholic university is only interested in *intellectus quaerens fidem,* it would be more authentic to redefine itself as a religious center, if not actually a mission. Indeed, one of the chief factors of Catholic proselytizing efforts (as opposed to most similar evangelical efforts) has been the attempt to show those who are now outside the church that the intellectual pursuit of truth is really a desire to know God, and that the church is best able to take over after intellect has run its natural course in that pursuit. (*Gratia non tollit naturam sed perficit,* or to paraphrase Aquinas, *fides non tollit intellectum sed perficit.*)[2] However, here too, by contemporary standards, a *sine qua non* of a university is that it not engage in proselytizing of any overt kind. For if this were the case, non-Catholic students who have no desire to change their own religious faith could hardly come to a Catholic university in good faith—as I came to Georgetown a generation ago.

Two other alternatives to the "quests" discussed above are: faith seeking faith *(fides quaerens fidem)* and knowledge seeking knowledge *(intellectus quaerens intellectum).* The first quest is what we would call "fideism," and it is one that the whole scholastic tendency of the Catholic tradition has usually been successful in resisting. And when it has been pursued outside the Catholic tradition (as in forms of Protestant pietism), it has been regarded as no real intellectual challenge by most Catholics inasmuch as it is usually so antiintellectual. However, the second quest, knowledge seeking knowledge, has characterized much of the secularist alternative to Catholicism, and indeed to other traditions, such as Judaism, that take the truth of revelation with utmost seriousness. And, unlike fideism, this secularist belief in the full sufficiency of human intellect to attain truth has posed the great intellectual challenge to Catholicism, to other forms of Christianity, and to Judaism. (Confining my attention to the West, Europe, and especially America, I leave the question of the secularist challenge to Islam aside.)

From the time of the Enlightenment until fairly recent times, the challenge that a tradition like Catholicism faced from secularism could be located in the question of what is the proper form of spiritual seeking for modern persons. Or where is truth to be found, and where is it not to be found? Catholics have asserted that faith and intellect are complementary in the quest for truth. The type of secularism that came to dominate the non-Catholic universities just as assuredly asserted that faith and intellect are contradictory in the quest for truth, that faith impedes rather than completes that quest. Virtually the whole thrust of such modern Catholic responses to modernity as those of Jacques Maritain or Bernard Lonergan, for example, has been to argue that secularism wrongly narrows the human quest for truth to human intellect alone, indeed to certain limited functions of human intellect.

At this point we can see how Catholic philosophy has played a more major role than Catholic theology per se. For in the strict sense discussed above, both *fides quaerens intellectum* and *intellectus quaerens fidem* are theological enterprises. The former can be seen as the domain of dogmatic theology; the latter the domain of apologetic theology. And as we have seen, neither enterprise, or even both of them in concert, really requires a university in the contemporary sense at all. However, if we broaden the role of the quest both between faith and intellect and intellect and faith, we can begin to find a modern justification for a Catholic university. This is what I see as the quest of Father Buckley's paper, and upon which my comment is, I trust, a creative reflection acceptable to him and to you.

In terms of *fides quaerens intellectum,* it is essentially an exercise in dogmatic theology (where one thinks of Karl Barth as the modern master) to think of this quest as being for self-understanding. In this enterprise one avoids as much as possible the attempt to bring the insights of theology to bear on issues that are not themselves strictly theological. But it becomes a more philosophical enterprise when faith seeks to inform a world of discourse outside its theological circle, when it enters its insights into conversations that it does not basically control in advance by ready appeals to the authority of revelation and tradition. This seems to be what Father Buckley means by taking pride in the greater sophistication and subtlety he sees in the contemporary academic enterprise of Catholic theology. In effect, he is implying that Catholic theology, especially as studied and taught in Catholic universities, has become more philosophical. (Questions of its greater orthodoxy or heterodoxy I will leave for Catholics themselves to decide.) In this type of functioning, theology becomes more philosophical by becoming what Paul Tillich used to call "theology of culture," which in fact is more "theology *in* culture." The enterprise is made more challenging by the greater secularity of Western civilization and culture as compared with the period when the classical sources of Christian (and Jewish) theology were written. I submit that this enterprise is best conducted in an atmosphere where Catholicism is a very real presence but not the solely dominating presence; that is, in the atmosphere of a modern university.

In terms of *intellectus quaerens fidem,* it is essentially an exercise in apologetic theology to think of this quest as being one designed to bring inquiring intellects into the church. In this enterprise the goal, the *telos,* is known in advance. It is simply a matter of deliberating about the best means to that end. This being an intellectual quest, overtly emotional appeals, such as one finds in many forms of Protestant proselytizing, are inappropriate. Yet it is still proselytizing, of a more intelligent variety to be sure. But the quest becomes a more philosophical enterprise when the goal is not known in advance. Here what one is seeking is the transcendent horizon implicit in intellectual seeking. The realization that this horizon cannot be denied is what the religious philosopher— in this case the religious Catholic philosopher—shows intellectually (usually *via negativa).* Nevertheless, it must be emphasized that this type of philosophical reflection could just as easily lead one to an affirmation of Judaism or more intellectually open forms of Protestantism or to the transcendent awareness of such nontheists as Karl Jaspers. It is only an antidote to the type of positivism that seems to regard the human quest for truth over and above the quest for facts as being futile. I submit that such a quest is well conducted in the atmosphere of a university like a Catholic university that draws its historical nourishment from someone like Thomas Aquinas who was in conversation (literarily, of course) with Aristotle who was not a theist in the Judeo-Christian-Islamic sense, Avicenna who was a Muslim theist, and Maimonides who was a Jewish theist.

Finally, I would submit that there is a new role for a Catholic university in our contemporary culture. That role is more basic than its role in earlier modernity and more important culturally as well.

In earlier modernity it could be assumed that the difference between a Catholic university and a secular one was located in the proper object of the spiritual quest for truth. The quest itself was assumed to be common to all, however. Thus it was commonly held that human persons are beings engaged in a search for truth that is proper to both their own nature and the nature of the things they seek to know (*veritas sequitur esse rerum*). Today such an assumption can no longer be made. There are large segments of the university world, especially in the humanities (which is the modern location of the study and teaching of philosophy), who do not believe that there is any real truth, either within humans or within the world, and that any search for it, by whatever means, is therefore quite futile. Human intellect, then, is simply a function of the power interests of the particular group one happens to be part of. Only power, not truth, is real and worth dealing with. In this world, there is no longer any tension between faith and intellect because there is no longer any truth over which they can even quarrel. Without the assumption of the reality of truth, neither faith nor intellect can really desire (*quaerere*) anything. The only thing left then is either at best compromise or at worst conquest. But neither compromise nor conquest is an act of faith or of intellect. Thus we are left today with neither theology nor philosophy but only ideology. And, of course, in this kind of world, there is no need for a university anymore, whether a Catholic university or even a secular one.

Into this empty cultural situation both faith and intellect must forcefully reinsert and reassert themselves. That cannot be by argument, because there is nothing outside of them to argue with anymore. Instead, it must be by demonstration, by showing that human life and culture, as Aristotle said about nature, cannot stand a vacuum, in our case the intellectual vacuum that the denial of truth necessarily entails. For Catholics, this reassertion can perhaps best come through the revitalization and rededication of one of the greatest contributions your tradition has made to our civilization: the university as *universitas magistrorum et scholarium*. Such a community seems to be possible only when truth is accepted from one's background and hoped for on the horizon.

NOTES

1. Mishnah, Avot 2.5.
2. Thomas Aquinas, *Summa Theologiae* I.i.8.

DISCUSSION

Discussion initially concerned key terms in Michael Buckley's paper and the commentaries and then an additional category raised in discussion: perspectivalism.

The ideal of a philosophical perspective *might* be possible, but that is not the perceived role of philosophy or theology in *Ex corde Ecclesiae,* which suggests a sectarian theology and philosophy. On the contrary, paragraph 19 of the apostolic constitution is a relatively thoughtful and nondogmatic statement about theology. But the role of the local ordinary is to scrutinize orthodoxy. No, it begs the question to say the perspective of *Ex corde Ecclesiae* is sectarian. The fundamental obligation of a theologian is allegiance to the truth. It is conceivable that in pursuing the truth the theologian may move beyond the faith and may have to leave the faith. This has to be recognized. But the local bishop certainly has the right to say that the theologian is no longer Catholic.

Is Buckley's distinction between *intrinsic* and *extrinsic* the same as Hollenbach's *complementarity?* Hollenbach previously cited John Courtney Murray about the importance of differentiation and a higher synthesis that does not destroy differentiation. This means that complementarity is not the same thing as collapsing the distinction between extrinsic and intrinsic, even though faith and reason are interconnected. Does *extrinsic* mean differentiation and *intrinsic* mean synthesis? Buckley's use of the word *intrinsic* is not the same as an integralist notion, just as Murray resisted an integralist idea of the church having a privileged position in the polis. A seventeenth- and eighteenth-century concept of grace is that it was added to humanity, thus grace is extrinsic. But if grace is intrinsic, the purpose of creation is grace-enhancing. Grace draws nature to its completion and involves all the disciplines. This is reminiscent of Maritain's comment that we distinguish in order to unite.

These ideas of grace and nature are abstractions. We need a more complete understanding, starting with Hollenbach's three elements: nature, grace, and sin. If we apply this idea to the academy, it becomes clear that human creations *101*

are easily destroyed. A problem of the contemporary academy is the disqualifi-
cation of the idea of the search for truth. Thus, if we are going to claim there
is the pride of ecclesiastical authority, we also have to acknowledge the pride
of reason. What are the implications of this? We need to restore Newman's
idea of the university as the culture of the intellect. We need to recognize
there can be a clouding of intellect in the university in its contemporary self-
understanding.

In addition to nature, grace, and sin, is there not a fourth element,
which could be described as perspectivalism? Perspectivalism is a disciplinary
perspective that implies a search, either a search for language in which the
disciplines can be reconciled among themselves or a search for honest discourse
among the various perspectives. There is a certain corruption in the modern
university: perspectives often degenerate into ideologies—the claim that there
is no understanding but my own. Feminism is a powerful perspective, which
has the power to destroy many classical certainties about the possibilities of
integrating truth conceived as a single language.

Perspectivalism may simply be a revival of sophistic tradition claiming that
there is no truth. On the other hand, it may offer something beyond various
perspectives, as in the dialogues of Plato, where, like the contemporary university, the unity is a unity of conversation.

Perspectivalism is not the same as sophism because it maintains a search
for unity. But to the extent to which Christianity identifies truth as a kind of
objectivism independent of culture and history, perspectivalism suggests that
the nature of truth is a function of our times. It is true that perspectivalism
can become ideology, that even valid perspectives can be converted into
ideology, but Lonergan recognized the destruction of the classical point of
view as probably irreparable. But that classical point of view really owes more
to the Enlightenment than it does to Aquinas and earlier classical thinkers.

Perspectivalism is an important element of the picture. It is important
not to reach a premature closure of perspective, which turns into ideology.
Certain assumptions of the Enlightenment are now denied by everybody. One
assumption is that intellect can be an island of intelligence that leads to
autonomy that can survive through the application of technology. This is the
delusion of the island of intelligence in an absurd universe. The faith assertion
is that there is an intelligible order, but it has to be integrated with one's own
intellect: the results are not known in advance. Faith saves perspectivalism; it
holds it off from being ideology.

Buckley's point was that we need a vision of the Catholic university. This
involves struggle and social solidarity. All prior programs with vision (Plato,
Robert Maynard Hutchins, and so forth) have failed. What difference would
it make if Buckley's vision were in operation? What is practically different
about it?

Following a reading of an advertisement for a prominent Catholic univer-
sity's MBA program, touting it as promoting "the survival of the fittest," it
was agreed with much laughter that this description was "not a higher
synthesis." Discussion then turned to the mission statements of Catholic
universities. Questions were raised about their purpose, formulation, and
impact; concern was expressed about their limitations.

The mission statements cited in Buckley's paper—how did they get to
be this way? This question is less intellectually challenging and stimulating than
our current discussion but very important. Who makes these decisions? How
did they happen?

Bureaucrats could fashion mission statements out of the rhetoric of our
own discussion. It is a special genre. There is no real model.

These mission statements are efforts to combine the blandness of consensus
with the vigor of commitment. These statements are designed to convey the
impression that we're changing, but we're protecting every element of tradition;
to give the idea that there are new things underway without frightening the
faculty; to stimulate discussion in a way that does not raise the specter of the
fires of the Inquisition.

These mission statements are made, presumably, by committees that are
supposedly representative. Presumably they are consensus statements. Why,
for example, don't the Jesuits draft a statement and put it out?

Are these mission statements just poorly done, or do they reflect the
reality of the contemporary university?

We need to talk more clearly about the role these statements have among
Catholics, where there is great pluralism of view. Is there support for these
missions of the universities among Catholics? What are they expecting? What
does it mean to be committed to mission? The experience of at least one
university is that non-Catholics often think about these matters much more
deeply than Catholics.

A third theme of the discussion was the problem of specialization.

There is a practical problem to all this, namely the drive toward narrow
specialization, which has a huge effect on the modern university. Does this
new integrating vision imply the reformation of the university structure which
is, in fact, going in the opposite direction?

Much depends on the university, how specifically reform is accomplished
in a given place with given people. It is clear we need to challenge, or modify,
specialization. We do this already with respect to the core curriculum and the
particular ethos of an institution.

The problem of greater specialization is in part resolved by the core
curriculum at the undergraduate level, but graduate schools are pulling in

entirely the opposite direction. It is most unfair to undergraduates to force them to juggle disparate courses and make some coherence out of the curriculum of their upperclass years.

One area that may bear integrative promise is the ethical component in a variety of decisions in different disciplines. This is a more pragmatic approach. People recognize this as an important theme of the university, an essential part of citizenship and culture—and it is less likely to alarm the faculty.

At the University of Chicago, there was a very distinct creation of a college that had its own role in that university.

Finally, several closing comments.

Ex corde Ecclesiae represents both a challenge and a threat. There appears to be a sense in the group that they are unwilling to take up the challenge as long as they consider it a threat.

With respect to the whole question of integration, this is clearly dependent on relationships and networks and people in the institutions. But what do the faculty bring to this question? What are the advertising copywriters doing? There seems to be some confusion and diffusion of what people are doing and thinking.

The American university has difficulty dealing with the power and authority questions that arise from being part of the Catholic church.

Let us return to the example of a medical center in an American Catholic university. It seems not useful to speak of the medical institution as "in" the church. Medical research is not fundamentally influenced by the wisdom of the church. It is not clear that Buckley's concepts are helpful in coming to grips with the Catholic nature of such a medical school.

Rev. James H. Provost, *The Catholic University of America*

A Canonical Commentary on
Ex corde Ecclesiae

Ex corde Ecclesiae is fundamentally a teaching document. It proposes to continue the teaching of the Second Vatican Council's declaration on Catholic education *Gravissimum educationis* and to be "a sort of 'magna carta' " for Catholic universities (nn. 8-9). As such it is appropriately understood from a doctrinal and theological perspective. But it also contains several norms that are to guide its implementation in various regions of the world, and it was promulgated both as a law and as a teaching document. It is therefore appropriate to address it from the perspective of canon law and to analyze it as church law.

There are seven "general norms" and four "transitional norms" in part 2 of the document. This paper is organized as a commentary on these norms. It will be useful, however, to recall some general principles of interpretation of law as we approach this task. Thus there are three general sections to this paper: a brief introduction concerning interpretation of this kind of document; a longer section dealing with the norms in the constitution; and concluding reflections on some remaining issues.

TOOLS FOR INTERPRETATION

The Text

A first consideration is the text to be interpreted. The official text of the constitution is the Latin text as promulgated in the *Acta Apostolicae Sedis*.[1] This is the controlling document, and any questions about the meaning of the text must be referred to the official Latin version.

It is a common practice today, however, for official church documents to be drafted in a modern language. This is all the more true of a document such **105** as *Ex corde Ecclesiae*, which was preceded by a worldwide consultation extending over several years. The drafts, observations on them, and responses to these observations were communicated in modern languages. There is reason to believe that the draft on which the official text is based was in English. Yet any differences between the English translation provided by the Vatican (presumably, the final draft text prior to translation into Latin) and the promulgated Latin text must be resolved by reference to the Latin text. It alone is the official legal text.

Text and Context

"Ecclesiastical laws are to be understood in accord with the proper meaning of the words considered in their text and context."[2] This canon directs us to work with care on a legal text, to pay attention to the words that are used, and to set them in their proper context. All of this is intended to help our understanding of what the legislator had in mind in promulgating the law.

Terms that have a technical meaning are to be understood according to this technical, or "proper," meaning. This has several implications. Where there is a technical term in canon law, and the constitution uses such a term in one of the norms, the presumption is that the document means the technical, legal use of the term.[3] On the other hand, where there is a technical term in canon law for something, and the constitution uses a different term where the technical one is to be expected, then it is legitimate to conclude that the legislator decided not to impose what is usually required, but has introduced a different course of action or set a different requirement than is usual.[4] The same goes for the use of verb forms: the use of *debet* indicates a stronger obligation, for example, than the use of the indicative or even the subjunctive verb form.[5]

Laws do not appear in a vacuum; they have a context. Placing them in their context will keep the interpreter from falling into a rigid legalism or formalism and will maintain the law as a servant to the ongoing life of the church. In our case, *Ex corde Ecclesiae* itself is rich in drawing our attention to the proper context.

Most immediately there is part 1 of the apostolic constitution. It is certainly the longest part of the document (twenty-seven pages in the *Acta*, compared with eight for the norms and promulgation section). It clearly is intended to set forth the intention of the legislator. As the substantive teaching part of the document, it provides the criteria for interpreting the norms that are intended to implement it.

The constitution itself (n. 9) states that it is an effort to continue the teaching of the Second Vatican Council, so the conciliar texts are part of the context in which the norms of *Ex corde Ecclesiae* are to be interpreted. Moreover, the general norms are presented as rooted in the Code of Canon Law and as providing a further "explication" of the canons and related church legislation (art. 1, sec. 1). The code provides another part of the context.

Finally, the constitution is directed toward a specific topic, Catholic universities. It locates them within the setting of universities generally, upholds their rights within this setting, and addresses the specifically "Catholic" dimension of Catholic universities. Thus the academic world provides a context within which this particular document is to be interpreted. It is not intended for seminaries or even for ecclesiastical universities and faculties (n. 8; art. 1, sec. 2). It addresses higher education, not primary or secondary schools.

Law as Law

Law needs to be interpreted as law. Hence, insofar as the norms in part 2 of *Ex corde Ecclesiae* are laws, they are to be interpreted not only in text and context, but also in keeping with all the other tools of interpretation that are used to understand and apply church laws in practice.

As with other interpretations of texts, there are definite rules to be followed and careful nuances to be applied in the interpretation of canon law texts. The Code of Canon Law provides some of these. For example, "custom is the best interpreter of laws" (c. 27). "Laws deal with the future and not the past, unless specific provision be made in the laws concerning the past" (c. 9). Authoritative interpretations of law are given only by a legislator or someone designated by the legislator to do this (c. 16, sec. 1). If a text remains doubtful and obscure, turn to parallel passages, to the purpose and circumstances of the law, and the *mens legislatoris* to resolve the doubt or obscurity (c. 17). Give a strict interpretation (i.e., a narrow one, one which binds only insofar as the text itself indicates) to laws that penalize, restrict the free exercise of rights, or contain an exception to the law (c. 18). If there is no provision in the law to help resolve a particular case, then look to the sources of suppletory law (c. 19).[6]

This brief discussion of interpretation leaves aside many other very significant considerations, such as the relationship of canon law to the civil law of the area, or the more fundamental issues related to the values that inform a law. But this would take us beyond the scope of the present study, and it is now time to turn to the norms within *Ex corde Ecclesiae* to see what we can learn from them.

NORMS IN THE CONSTITUTION

The norms are divided into seven general norms, each with several sections, and four transitional norms, which are much shorter.[7]

Article 1. The Nature of These General Norms[8]

The norms themselves are contained in an apostolic constitution. This is one of the more important types of documents in the church. Apostolic constitutions are used to present solemn teaching (the dogma of the Assumption of Mary), to promulgate laws (including codes of laws), and to make other enactments of major significance to the church.[9] They are therefore significant legislative enactments. Article 1 of the general norms sets them in relationship to other laws and to the enactments of various authorities in the church and in universities.

Relationship to Existing Law (art. 1, sec. 1)

The general norms are based in and provide further explicitation to the canons of the 1983 code (n. 11). Canons 807-814 of that code provide the norms for Catholic universities and other institutes of higher studies. The general norms do not replace those canons, nor do they cover all the matter contained in the canons. When *Ex corde Ecclesiae* was promulgated, the Code of Canons of the Eastern Churches had not yet appeared; it was promulgated two years later.[10] The Eastern code contains six canons on Catholic universities. These are not the same as those in the 1983 code for the Latin church, they more explicitly reflect Vatican II texts, and they are more restrictive in their understanding of a "Catholic university."[11] *Ex corde Ecclesiae* is explicitly related to the code for the Latin church, although when the apostolic constitution was promulgated, the Latin code's provisions did provide suppletory law for Eastern churches as needed. The two codes are distinct, but they do have some relationship to each other.[12] The applicability of *Ex corde Ecclesiae* to Catholic universities in Eastern Catholic churches remains an issue to be explored. For the purposes of the analysis in this paper, attention will be focused on Catholic universities in the Latin church, primarily with reference to the United States.

The general norms are also said to be rooted in and provide further explicitation to "complementary" church legislation. There is no indication in the text or in a note to indicate what this legislation may be. An example could be the directory on ecumenism in higher education.[13]

The norm is also careful to reaffirm the right of the Holy See to intervene when it considers this necessary. This is a practical application of the primacy of the pope, which extends "over all particular churches" as well as the church universal (c. 333, sec. 1).

Extent of Application (art. 1, sec. 1)

The norms apply to all Catholic universities and Catholic institutes of higher studies throughout the world. There is no exception for universities or institutes located in missionary territories, for example.[14]

This norm does not determine which institutions of higher learning are included as "Catholic universities" and "Catholic institutes of higher studies." It merely asserts that whatever institutions fall within these categories are bound by these norms.

Episcopal Conference Ordinationes *(art. 1, sec. 2)*

Directions for the application of the general norms to various localities are placed in the hands of the episcopal conferences. This is a practical recognition that "the situation of Catholic Universities differs from region to region," and that "in such diversity of situation a precise law for application to all Catholic Universities appears impossible."[15] This provision is a clear example of a healthy subsidiarity within the church, as desired in the principles for the revision of church law and as encouraged by various scholars.[16] It implies that the *ordinationes* will be more than a repetition of existing canon law or the general norms themselves but will genuinely address the application of the law to local circumstances.

There are several restrictions on the options available to episcopal conferences in drawing up their *ordinationes*. First, they are to respect the existing statutes of the various universities and institutes. The *ordinationes* are not to replace these statutes, nor do they override them. This is an expression of respect for the autonomy of the institutions, which received such positive affirmation in the first part of *Ex corde Ecclesiae* (nn. 12, 37). The *ordinationes*, then, must leave room for diversity among the various institutes in keeping with their own statutes; even within the same region, there can be considerable diversity among Catholic universities.[17]

Second, insofar as this is possible and to the extent it is opportune, the *ordinationes* are to respect civil laws. This is especially pertinent in view of the diversity of civil legislation affecting higher education, which differs from one country to another. In the United States it is even more complex, where Catholic universities may be subject not only to federal laws, but also to the legislation of one or more of the fifty states or the District of Columbia. Moreover, in this country accreditation of degrees depends on voluntary accrediting associations, but there are civil consequences if a university's degrees are not so recognized. Failure to respect this diversity of civil legislation could put Catholic universities in the impossible situation of having to choose between failure to observe civil law in order to retain their recognition as Catholic, with the danger of going out of existence, or failure to observe the *ordinationes*, with the possible consequence of being disowned by the church. Wisely, therefore, the general norms call on the episcopal conferences to work very carefully in this area so as not to endanger the very existence of these universities.

Third, the bishops are not authorized to act entirely on their own. Their *ordinationes*, once adopted by the conference, are subject to "inspection" (*inspectio*) by the Holy See. Note 44 of the general norms makes reference to canon 455, section 2, of the 1983 code. This canon requires that general decrees adopted by a bishops' conference be "reviewed" (*recognita*) by the Apostolic See. *Recognitio* has a technical meaning in canon law, going back to Sixtus V.[18] It means a document is reviewed by the Apostolic See, can be changed (by additions, changes, omissions, etc.), and is returned for the authority that originally adopted the document to promulgate. Even though the Apostolic See has modified the document, it does not become a document of the Apostolic See. It remains at the level of the authority that adopted it. Moreover, *recognitio* is no guarantee that in the future the Apostolic See may not still object to the contents of the document.[19]

Recognitio is distinguished from *approbatio*, which entails a greater degree of commitment by the Apostolic See to the document approved.[20] *Inspectio* ("examination," "inspection") is used in law for determining what the factual situation is.[21] In none of these situations does *inspectio* carry with it the technical possibilities of changing a document that *recognitio* involves, much less the commitment of the higher authority that *approbatio* implies.

Does the use of *inspectio* carry a significant meaning, given the reference in the note to canon 455, section 2? The reference to the canon does indicate the procedure to be followed: namely, that a two-thirds majority of the members having a deliberative vote must approve the *ordinationes*; that the *ordinationes* must be submitted to the Apostolic See; and that after they have been "examined" or "inspected" there, they are to be promulgated by the conference. Whether it says more, namely that *inspectio* is to be interpreted as *recognitio*, is not certain. Moreover, in the context of the exercise of subsidiarity so evident in this norm, and in light of the careful use of a term other than *recognitio* or *approbatio*, it appears the legislator is indicating in advance that the *ordinationes* will be examined (*inspectio*) but not changed (*recognitio*) by higher authority, further emphasizing the respect for differing local conditions which underlies this norm.

Finally, the bishops are not authorized to adopt *ordinationes* affecting ecclesiastical universities or faculties. This special classification of institutions (see cc. 815-821) are more immediately subject to the Apostolic See itself, which issued the apostolic constitution *Sapientia christiana* for them.[22] Indeed, the implementation norms comparable to the *ordinationes* discussed here were issued by the Apostolic See itself.[23]

Application to Universities (art. 1, sec. 3)

Here is an instance where the general norms provide for a retroactive application, an explicit exception to the general rule that laws deal with the future and not the past (c. 9). As an exception to the law, it must be interpreted strictly (c. 18); that is, only what is precisely required by the norms to be applied to existing institutions is to be required. Where the norms are not clear, where an interpretation could be broadened to include other institutions under its scope beyond those explicitly mentioned in the law, the law draws a line: the norms cannot be given a broader interpretation than the meaning of the words in their text and context clearly warrant.

Two different classifications of Catholic universities are identified when it comes to applying the *ordinationes* to existing Catholic universities. The first classification are those universities constituted or approved by the Holy See, an episcopal conference, or a diocesan bishop. All other Catholic universities are in the second classification.

The distinction is based on the authority that constituted (established, founded) the institution or that has given it formal *approbatio*. While all Catholic universities have some bond with the church (n. 27), those for whom this was done by a competent authority within the hierarchical structure of the church are considered to have a closer bond. They are more immediately subject to competent church authority, and therefore are required (*insere debet*) to incorporate the general norms and the *ordinationes* into their governing documents and to conform their existing statutes to these. Moreover, they must submit all this for the approval (*approbatio*) of the competent ecclesiastical authority.

The other classification of Catholic universities is those that were not founded by or have not received formal *approbatio* by these hierarchical authorities. They may include universities founded by religious institutes, by associations, by individual lay persons or clergy, etc. They may be among those considered "truly" Catholic even though they do not bear the word *Catholic* in their title (cf. c. 808). While they have some bond with the church, it is not so close as the previous classification, nor are they so tightly bound to incorporate the general norms and *ordinationes*. They are clearly expected to take these documents seriously in reference to their governing documents. The requirement to adjust their statutes is less stringent—it is to be done "as far as possible." They are not required to submit any of this for the *approbatio* of any ecclesiastical authority, but they are expected to carry out any adjustments in agreement with the local church authority.

Who is the "competent ecclesiastical authority" (or the "local ecclesiastical authority" for the second classification)? The term "competent ecclesiastical authority" appears many times in the code, but only once is its meaning specified. Canon 312 states that the authority competent to erect public associations is determined by the scope of the association: the Holy See for universal and international ones; the bishops' conference for national ones; the diocesan bishop for associations whose founding purpose is directed toward work within the diocese but not nationally. A similar gradation is implied in the reference to these three levels in this norm.

"Local ecclesiastical authority" clearly includes the diocesan bishop, who is a "local ordinary" (c. 134, sec. 2). In some instances it also includes the episcopal conference, if the university is national in scope, because a nation is still a "locality."[24]

To repeat, the specific requirements that bind Catholic universities constituted or approved by competent ecclesiastical authorities bind only those universities; they are not equally applicable to any other Catholic universities. Only those obligations that are spelled out for these other universities bind them.

Article 2. The Nature of a Catholic University

A major portion of part 1 of *Ex corde Ecclesiae* is devoted to discussing the nature of a Catholic university as a university and as Catholic. This article attempts to distill some of the richness of that teaching, without in any way supplanting or substituting for it. In other words, the norms in article 2 must be read with all the nuances and distinctions with which part 1 of the document approaches the same topic. The following comments presume this and will only allude to or briefly refer to the teaching of part 1 in commenting on the norms.

University (art. 2, sec. 1)

Four elements identify an entity as a university in this norm. First, it is a community of scholars. This community is composed of faculty, students, and administrators (nn. 21-23). Second, these scholars investigate various branches of human knowledge. One of the defining characteristics of a university (as contrasted to other institutions of higher education) is the presence of several distinct graduate schools. The interaction of these distinct disciplines, whether in the undergraduate or graduate level, provides one of the distinguishing characteristics of a genuine university education (nn. 15-17).

Third, universities are engaged in a variety of activities: research, teaching, and service. The interaction of all three activities provides the full complement of university life and characterizes the role of a university in the broader community (nn. 12, 15, 31-37). Fourth, the cultural mission is something part 1 considers crucial for any university, and in a special way for a Catholic university (nn. 43-47). A major reason for the diversity among Catholic universities arises from this need to relate to diverse cultures.

Catholic University (art. 2, sec. 2)

There are two aspects of Catholic identity for a university: *being* Catholic, in terms of implementing Catholic ideals, principles, and values in its research, teaching, and service; and *committing* itself to some relationship with the Catholic church. Both are essential for the university to be Catholic.[25]

Being Catholic evidences itself in many ways, no one of which is sufficient to identify, as an isolated element, an institution as Catholic. For example, a Catholic university does not limit itself to the investigation of "Catholic" issues, whatever this might mean, but is called on to address all the questions appropriate to a university (n. 15). It does attempt an integration of knowledge, incorporating insights of the gospel with the advances of human sciences, promoting a dialogue between faith and reason, showing a concern for ethical and moral implications of its methods and discoveries, and recognizing the distinct role of theology within this interaction (nn. 16-19).

Commitment to the Catholic church is presented as involving two distinct approaches.[26] One consists in certain, constitutive, and legal bonds (*certo vinculo constitutivo et legitimo*). Such bonds appear to be bilateral; i.e., not only is this commitment expressed in the governing documents of the institution, but these have been accepted and approved by competent ecclesiastical authority. This makes the bond certain and legal and is constitutive of this kind of university as Catholic.[27]

The second approach is a commitment from within the institution itself (*ex officio institutionali*), but not entailing a corresponding commitment from competent church authorities. This commitment is to be made by those who sponsor the university (*ab eius sponsoribus sumpto*), indicating a basic commitment by those who are competent to commit the institution as such. These would certainly include those universities canon 808 refers to as "truly Catholic" (*reapse catholica*) even though "Catholic" does not appear in their name or title. It could also include those universities that do include "Catholic" in their name or title, since the "consent" of competent ecclesiastical authority required to do this does not necessarily involve that certain, constitutive, and legal bond that the first approach involves.[28]

In light of the distinction in the previous norm (art. 1, sec. 3), all existing Catholic universities except those founded by or approved by competent ecclesiastical authority are included within this second category. Thus those already founded by a public juridic person (such as a religious institute or a public association in the church), as well as universities founded by clergy or laity as individuals or in private associations, come under this category. For these institutions to be Catholic universities, in addition to *being* Catholic they are to make an institutional commitment to the Catholic church. How this is to be expressed is the topic of the next section of this norm.

Expression of Catholic Character (art. 2, sec. 3)

There are two actions required of Catholic universities for the expression of their Catholic character. The first looks to the public articulation of this character in some document; the second looks to developing effective means to assure that the Catholic character is realized in practice.

As a general rule, the institutional commitment to being Catholic and to a relationship with the Catholic church is to be expressed in some public document. The norm provides several alternatives for this expression, in keeping with the two approaches discussed in relation to article 2, section 2, above. For example, this commitment for those with certain, constitutive, and legal bonds will be found in the governing documents or other instrument approved by the competent ecclesiastical authority. For the other types of Catholic universities, it may be in any variety of documents, e.g., a mission statement, a statement of identity, the charter of the institution as approved by the proper secular authorities, etc. The only condition is that the document must be one adopted by those with the authority to commit the institution as such, its "sponsors."

Exceptions to this general rule are permitted but must be authorized by competent ecclesiastical authority. Such, for example, may be advisable in situations where the church is being persecuted and any mention of Catholic identity in a public document would be to the detriment of the institution. It may also be appropriate in situations where financial support for the institution would be seriously affected.

The other action required of the university is to provide practical means for guaranteeing the expression and preservation of its Catholic identity in its research, teaching, and service. All Catholic universities are bound to do this, even those with an exemption from expressing the Catholic identity in their documents. The norm suggests some ways this can be done (through the institutional structure, inner regulations, etc.). Given the diversity among Catholic universities and the requirement that even the *ordinationes* respect the role of statutes of individual institutions, the practical details for this are properly left to each institution. What the norm insists on is that the institution attend to this issue.

Respect for Catholic Teaching and Discipline (art. 2, sec. 4)

There are three aspects to this norm. First, Catholic teaching and discipline are to influence the entire life of the university. Second, this must be done in a way that fully respects the freedom of conscience of each individual in the university. Third, the public actions of the university must be in keeping with its Catholic character.

The requirement of Catholic influence on the entire life of the university reaffirms what was covered above concerning *being* Catholic. It is not possible to state in detail, either in the general norms or in the *ordinationes* of each episcopal conference, what this means. It truly belongs to the inner life of the university and is effected not only by documents and position statements, but also by the climate, "spirit," and other intangibles that are frequently the concern of the university community.

Respect for the freedom of conscience of each individual makes no distinction between active or inactive Catholics, between Catholics and non-Catholics, between believers and nonbelievers in the university community. The freedom of conscience of each person is to be respected. The norm even qualifies this as something to be done "fully" (*omnino*). The norm applies not only to the private beliefs in conscience of an individual, but also, in keeping with Catholic teaching, to the expression of one's beliefs in conscience, provided this is done with due respect for the common good (which in the situation of a Catholic university, includes the Catholic character of the institution).[29]

Balancing these two requirements is no easy task. The norms do not attempt to dictate how this is to be done, and given the diversity among universities, it would seem this is one of those areas where the *ordinationes* are called upon to respect the competence of the statutes of individual universities.

When the university acts as an institution, its commitment to a Catholic character calls for it to respect its own institutional "conscience" in its official actions and commitments. This norm is a claim over against those who would force the institution to act contrary to its Catholic commitment, whether through civil laws or through public or private pressures. It is also a reminder to the institutions themselves that their commitment is to be more than words on paper, but as called for in article 2, section 2, it must *be* Catholic as well as proclaim itself to be such.

Given the diversity of social and legal situations in which Catholic universities find themselves, the general norms do not attempt more than to state this general principle. If the *ordinationes* attempt to specify the application of this principle further, they must respect the competence of each university's statutes in the matter, and ought to attend to civil laws as well.

Institutional Autonomy (art. 2, sec. 5)

The very notion of a university includes "that institutional autonomy necessary to perform its functions effectively" (n. 12). The norm reaffirms this principle for Catholic universities and sets it as a standard that must be observed by all who deal with these universities. In drawing up their *ordinationes,* for example, bishops' conferences must keep this in mind. This is one of the ways that Catholic universities differ from other formation and educational institutions in the church, such as seminaries and Catholic schools, which are under much closer control of competent ecclesiastical authority.[30]

Institutional autonomy, however, exists not for its own sake, but for the sake of pursuing the purposes of the university. It is one of the guarantees of academic freedom. It is for the institution itself, within its autonomy, to put this guarantee to work, recognizing and respecting freedom in teaching and research appropriate to a university. Similarly, others must recognize and respect this freedom. *Ex corde Ecclesiae* itself does this in several places (nn. 12, 29); the *ordinationes* adopted by episcopal conferences must also recognize and respect this freedom, at least by not adopting any provisions to the contrary.

Academic freedom, like all human freedoms, is not unlimited; it exists within certain boundaries. The norm expresses three elements of these boundaries: respect for the rights of others (individuals and community); respect for the confines of truth; respect for the common good. These are drawn from *Gaudium et spes* (n. 59), which spells them out more in detail.

First, the just freedom to develop culture enjoys inviolability provided "the rights of the individual and the community, whether particular or universal, are preserved within the context of the common good."[31] The common good consists in "the sum of those conditions of social life by which individuals, families, and groups can achieve their own fulfillment in a relatively thorough and ready way."[32] The restrictions on academic freedom, then, are in the first place the usual restrictions on the exercise of any rights: the rights of others, and the common good.[33]

Second, respecting the confines of truth is dealt with separately in number 59 of *Gaudium et spes,* reaffirming the teaching of Vatican I that there are " 'two orders of knowledge' which are distinct, namely, faith and reason."[34] It concludes that "within the limits of morality and the general welfare, a man [must] be free to search for the truth, voice his mind, and publicize it."[35] The confines of the truth are not so easily set in these matters; the Council recognized "it is sometimes difficult to harmonize culture with Christian teaching" but went on to affirm that "these difficulties do not necessarily harm the life of faith. Indeed they can stimulate the mind to a more accurate and penetrating grasp of the faith. For recent studies and findings of science, history, and philosophy raise new questions which influence life and demand new theological investigations."[36]

Even within a particular science it is not always a simple matter to determine when one has gone beyond the "truth"; many modern discoveries have resulted precisely from questioning the accepted "truth" in a particular discipline. The statement in the norm, therefore, sets a goal, but one that is difficult to particularize in practice beyond recognizing the illegitimacy of a gross violation of the truth. Practical judgments in this matter must obviously be left to competent persons in the field, exercising due caution.

Article 3. The Establishment of a Catholic University

Here the general norms are looking toward the future. They address the establishment of future Catholic universities and not the establishment of those already in existence (which were considered under art. 1, sec. 3). Three different classifications of founders are considered.

Competent Ecclesiastical Authority (art. 3, sec. 1)

The Holy See, a conference of bishops, or a diocesan bishop can establish a Catholic university. They are competent ecclesiastical authorities, as discussed earlier. When they do establish a Catholic university, its statutes must be approved by them (art. 3, sec. 4). This is the same situation as the first classification of existing Catholic universities in article 1, section 3.

Religious Institute or Other Public Juridic Person (art. 3, sec. 2)

By the law itself a religious institute is a public juridic person; so, too, are its houses and provinces (c. 634, sec. 1). The norm specifies that a Catholic university could be founded by any of these juridic persons, not just the religious institute itself. The law recognizes other entities as public juridic persons; for example, public associations of the faithful (c. 313), societies of apostolic life (c. 741), and parishes (c. 515, sec. 3). By implication, secular institutes are public juridic persons (c. 718) even though the law does not expressly state they are. Other entities can be erected as public juridic persons by decree of competent ecclesiastical authority (c. 114); for example, a personal prelature is not identified in the law as a public juridic person, but it is likely it would be constituted as such by the decree of the Apostolic See erecting it.[37]

For any of these public juridic persons to erect a Catholic university the consent of the diocesan bishop is required. No exception is made here for pontifical institutes or for national or international organizations that are public juridic persons.

The consent of the diocesan bishop for a religious institute to found a Catholic university could be contained in his consent to erect a religious house.[38] If erecting and conducting Catholic universities falls within the apostolate of the institute, the bishop's consent to erect a house brings with it the consent to carry out the works of the institute (c. 611, 2°). Only if he explicitly restricted this aspect of the institute's apostolate when he gave permission to erect the house would the bishop's explicit permission later be required to erect a Catholic university.

The statutes of Catholic universities founded by public juridic persons in the future will have to be approved by the competent ecclesiastical authority (art. 3, sec. 4). It is not immediately evident that this authority will always be the local diocesan bishop, since the competent ecclesiastical authority could also be the Apostolic See or the episcopal conference, depending on the case. This is something the *ordinationes* might further specify, although care must be exercised to respect the diverse possibilities assured under canon law.

Other Persons (art. 3, sec. 3)

Clergy or lay persons can also erect universities. They can do this either as individuals or in private associations. The associations could be recognized in the church or could be what are called "de facto" associations (associations which exist, but which have not sought recognition in the church).[39] Similarly, various movements of Catholics may erect universities.[40]

The norm stipulates that for any of these universities to be considered Catholic (*poterit Universitas Catholica haberi*), the competent ecclesiastical authority must approve this designation. The conditions for obtaining such an approval are to be agreed upon by both the founders of the university and the respective church authority. In a note, the norm further specifies that the erection of these universities and the conditions according to which they can be considered Catholic universities must correspond to the directive norms established by the Apostolic See and by the bishops' conference.

What is involved here? The underlying concern is that before an institution presents itself to the public as a "Catholic university" it give evidence that it is the genuine article. The responsibility for evaluating this evidence is placed in the hands of the competent ecclesiastical authority—whether the diocesan bishop, the episcopal conference, or the Holy See.

Does the norm merely repeat the provisions of canon 808, which acknowledges the existence of universities that are "truly Catholic" even though they do not carry the word *Catholic* in their title or name? Or does this norm go beyond the canon and impose a new obligation that, in the future, to found a university that is "truly Catholic" will require approval from the competent authority? I have argued elsewhere that the norm is to be interpreted in light of the code, and that it appears to be a reaffirmation that universities are not to title themselves "Catholic" (in their name) without approval.[41] The issue, however, remains a complex one and admits of varying views.

Article 4. The University Community

The primary responsibility for maintaining and developing a university's Catholic character belongs to the university community itself. This is in keeping with the autonomy of the institution and the understanding of its Catholic character as rooted in *being* Catholic and in publicly identifying itself in relationship to the Catholic church, as discussed earlier. The general norms address several dimensions of the role of the community and its members: the community itself; teachers and administrators in general; teachers and Catholic doctrine; Catholic theologians; non-Catholic teachers and administrators; and students.

The Community Itself (art. 4, sec. 1)

The norm first states the general obligation of the university community, and then addresses the gradation of obligations within the community. The university authorities have a primary responsibility. The structuring of university authorities varies among universities, so the norm leaves the precise determination of this up to the statutes of the university itself. It does mention that if there is a chancellor, a board of trustees, or some other corporate body with ultimate responsibility for the institution, these must of course be included among the university authorities responsible for its Catholic character.

Next, there are varying degrees of responsibility for its Catholic character among other members of the university community. Special attention is given to teachers and administrators, who must be ready and competent to foster this character.

A third general observation about the community itself is that there are two keys to the Catholic character of the university: the quality of the teachers, and the observance of Catholic doctrine. It is especially in regard to these two factors that legitimate authorities are to be vigilant. In a note, the "legitimate authorities" are identified with those addressed by canon 810.

Canon 810 is a very carefully drawn law. It is intended to respect the legitimate autonomy of a Catholic university, the Catholic character of the university, and the responsibility of competent ecclesiastical authorities (especially diocesan bishops and bishops' conferences) to be vigilant concerning the observance of Catholic doctrine in Catholic universities. The canon is important for what it says, and for what it does not say.[42]

a. The selection and quality of teachers. The canon places this responsibility in the hands of the internal authorities of the university, as specified in each institution's own statutes. At a Catholic university, these authorities are to take into consideration the scientific and pedagogical suitability of applicants, and also their "integrity of doctrine and probity of life." The statutes of the institution are also to determine how a teacher who lacks these qualities is to be removed. Thus the specific criteria and procedures are left by the canons in the hands of the individual institutions.

Here is where Catholic universities quite clearly differ from other Catholic institutions for formation or education. The appointment and removal of teachers in seminaries is the prerogative of the bishop (c. 253). The appointment or approval of religion teachers in Catholic grade and high schools is also the prerogative of the diocesan bishop (c. 805). But when it comes to higher education, this prerogative shifts to the authorities internal to the institution, in keeping with the distinct autonomy of these institutions. This does not mean these authorities will be insensitive to the same concerns for the church and academic competence that guide a diocesan bishop, but it does mean the law places the responsibility not in the bishop's hands, but in those of the academic authorities.

b. The observance of Catholic doctrine. The canon places overall concern for this in the hands of the diocesan bishop and the episcopal conference.

Bishops are authoritative teachers of the faith, and judgment concerning Catholic doctrine belongs ultimately to those who hold the episcopal office as successors to the apostles (cc. 753-754). The bishops' role here, however, is one of vigilance, similar to the vigilance they exercise over all the pastoral life of the churches committed to their care (cf. cc. 383, 386, 392, 394). Unlike their role in other institutions, they are not authorized to intervene in the internal affairs of a Catholic university but are to work closely with the internal authorities if, in their vigilance, they detect that Catholic doctrine is not being observed (art. 5, sec. 2).

The canon deals with Catholic doctrine, which includes matters of faith and morals, as well as the practice of Catholic social doctrine. Thus bishops have a responsibility to see that Catholic universities, as well as other Catholic institutions in their dioceses, observe the teaching of the church on respect for human dignity, working relations with employees, wages, etc., as well as that what is taught in the university is consistent with Catholic doctrine. Their vigilance is directed toward observance by the institution as such as well as by individuals who make up the university community.

Teachers and Administrators in General (art. 4, sec. 2)

The norm explicitly requires that new teachers and administrators be informed about the Catholic character of the institution and the implications of this character. It also requires that they be informed of their responsibility for promoting this character, or at least of observing it. This last provision appears to apply in a particular way to non-Catholics serving in a Catholic university (n. 26).

Teachers and Catholic Doctrine (art. 4, sec. 3)

In addition to promoting or at least observing the Catholic character of the university, in their research and teaching Catholic teachers are to receive Catholic doctrine and discipline on morals, in keeping with the ways appropriate to their various academic disciplines. Non-Catholic teachers are to respect church teaching even if they are not bound to receive it.

The responsibility of Catholic teachers here is part of the overall project of the university to explore the relationship between faith and reason, to bring the gospel to bear on all aspects of human culture, and "to try to communicate to society those ethical and religious principles which give full meaning to human life" (n. 33; cf. nn. 17, 43). This does not deny the role non-Catholic teachers may also exercise in this regard, but it places the active responsibility only on those who are Catholics.

Catholic Theologians (art. 4, sec. 3)

Catholic theologians have a special responsibility in this context. They have already been assured of academic freedom in part 1 and have been encouraged to be creative in their work, conducting their research in a way that respects theological method and seeking "to understand better, further develop and more effectively communicate the meaning of Christian Revelation as transmitted in Scripture and Tradition and in the Church's Magisterium" (n. 29). Because bishops are the authoritative interpreters of revelation, theological method itself includes respect for the bishops' authority and assent to Catholic doctrine according to the degree of authority with which it is taught (n. 29). The norm must be understood in this context, for it focuses on only one aspect of the work of Catholic theologians, their fidelity toward the church's magisterium.

The norm also makes reference to theologians carrying out a "mandate" (*mandatum*) of the church, and in a note refers to canon 812.[43] This raises a very complex issue in the canon law on Catholic higher education.[44] Without attempting to resolve disputed questions, it is possible to analyze the issue in four stages: the meaning of the mandate; those who are to receive one; those who grant it; and the implications for Catholic universities.

a. The mandate. The requirement of a "canonical mission" to preach has a long history in the church.[45] The concept was applied to teaching religion at any level of education when schools and universities were secularized in Germany in 1848, as a means of protecting the teaching of Catholic religion from control by state authorities.[46] Gradually the term was introduced into concordats, particularly with German states, to protect the church's role in the teaching of Catholic religion in state-run schools. The concept was also taken over in the norms for ecclesiastical universities promulgated by Pius XI.[47] When John Paul II revised this legislation, the requirement of a "canonical mission" was retained for those who teach disciplines touching on faith and morals.[48] Early drafts of the 1983 code retained the same language, as a new requirement for those who taught theological or related disciplines in any kind of institutions of higher learning, not just ecclesiastical faculties.

Responding to concerns expressed about this requirement, the secretariat of the code commission changed the term to "mandate" instead of "mission," reasoning that what was under consideration was not fully equivalent to a true canonical mission.[49] In canonical usage today, canonical mission refers primarily to the assignment of people or territory for a bishop to exercise his office authoritatively.[50] In an applied sense it relates to various other authorizations to act in the name of the church.

Since "mandate" was selected to avoid the possible misinterpretations to which "mission" could give rise, it is evident that "mandate" at least is not a delegation or granting of jurisdiction. It does not establish the one who is mandated in a position of disciplinary authority over others in the church. It does not confer an ecclesiastical office.

On a more positive note, some have sought the meaning of mandate in the mandate for Catholic Action, particularly the rather nuanced presentation of this in the Second Vatican Council's Decree on the Apostolate of the Laity. Here it is used in the context of the varying degrees of relationship between lay apostolic activity and the hierarchy. Laity can exercise their own initiative in undertaking apostolic activity. Some of these initiatives are given explicit recognition by the hierarchy, and in various ways. The hierarchy gives special encouragement or endorsement to some apostolic associations and projects. Others receive a "mandate" that joins some particular form of the apostolate "more closely with its [the hierarchy's] own apostolic function," but at the same time "the proper nature and individuality of each apostolate must be preserved, and the laity must not be deprived of the possibility of acting on their own accord."[51] Some laity receive a "mission" to be involved in pastoral duties such as teaching Christian doctrine, conducting certain liturgical actions, and exercising care of souls.

Because of the distinction between "mission" and "mandate" in this passage, it has been taken as a way to explain canon 812.[52] Under this perspective, theologians receiving the mandate would be brought into a closer relationship with the hierarchy's own apostolic function, while retaining the proper nature and individuality of theologians and the right to their own initiatives. In a similar perspective but without reference to the decree on the apostolate of the laity, Örsy proposes that the mandate "is a commission to teach. It is less weighty than a canonical mission, which is needed for obtaining an ecclesiastical office, but it is more than a mere permission, because 'mandate' includes an element of acting in the name of someone else."[53]

Yet great caution needs to be exercised here. If the mandate could be interpreted at civil law as in any way making a theologian an "agent" ("acting in the name") of the bishop, bishops who are already faced with major legal problems because of misconduct by their clergy may have a whole new class of persons whose behavior may involve bishops in expensive litigation. It does not seem likely that diocesan bishops want to add to their potential liability in this way.

Moreover, such a closer involvement with the work of the hierarchy does not seem to be *Ex corde Ecclesiae*'s understanding of the work of theologians who are said to "serve the Church through research done in a way that respects theological method" (n. 29). There is no mention here of a special closeness to the hierarchy's apostolic function, but of doing their own proper work "alongside other disciplines" in the university. Their roles interrelate with the bishops not because theologians are involved in the bishops' work, but because theologians are to respect the authority of bishops as integral to their theological method. The relationship between bishops and theologians is characterized as one of "dialogue," not one of participating in the bishops' own apostolic function.

The mandate comes from a competent ecclesiastical authority, so it could be considered a statement by that authority that the theologian is in ecclesiastical communion. Or, since competent ecclesiastical authority has a central role in the teaching function of the church, it could be considered an assurance about the theologian's orthodoxy. On the other hand, it is a theologian who receives the mandate; some have suggested it represents a judgment that the theologian is competent in the theological sciences.[54] The code commission rejected the proposal to replace mandate, viewed as a positive act of ecclesiastical authority, with that authority's traditional role of negative vigilance;[55] yet eventually this may be what the mandate means in practice, at least in areas where there are no other considerations requiring the mandate.[56]

b. Recipients of mandate. The norm requires Catholic theologians to receive the mandate. Canon 812 refers to "those who teach theological disciplines." In either sense, the person must be a Catholic to be obliged to receive the mandate; canon law normally does not apply to non-Catholics (c. 11). The requirement is clearly on the individual, not on an institution of some kind.

Theologians do not need the mandate, however, if they are not engaged in teaching in institutes of higher studies. It is not clear if they can request the mandate without a teaching position in prospect, although in Germany this is reportedly done as the theologian completes advanced studies and prior to seeking a position.[57] However, to teach in Catholic universities of whichever classification (the two types in art. 1 or the three types in art. 3), Catholic . theologians need the mandate.

c. Competent ecclesiastical authority. The mandate is to be given by the competent ecclesiastical authority. The earlier discussion of this topic makes it clear that the Apostolic See is always competent to grant the mandate to teach; similarly, the diocesan bishop is competent. So, too, the episcopal conference appears to be competent for a mandate having effect nationwide.

The granting of the mandate is an administrative act, a disciplinary activity. The authority to issue such acts includes all local ordinaries (vicars general and episcopal vicars), and for their subjects, religious ordinaries. Some deny that religious ordinaries should be considered competent authorities here, arguing that the mandate is related to the office of teaching in the church and that this pertains to the hierarchy.[58] However, since the mandate is not a grant of power over others, it would seem religious ordinaries are not excluded on that basis.

The law does not restrict the granting of the mandate to bishops or religious ordinaries personally. It can, therefore, be delegated to others, arguably to lay persons as well as to clerics, to grant the mandate. In Germany, for example, canonical missions to teach (as required by concordat) are granted by the chancery in the bishop's name, but he is involved personally only in special cases.

Once granted, is the mandate "portable"? It is not tied to a specific appointment at a given university but is required for any kind of university. If a theologian moves from one Catholic university to another within the jurisdiction of the authority that granted the mandate, there would appear to be no reason to need another mandate; it is the theologian, not the institution, that needs it. In Germany, by particular law, mandates are valid within an ecclesiastical province; if one bishop in the province grants it, all the others accept it. It would be possible for the *ordinationes* of a bishops' conference to achieve a comparable effect in other countries.

There is a legitimate concern among theologians that one bishop could deny a mandate that another bishop might grant; moreover, currently there are no standard procedures for the granting of the mandate. Again, because of their concordat situation, the German bishops have designed a common procedure with standard criteria for the granting of the "canonical mission" there; something similar could be adopted by bishops' conferences in other countries as part of their *ordinationes*.

The extent to which the implementation of canon 812 may affect the standing of Catholic universities has been studied by others. This could be a situation where the bishops' conference of a country could take civil law into consideration in developing their *ordinationes,* but the question goes beyond the strictly canonical perspective of this present study.

d. Implications for Catholic universities.

d. Implications for Catholic universities. The mandate obliges the theologian, not the institution. But the mandate could be one way in which university authorities are assured of the "integrity of doctrine and probity of life" of theologians. The problem arises if a mandate is withdrawn from an existing faculty member, in keeping with the exercise of negative vigilance by competent ecclesiastical authority.

Catholic universities dependent on competent ecclesiastical authorities (the first types in both art. 1 and art. 3) should make provisions in their statutes for what to do in this eventuality, including procedures to be followed. It would be in the self-interests of other Catholic universities to make similar provisions.

It is also important for Catholic university authorities, theologians, and bishops to work out mutually acceptable standards and procedures for the granting of the mandate and its withdrawal. As *Ex corde Ecclesiae* and the conference's *ordinationes* are implemented, the absence of mutually acceptable standards and procedures would create an unnecessary uncertainty and tension in the theological and academic communities.

Non-Catholic Teachers and Administrators (art. 4, sec. 4)

Two concerns are expressed in this norm. The first is the support of the Catholic character of the university by everyone in it; the second addresses the issue of "critical mass."

A proper respect for the Catholic character of the university is called for by those who are not Catholics among the teachers and administrators, and by all students (Catholic as well as non-Catholic). *Ex corde Ecclesiae* (n. 26) also calls for a positive value to be placed on the contribution of non-Catholics within the university.

The issue of "critical mass," however, is new in this norm. This question is often discussed: What is necessary for any Catholic institution to maintain its Catholic identity? At one time the impression was that clergy and religious guaranteed this, and there is still a tendency to think that when Catholic lay persons take over the institution, its Catholic character is somehow lessened. *Ex corde Ecclesiae* (n. 25) rejects this view and emphasizes the important contribution Catholic lay persons make to Catholic universities.

It is not enough for an institution to affirm its Catholic identity in its governing documents, policies, and programs. There also has to be a sufficient Catholic presence to assure these are put into practice. The norm locates this presence not among the administrators or governing officials, and not among the student body, but among the teachers. There must be a sufficient number of Catholics among the teachers to assure the university lives out its Catholic identity.

The norm cautions against non-Catholics becoming the *pars maior* on the faculty. Does this have to be taken in a numerical sense (i.e., more than 50 percent), or does it have a qualitative meaning? In some cultural settings, the majority of faculty may well be non-Catholics, but those who set the tone for the institution are Catholic. Consideration needs to be given to the cultural setting of each university; even the norm does not set an absolute rule, but provides a caution (*caveatur*).

Article 5. The Catholic University within the Church

All Catholics have an obligation to maintain communion with the universal church and the particular church (c. 209). Similarly, all are called to participate in the work of evangelization (c. 211). Section 1 reaffirms these obligations for Catholic universities as institutions.

Bishops have the responsibility to be vigilant, as discussed earlier. Article 2 applies this responsibility to exercising vigilance that the Catholic character of local Catholic universities be preserved and strengthened. *Ex corde Ecclesiae* (n. 28) also calls on bishops to protect this Catholic identity relative to civil authorities, where this is needed. It follows that the vigilance of a bishop must be exercised in such a way that it does not threaten the existence or the Catholic identity of a university relative to civil authorities.

The article places with the bishop the responsibility for taking initiatives if his vigilance uncovers difficulties, but it also emphasizes the respect due to the institution's autonomy. Thus the bishop is to take the matter up with the competent university authorities, and the article calls for procedures to be established that will facilitate this work. A note calls for new Catholic universities established by competent ecclesiastical authority or by public juridic persons to include these procedures in their statutes. The same would appear to apply to existing universities founded or approved by competent ecclesiastical authority whose statutes are to be revised and given new approval (art. 1, sec. 3). Other universities already in existence and those that are to be founded in the future according to article 3, section 3, are to follow the procedures adopted by the bishops' conference. These would most conveniently be found in the *ordinationes* adopted by the conference but could be adopted separately since the norm does not mandate that they be included in the *ordinationes*.

Section 3 states that new universities founded by competent ecclesiastical authority or by public juridic persons must (*debet*) submit periodic reports to competent ecclesiastical authority. The same would seem to apply to existing universities founded or approved by competent ecclesiastical authorities, given the requirement that they conform their statutes to the constitution, norms, and *ordinationes*. Other Catholic universities, whether already in existence or new ones formed according to article 3, section 3, must (*debent*) provide information to the diocesan bishop where their principal seat is located. The norm does not state how frequently these reports are to be submitted; this could be specified by a bishops' conference in its *ordinationes*. What these reports are to contain and how they are to be submitted might also be described in the *ordinationes*, always respecting the autonomy of the universities and sensitive to any possible impact such reporting may have on the university's status in civil law.

Article 6. Pastoral Ministry

Ex corde Ecclesiae (n. 38) considers pastoral ministry to be an activity of and within the university; it is not something added on from outside or extraneous to the overall commitment of the university community. The purpose for pastoral ministry is to assist in integrating faith with life, providing the community with an opportunity for demonstrating its faith in its daily activities and enriching the lives of Catholic and non-Catholic members alike.

The organization of pastoral ministry on campus is primarily the responsibility of the university. Section 2 of this norm calls for a sufficient number of priests, religious, and lay persons to be appointed to assure pastoral ministry.

It is the Catholic university that selects and appoints these individuals. The constitution does not address the role of the diocesan bishop in the selection or appointment of these individuals, and there is the potential for some misunderstanding here.

If the diocesan bishop has erected a parish for campus ministry (c. 813), then it belongs to the bishop to confer the office of pastor on the priest who will fill that position (c. 523). It would appear that *Ex corde Ecclesiae*, particularly in article 6, section 2, is conferring the right of presentation on Catholic universities so that the individual priest who is proposed for this position is selected by the university. If this is so, the bishop is not free to select which priest will have this office, but the university must obtain the bishop's conferral before its candidate is named pastor of the university parish (cf. cc. 158-163).

Where campus ministry has not been erected as a parish, the bishop's permission is needed for a priest of that diocese to function in campus ministry (c. 274, sec. 2), and the bishop may indeed assign him to the work (c. 813). But the university still has the option of determining whether to accept him in campus ministry since pastoral ministry within the university is the prerogative of the Catholic university. While priests from other dioceses or religious institutes may not need faculties of the diocese where the university is located,[59] cooperation with the diocesan bishop includes at least notifying the bishop of the extern priests who may be involved in campus ministry. The diocese may impose other requirements for priests to minister in the diocese.[60]

Pastoral ministry in a Catholic university is not limited to the campus but should cooperate with the pastoral activity of the local diocese, assist in addressing social justice needs of the community, and promote ecumenical and interreligious dialogue.[61] Because of this impact on the local church community, section 2 requires campus pastoral ministry to work "in harmony and cooperation with the pastoral activities of the local church under the guidance or with the approval of the diocesan bishop." How this is to be worked out in practice needs to be developed through mutual exchanges between the university community and the bishop. The *ordinationes* of an episcopal conference may provide further details for such exchanges.

Article 7. Cooperation

This "norm" is really an encouragement rather than a strict legal obligation. It calls for cooperation in three dimensions: with other Catholic universities, including ecclesiastical ones; with other universities, with research institutions, and other educational institutions; and with governmental and other programs, particularly in regard to justice, development, and progress.

Unlike episcopal conferences, which must consult the Apostolic See before undertaking actions or programs on an international level (c. 459, sec. 2), no advance approval of ecclesiastical authority is required for Catholic universities to engage in national and even international cooperation. Similar encouragement is given to ecclesiastical universities in the code (c. 820).

Transitional Norms

These transitional norms (*normae temporariae*) make the legal character of the general norms more evident. They establish the *vacatio legis* for *Ex corde Ecclesiae* (art. 8), authorize the Congregation for Catholic Education to publish norms for the application of the constitution (art. 9) and to propose changes to the pope as experience may indicate (art. 10). It also establishes the binding force of *Ex corde Ecclesiae* despite any particular laws or customs to the contrary (art. 11), an exceptional provision provided for by canon 20.

The *vacatio legis* is interesting because it is not a fixed period of time. The "first day of the academic year" varies from place to place, hemisphere to hemisphere. By setting the first day of the academic year 1991 (art. 8), the constitution reaffirms the emphasis on subsidiarity evident earlier in the document.

The Congregation for Catholic Education has a double charge. It is to look after (*prospicere*) the execution of the constitution and to issue any necessary norms for this (*normas prodere*). The general norms (art. 2) have placed the major responsibility for developing *ordinationes* for the application of the constitution at the local and regional levels. The congregation's norms may be in the form of instructions to guide episcopal conferences in drafting their *ordinationes*.[62] The scope of the congregation's concern is limited by the provisions of the apostolic constitution itself, including the proper responsibility of episcopal conferences and the appropriate institutional autonomy of Catholic universities.

The second charge of the congregation is to propose future modifications to *Ex corde Ecclesiae* in light of experience. This is not an authorization for the congregation to issue new laws, however. Article 10 indicates the congregation is to propose (*proponere*) these changes; it will be for the legislator to determine what to do with the proposals.

CONCLUDING REFLECTIONS

Ex corde Ecclesiae is an important document containing both a teaching component and laws (general norms). It reaffirms the church's recognition and support for Catholic universities, their proper autonomy and academic freedom. It addresses the issue of Catholic identity in these institutions and recognizes the considerable diversity that exists among them. Three areas for continued study have surfaced from this canonical analysis.

Classifications of Catholic Universities

The document locates the distinctions among Catholic universities not on whether they are themselves juridic persons (a topic debated by commentators on the drafts and final version of the code), but on the nature of the person or entity that founded or approved them. It is important to note this approach, but also to recognize that there may be an inconsistency within the document in its use of this classification scheme.

As the constitution's norms are worded, there are two distinct classifications. The first concerns those which already exist (art. 1); these are divided into two types, universities founded or approved by competent ecclesiastical authority, and all other universities. The second classification is for Catholic universities that will be founded in the future (art. 3); these are divided into three types: universities founded or approved by competent ecclesiastical authority, universities founded by public juridic persons in the church, and universities founded by other people.

A first question appeared in analyzing article 5, section 3, on regular reports; it appears that Catholic universities founded by religious institutes in the future will have to report regularly to a competent ecclesiastical authority (who may or may not be the diocesan bishop), but existing Catholic universities founded by religious institutes report only to the diocesan bishop.

A second question appears in the instructions from the Congregation for Catholic Education to the bishops of the United States, which appear to utilize only the classifications in article 3, even when dealing with existing universities.

Subsidiarity

One of the major features of *Ex corde Ecclesiae* is its effort to utilize subsidiarity. The episcopal conferences are charged with seeing to its application in the various regions of the world. Even in doing this, they are to respect the role of statutes for each individual university. Frequently the constitution's norms remain quite general, recognizing that the practical decisions at a much more local level will have to be taken in order to address the concerns that underlie the apostolic constitution.

The difficulty with subsidiarity is that it means different things to different people. What is one person's "appropriate level of responsibility" may be seen by another as inappropriate intervention. Catholic universities have recognized the need to affirm their Catholic identity; they have been less happy about perceived efforts of ecclesiastical authorities to control their activities. Church officials, on the other hand, recognize in Catholic universities an important dimension of the church's mission to the world of science and culture, and an important witness of the church in the modern world generally. These universities are also important for the future of the church given their impact on their students. Ecclesiastical authorities have been concerned about perceived drifting away from a Catholic commitment by some institutions and by activities on the part of some in the universities that may not be wholly consistent with official church policy.

The constitution has taken an important step toward attempting to address this situation. But as the general norms recognize, it is not the only step or even the last step. The application of the constitution, if carried out in the spirit of subsidiarity that characterizes its norms, provides an opportunity to continue this process.

Eastern Catholic Churches

As indicated earlier, there are several problems in relating *Ex corde Ecclesiae* with the Eastern Catholic churches, even though the constitution apparently intends to apply to them as well (hence the repeated references to *cetera Consilia Hierarchiae Catholicae*). A note to article 1, section 2, explains these *consilia* exist in "rites" (*Ritus*) other than the "Latin rite" (*Latino Ritu*).

The Latin code refers to Ritual churches *sui iuris* (cc. 111-112); the Eastern code, even in the draft form published in 1987, referred to churches *sui iuris*. "Rite" was retained for the five liturgical rites, but not for the ecclesiastical structures. *Ex corde Ecclesiae* uses a terminology that is not consistent with either of these documents. Moreover, the *Consilia Catholicae Hierarchicae* in the Eastern code exist only in Metropolitan churches *sui iuris* (*CCEO*, cc. 164-171); Patriarchal churches *sui iuris* have a Patriarchal synod. Both of these bodies are the highest administrative authority of the respective churches; only the highest administrative authorities can erect a Catholic university in the Eastern churches (*CCEO*, c. 642).

More comparable to episcopal conferences of the Latin church are the "assemblies of hierarchs of several Churches *sui iuris*" (*conventus Hierarcarum plurium Ecclesiarum sui iuris*) which meet for purposes similar to those of episcopal conferences, and whose decisions must be adopted by a two-thirds vote and receive the *approbatio* of the Roman pontiff (*CCEO*, c. 322). If the *cetera Consilia Hierarchicae Catholicae* of *Ex corde Ecclesiae* mean these *conventus*, the parallel is quite close, but these bodies have little authority over Catholic universities compared to the *Consilia* of the Metropolitan church₋ *sui iuris* or the Patriarchal synods. If the *Consilia* of *Ex corde Ecclesiae* are meant to apply to the *Consilia* of the Metropolitan churches *sui iuris* and to the Patriarchal synods, the reported parallel is not very close at all.

Further complicating the situation is the competence of various Roman departments. While it is not explicitly stated, the Congregation for Eastern Churches appears to have competence over Catholic universities in Eastern Catholic churches,[63] yet *Ex corde Ecclesiae* gives the Congregation for Catholic Education the responsibility for seeing to the constitution's implementation.

It could be that despite the occasional references to the Eastern churches, *Ex corde Ecclesiae* really addresses the Latin church, which has the greatest number of Catholic universities. While the issue is important, it is not crucial to the present study since there are no Catholic universities in the United States that pertain to an Eastern Catholic church.

In light of these concerns and the overall analysis of this study, it seems appropriate to close on a note of caution. If *Ex corde Ecclesiae* is to be a "magna carta" for Catholic universities, a proper understanding of its content requires more than a casual reading. Careful analysis and interpretation must be brought to bear on the text, seen in itself and in its context. The document's implementation requires careful work by all concerned—the universities, their various levels of authority, the entire university community, competent ecclesiastical authorities, and all in the church who share with the pope the hope that these institutions will fulfill their distinct and unique mission.

NOTES

1. John Paul II, apostolic constitution *Ex corde Ecclesiae,* 15 August 1990: *AAS* 82 (1990): 1475-509.

2. 1983 code, c. 17. All translations of the code are taken from *The Code of Canon Law, Latin-English Edition* (Washington D.C.: CLSA, 1983). Citation of canons within the text is indicated by (c.).

3. For example, art. 1, sec. 3, speaks of universities "constituta vel approbata." These are technical terms, and must be interpreted according to their technical uses. Technically, a document that simply "praises" such an institution does not constitute or approve it.

4. For example, art. 1, sec. 2, speaks of the "inspectionem Sanctae Sedis" rather than "recognitionem" by the Apostolic See. As discussed below, the choice of a different technical term here is significant from a canon law point of view.

5. See, for example, the different degrees of obligation evident for different types of universities in art. 1, sec. 3: some "inserere debet," while others "convertent . . . inserent." Concerning the various kinds of expressions in the code, see Peter Erdö, "Expressiones obligationis et exhortationis in Codice Iuris Canonici," *Periodica* 76 (1987): 3-27; John J. O'Rourke, "Expressions of Command in the New Code," *The Jurist* 43 (1983): 385-86.

6. This is not the place to enter into a lengthy explanation of these traditional norms for interpretation. See, for example, James A. Coriden, Ellsworth Kneal, Richard A. Hill, and Ladislas Örsy, *The Art of Interpretation: Selected Studies on the Interpretation of Canon Law* (Washington, D.C.: CLSA, 1982), and the standard canon law commentaries.

7. Only a few canonical commentaries on *Ex corde Ecclesiae* have appeared. See, for example, Peter Krämer, "Die katholische Universität," *Archiv für katholisches Kirchenrecht* 160 (1991): 25-47 (dealing primarily with the unique situation in Germany); Patrick de Pooter, "L'Université catholique: au service de l'Église et de la société," *Ius Ecclesiae* 4 (1992): 45-78.

8. Subheadings are those used in the Vatican's English translation of the constitution.

9. See Francis G. Morrisey, "Papal and Curial Pronouncements: Their Canonical Significance in Light of the 1983 Code of Canon Law," *The Jurist* 50 (1990): 107-108; also Lothar Wächter, *Gesetz im kanonischen Rechts* (St. Ottilien: EOS Verlag, 1989): 20-21.

10. *Codex Canonum Ecclesiarum Orientalium* [*CCEO*], 18 October 1990: *AAS* 82 (1990): 1033-363; English translation, *Code of Canons of the Eastern Churches, Latin-English Edition* (Washington, D.C.: CLSA, 1992).

11. *CCEO,* cc. 640-45. In the Eastern Catholic churches a Catholic university can only be founded by the Apostolic See or in consultation with it (*CCEO,* c. 642, sec. 1).

12. See Jobe Abbass, "Canonical Interpretation by Recourse to 'Parallel Passages': A Comparative Study of the Latin and Eastern Codes," *The Jurist* 51 (1991): 293-310; James H. Provost, "Some Practical Issues for Latin Canon Lawyers from the Code of Canons of Eastern Churches," *The Jurist* 51 (1991): 38-66.

13. Secretariat for Promoting Christian Unity, directory *Spiritus Domini,* 16 April 1970: *AAS* 62 (1970): 705-24.

14. This is further confirmed by the regulations governing the Roman Curia. The Congregation for Catholic Education has exclusive competence over Catholic universities in the Latin church, including missionary areas. See John Paul II, apostolic constitution *Pastor bonus,* 28 June 1988, art. 88, sec. 2, and art. 116, sec. 3: *AAS* 80 (1988): 882, 889.

15. Congregation for Catholic Education, "Proposed Schema [Draft] for a Pontifical Document on Catholic Universities," 15 April 1985, nn. 46, 48: *Origins* 15, no. 43 (April 10, 1986): 708.

16. See "Principia quae Codicis Iuris Canonici recognitionem dirigant," *Communicationes* 1 (1969): 80-82 (this principle was approved by the 1967 Synod of Bishops; ibid., p. 100); also Joseph A. Komonchak, "Subsidiarity in the Church: The State of the Question," *The Jurist* 48 (1988): 298-349.

17. Congregation for Catholic Education, "Proposed Schema," nn. 46-47.

18. See Sixtus V, constitution *Immensa Aeterni Dei,* 22 January 1588: *Bullarum, diplomatum et privilegiorum sanctorum Romanorum Pontificium taurinensis editio,* ed. Luigi Bilio (Turin: F & H Dalmazzo, 1857-1872), 8:991. For a thorough discussion of the practice and issues surrounding *recognitio* see Julio Manzanares, "Papal Reservation and *Recognitio*: Considerations and Proposals," *The Jurist* 52 (1992): 228-54.

19. See discussion in Manzanares, "Papal Reservation and *Recognitio*"; also Francis J. Murphy, *Legislative Powers of the Provincial Council: A Historical Synopsis and a Commentary,* Canon Law Studies 257 (Washington, D.C.: Catholic University of America, 1947), p. 48-52.

20. For example, *approbatio* by the Apostolic See is required before a bishops' conference can erect an interdiocesan seminary for its territory (c. 237, sec. 2), before it can issue its own catechism (c. 775, sec. 2), and before it can abolish holy days of obligation or transfer them to a Sunday (c. 1246, sec. 2).

21. The Roman pontiff examines all the circumstances (*inspectis adiunctis*) before making provisions for a bishop who submits his resignation (c. 401, sec. 1), as does a bishop when a pastor retires (c. 538, sec. 3) or when he appoints a dean (c. 554,

sec. 1). Before a non-Catholic is conditionally rebaptized in the Catholic church, the words and form of the reported prior baptism are to be examined (*inspecta*; c. 869, sec. 2). Sometimes documents are "inspected" (*actis inspectis*) prior to some action being taken: the defender of the bond in a marriage case (c. 1433) or a pastor who is threatened with removal (c. 1745, 1°).

22. John Paul II, apostolic constitution *Sapientia christiana*, 15 April 1979: *AAS* 71 (1979): 469-499.

23. Congregation for Catholic Education, norms *Universitatis vel facultatis*, 29 April 1979: *AAS* 71 (1979): 500-21.

24. Such is the case, for example, of the Catholic universities of Louvain/Leuven in Belgium, where the episcopal conference is also the governing board.

25. It is conceivable that a university could be composed of Catholic teachers and students, carry on its activities in a truly Catholic manner, but for some reason or other not adopt any kind of relationship with the Catholic church. For example, a state university in a predominantly Catholic country could fit this category and even be thought of in the popular mind as "the Catholic university." Yet it would not be considered a Catholic university because it would lack the second aspect required here.

26. The text considers these as either/or alternatives: "aut ... aut"; *AAS* 82 (1990): 1503.

27. This would appear to be the result of the founding or *approbatio* of a university by competent ecclesiastical authorities, or the *approbatio* of their governing documents and statutes, as described in art. 1, sec. 3. It is also the condition of Catholic universities in Eastern Catholic churches, where they can be established only by competent ecclesiastical authority, and always with the involvement of the Apostolic See (*CCEO*, c. 642, sec. 1).

28. That is, there is a difference between giving consent to use "Catholic" in the title of an organization and giving formal approval to that organization. For a parallel that clearly shows the different degrees of involvement by competent ecclesiastical authority, see the canons on associations of the faithful, especially cc. 299, sec. 3 (*recognitio* of statutes for an association to be recognized in the church); 300 (*consensu* to use the title "Catholic"); 322, sec. 2 (*approbatio* of statutes for a private association to become a private juridic person).

29. The norm cites the Second Vatican Council declaration on religious liberty *Dignitatis humanae*, n. 2, where freedom of conscience is viewed as an integral dimension of religious liberty; see also the pastoral constitution on the church in the modern world *Gaudium et spes*, nn. 16-17, on the basic role of freedom of conscience in Christian anthropology.

30. Seminaries, now considered institutions of formation rather than schools, are directly under the bishop or bishops involved (c. 259); schools are subject to regulation by the diocesan bishop, and religion teachers in schools are appointed by him or approved by him (cc. 805-806).

31. *Gaudium et spes*, n. 59, in *The Documents of Vatican II*, trans. and ed. Walter Abbott (New York: America Press, 1966), p. 265.

32. Ibid., n. 74, p. 284.

33. The code adopts this concerning the exercise of rights within the church; see c. 223, sec. 1: "In exercising their rights the Christian faithful, both as individuals

and when gathered in associations, must take account of the common good of the Church and of the rights of others as well as their own duties toward others."

34. *Gaudium et spes,* n. 59, p. 265.

35. Ibid.

36. *Gaudium et spes,* n. 62, p. 268.

37. For Opus Dei, erection into a public juridic person is found in the *Codex Iuris Particularis Operis Dei,* issued by John Paul II together with the erection of Opus Dei as a personal prelature through the apostolic constitution *Ut sit,* 28 November 1982: *AAS* 75 (1983): 423-25. The code of particular law for Opus Dei was not promulgated in the *AAS* but can be found in Amadeo de Fuenmayor et al., ed., *El itinerario jurídico del Opus Dei. Historia y defensa de un carisma,* 4th ed. (Pamplona: EUNSA, 1990), pp. 628-57. For juridic personality, see art. 129, sec. 1, on p. 647.

38. Religious "house" is used here in the technical sense of a *domus religiosa.* The written consent of the diocesan bishop is needed for the competent authority within the religious institute to erect a *domus religiosa* (c. 609, sec. 1).

39. See discussion in Roch Pagé, "Associations of the Christian Faithful," *The Jurist* 47 (1987): 165-203.

40. Such "movements" often do not seek recognition as an association of the faithful. See Jean Beyer, "Motus ecclesiales," *Periodica* 75 (1986): 613-37; Jean Beyer, "De motu ecclesiali quaesita et dubia," *Periodica* 78 (1989): 437-52.

41. See James H. Provost, "The Canonical Aspects of Catholic Identity in the Light of *Ex corde Ecclesiae,*" *Studia Canonica* 25 (1991): 176-79.

42. For commentaries on this canon, see Dario Composta in *Commento al Codice di Diritto Canonico,* ed. Pio V. Pinto (Rome: Urbaniana University Press, 1985), pp. 497-498; James A. Coriden in *Code of Canon Law: A Text and Commentary,* ed. James A. Coriden et al. (Mahwah, N.J.: Paulist Press, 1985), p. 574; Lamberto de Echeverría in *Código de Derecho Canónico, Edición bilingüe comentada,* ed. Lamberto de Echeverría, 5th ed. (Madrid: BAC, 1985), pp. 417-418; José M. González del Valle in *Código de Derecho Canónico, Edición anotada,* ed. Pedro Lombardía et al. (Pamplona: EUNSA, 1983), p. 503; Heinrich Mussinghoff in *Münsterischer Kommentar zum Codex Iuris Canonici,* ed. Klaus Lüdicke et al. (Essen: Ludgerus Verlag, 1985-), at c.810 Patrick Valdrini, "Les universités catholiques: exercise d'un droit et contrôle de son exercise (canons 807-814)," *Studia Canonica* 23 (1989): 445-58.

43. Canon 812: "Qui in studiorum superiorum institutis quibuslibet disciplinas tradunt theologicas, auctoritatis ecclesiasticae competentis mandatum habeant oportet." ["It is necessary that those who teach theological disciplines in any institute of higher studies have a mandate from the competent ecclesiastical authority."]

44. The literature here is quite extensive. Here are some of the more pertinent sources: James J. Conn, *Catholic Universities in the United States and Ecclesiastical Authority,* Analecta Gregoriana 259 (Rome: Editrice Pontificia Università Gregoriana), pp. 266-89; Robert P. Deeley, *The Mandate for Those Who Teach Theology in Institutes of Higher Studies,* J.C.D. diss. at the Gregorian University (Rome: Tipografia di Patrizio Graziani, 1986); Sharon A. Euart, *Church-State Implications in the United States of Canon 812 of the 1983 Code of Canon Law,* Canon Law Studies 526 (Washington, D.C.: Catholic University of America, 1988); Alice Gallin, "Catholic Higher Education and the 1983 Code of Canon Law," *CLSA Proceedings* 52 (1990): 134-51; Frederick R. McManus, "The Canons

on Catholic Higher Education, Prepared for the Association of Catholic Colleges and Universities" (Washington, D.C.: ACCU, 1983); L. Michaud, "The Code of Canon Law and the Catholic Universities," *Seminarium* 34 (1983): 583-89; Ladislas Örsy, "The Mandate to Teach Theological Disciplines: Glosses on Canon 812 of the New Code," *Theological Studies* 44 (1983): 476-88; Heribert Schmitz, "Die Entwicklung des kirchlichen Hochschulrechts von 1917-1980," *Archiv für katholisches Kirchenrecht* 151 (1982): 424-78; Heribert Schmitz, "Katholische Theologie in der Universität. Zur rechtliche Stellung theologischer Wissenschaftsinstitutionen ausserhalb theologischer Fakultäten unter kirchenrechtlichen Aspekt," *Archiv für katholisches Kirchenrecht* 156 (1987): 3-33; Heribert Schmitz, *Katholische Theologie und Kirchliches Hochschulrecht* (Bonn: Sekretariat der Deutschen Bischofskonferenz, 1992); John Strynkowski, "Theological Pluralism and Canonical Mandate," *The Jurist* 42 (1982): 524-33; Francis A. Sullivan, *Magisterium: Teaching Authority in the Catholic Church* (Ramsey, N.J.: Paulist Press, 1983), pp. 196-204; Knut Walf, "La relation des facultés de théologie catholique avec l'Etat et la société: le cas de la République fédéral d'Allemagne," *Studia Canonica* 23 (1989): 101-118. In addition, see Coriden in *Code of Canon Law: A Text and Commentary*, pp. 575-76; de Pooter, "L'Université catholique," pp. 67-73.

45. See Heinrich Flatten, "Missio Canonica," in *Verkundigung und Glaube. Festschrift für Franz X. Arnold*, ed. Theodor Filthaut and Josef A. Jungmann (Freiburg-Br.: Herder, 1958), pp. 123-41; Hugo Hellmuth, "Die missio canonica," *Archiv für katholisches Kirchenrecht* 91 (1911): 448-76, 601-37; M. Peuchmaurd, "Mission canonique et prédication," *Recherche de théologie ancienne et medievale* 30 (1963): 122-44, 251-76.

46. See Johann Haring, *Das Lehramt des katholischen Theologie. Festschrift des Grazer Universität für 1926* (Graz: Meyerhoff, 1926); Wilhelm Kahl, "Die Missio Canonica zum Religionsunterricht und zur Lehre des Theologie an Schulen bezw. Universitäten nach dem Rechte des katholischen Kirche und dem staatlichen Rechte in Preussen," *Deutsche Zeitschrift für Kirchenrecht*, 3rd ser., 18 (1908): 349-93.

47. Pius XI, apostolic constitution *Deus scientiarum Dominus*, 24 May 1931, art. 21, 5°: *AAS* 23 (1931): 251.

48. *Sapientia christiana*, art. 27, sec. 1: *AAS* 71 (1979): 483.

49. *Communicationes* 15 (1983): 105: "opportunius visum est sermonem instituere de mandato, quam de missione canonica quae in hoc casu non plene aequaretur cum vera canonica missione."

Despite the decision of the code commission, some scholars still hold there is no difference in reality between mission and mandate for theologians; see de Pooter, "L'Université catholique," p. 71, who cites Julio Manzanares, "Las Universidades y Facultades Eclesiasticas en la nueva codificación canónica," *Seminarium* 34 (1983): 588; and Strynkowski, "Theological Pluralism and Canonical Mandate," p. 533.

50. *Lumen gentium*, n. 24. See also *Nota explicativa praevia*, 2°.

51. *Apostolicam actuositatem*, n. 24, in Abbott, *The Documents of Vatican II*, p. 513.

52. This is the main thrust of Deeley's, *The Mandate for Those Who Teach Theology in Institutes of Higher Studies*.

53. Örsy, "The Mandate to Teach Theological Disciplines," p. 480.

54. Coriden, *Code of Canon Law*, p. 576: "The 'mandate' is simply a recognition that the person is properly engaged in teaching the theological discipline. It is not an empowerment, an appointment, or a formal commission. It is disciplinary, not doctrinal."

It does not grant approval of what is taught nor is it a formal association with the Church's mission or ministry of teaching."

55. See discussion in Sullivan, *Magisterium,* pp. 196-200; John A. Alesandro, "The Rights and Responsibilities of Theologians: A Canonical Perspective," in *Cooperation between Theologians and the Ecclesiastical Magisterium,* ed. Leo J. O'Donovan (Washington, D.C.: CLSA, 1982), pp. 106-109.

56. For example, in Germany the mandate—or mission—is required by concordat.

57. The German situation is rather complex because of the various concordats. See "Rahmenrichtlinien der Deutschen Bischofskonferenz vom 12 bis 15 März 1973 zur Erteilung der kirchlichen Unterrichtserlaubnis und der Missio canonica für Lehrkräfte mit der Fakultas 'Katholische Religionslehre' und Rahmengeschäftsordnung zu diesen Richtlinien," *Archiv für katholisches Kirchenrecht* 142 (1973): 491-93; and for an update and commentary, see Heribert Schmitz, *Katholische Theologie und Kirchliches Hochschulrecht.*

58. Conn, *Catholic Universities in the United States,* p. 284, seems to argue that the one who issues the mandate must have pastoral authority over the students in the university, since in his view the mandate is an attestation of ecclesial communion.

59. Priestly "faculties" are needed to celebrate the sacrament of penance, but if a priest has these from his diocese of incardination or domicile, they may be used anywhere in the world unless an individual exception is made for him by some other local bishop; see c. 967, sec. 2. Faculties are no longer required to preach (unless this is imposed by particular law—c. 764), nor are they needed to celebrate Mass (see cc. 900-903). Delegation to assist at marriages may be given, even habitually, by the local pastor as well as by the local ordinary (c. 1111).

60. Increasingly dioceses are requiring documentation on a priest's suitability, particularly in reference to sexual conduct, before he is permitted to minister in a diocese.

61. See *Ex corde Ecclesiae,* nn. 46-47.

62. See Prot. N. 1485/90, 21 January 1991, for instructions to the episcopal conference in the United States.

63. See *Pastor bonus,* art. 58, sec. 2, and art. 116, sec. 3: *AAS* 80 (1988): 875, 889.

COMMENT

SR. SHARON A. EUART, R.S.M.
National Conference of Catholic Bishops

THE CANONICAL IMPLICATIONS OF
"EX CORDE ECCLESIAE"

First, I wish to thank Father Provost for his clear and comprehensive commentary on the canonical implications of *Ex corde Ecclesiae*. His treatment of many of the complex canonical issues in the apostolic constitution provides a valuable resource for bishops, college and university presidents and faculty, as well as for canonists. We're grateful for his contribution to the discussion.

My comments following Father Provost's paper will focus on the *mandatum* referred to in article 4, section 3, of the general norms of *Ex corde Ecclesiae*[1] and required in canon 812 of the 1983 Code of Canon Law.[2] There is little doubt that the incorporation of the requirement of canon 812 in *Ex corde Ecclesiae*, namely that Catholic teachers of theological disciplines obtain a mandate from competent ecclesiastical authority, has evoked more debate and discussion, generated more fears and suspicion on the part of theologians, and raised more concerns and complexities than any other requirement in the apostolic constitution.

Among the many issues related to the mandate, two seem to me to warrant further consideration for their importance in interpreting and applying canon 812: (1) the distinction between canonical mission and mandate insofar as it affects the meaning and purpose of the mandate, and (2) the need for clear procedures for the granting, withdrawal, and denial of the mandate.

Canonical Mission and Mandate

To discuss the significance of the mandate in *Ex corde Ecclesiae* and canon 812 it is helpful to determine whether or not it differs from canonical mission, *137* and if so, how. That some difference exists would appear evident since, as Father Provost noted, the early drafts of canon 812 required a *canonical mission* for teachers of theological disciplines in institutes of higher learning. The textual change was reported in the *Relatio* prepared for the 1981 plenary session of the Pontifical Commission for the Revision of the Code.[3] Following urging from Cardinal G. Emmett Carter of Toronto and Archbishop Joseph Bernardin of the United States to omit the canon, the text was amended. The Relator stated that substituting "mandate" for the previously used "canonical mission" seemed opportune since "canonical mission . . . in this case is not fully equated with a true canonical mission."[4]

By a brief review of past usage of the terms *canonical mission* and *mandate,* some light might be shed on why the term *canonical mission* had been incorporated in the earlier drafts, why it was later thought not to be opportune, and why *mandate* was considered to be more suitable.

The notion of canonical mission (*missio canonica*) as applied to teaching in the church is rooted in conciliar legislation of the Middle Ages concerning requirements for preaching. For example, Lucius III, at the Council of Verona in 1184, condemned those who "presumed to preach" without "having been sent [*non missi*]" by the Holy See or a local bishop.[5] Similar condemnations were issued against positions that denied the necessity of ecclesiastical authorization for preaching by the Fourth Lateran Council, the Council of Constance, and the Council of Trent.[6] This conciliar legislation seems to have relied on the letter of Paul to the Romans, in which the author states, "But how are men to call upon him in whom they have not believed? And how are they to believe in him of whom they have never heard? And how are they to hear without a preacher? And how can men preach unless they are *sent?*" (Rom. 10:14 RSV; italics added). In so doing, the conciliar documents appear to have juridicized the biblical notion of "being sent" to preach the Word of God.

As Father Provost mentioned, later in the nineteenth century, canonical mission was applied more broadly to all public religious instruction with the federalization of schools and universities in Germany. The church required all teachers of theology, at whatever level of teaching, to have an ecclesiastical (canonical) mission from the bishop to ensure freedom from state intervention in the teaching of theology.

In the 1917 code the term *missio canonica* was used to denote the principal means of acquiring the power of jurisdiction. In the writings of many commentators on the 1917 code, however, it was also applied to liturgical preaching and to the entire ministry of teaching. The basis of this usage was canon 1328 which did not use the term *missio canonica*; it used simply the term *missio* to describe the authorization needed for the ministry of preaching.[7] The placement of canon 1328 in the 1917 code, and the organization of the section in which the canon appeared, supported the opinion that the required authorization called for in the canons applied to the broader ministry of teaching, including catechetical teaching as well as preaching.[8]

Although canon 1328 did not use the term *missio canonica,* many commentators interpreted the term *missio* in the canon to mean *missio canonica.* Much of the debate around the authorization of canon 1328 focused on the dispute over the relationship of ecclesiastical magisterium to the power of jurisdiction, namely whether or not ecclesiastical jurisdiction included the power to teach as well as the power to govern.[9] In recognizing the applicability of canon 1328 to the entire ministry of ecclesiastical teaching, commentators on the 1917 code had to grapple with the practical application of the *missio* to lay persons. For most, it was not a canonical mission in the strict sense of participation in the church's power of jurisdiction since only clergy were capable of such power. It could more precisely be called a "mandate" or an "assignment" from ecclesiastical authority. As a "mandate without jurisdiction," such a "commission" was not an ecclesiastical office, but rather an appointment of a lay person by competent ecclesiastical authority to perform a special function.

In light of this canonical history, it might be argued that the roots of the mandate of canon 812 include the *missio* of canon 1328 of the 1917 code as it was understood to be some form of ecclesiastical authorization distinct from the *missio canonica* of the same code.

In 1931 the requirement of a canonical mission for some public ecclesiastical teaching became an explicit part of the universal law in the norms governing ecclesiastical faculties and universities.[10] Article 21 of the apostolic constitution listed five requirements for faculty selection, the fifth of which required that each professor "receive a canonical mission for teaching from the chancellor after having obtained the *nihil obstat* from the Holy See." A second reference to canonical mission was found in article 22 which authorized the chancellor to withdraw the canonical mission where a professor had been shown to have departed from doctrinal integrity.[11]

In 1979 Pope John Paul II promulgated *Sapientia christiana* replacing the previous norms regulating ecclesiastical faculties and universities.[12] *Sapientia christiana* retains the requirement of a canonical mission for teachers of disciplines related to faith and morals; other teachers require "permission" to teach (*venia docendi*).

While the term *missio canonica* had been incorporated into the early drafts of canon 812, the reason for its inclusion does not appear in the published legislative history of the canon. It would seem reasonable that the drafters of canon 812, intending to uphold the integrity of Catholic doctrine by requiring ecclesiastical authorization for the teaching of theology in institutes of higher studies, introduced a term whose past usage could be said to lend legitimacy to such a contemporary application.

When it was later determined that the *missio canonica* was not opportune terminology, the drafters were not suggesting that ecclesiastical authorization was unnecessary. Rather, the deletion of *missio canonica* simply reflected concern over the nature of the authorization required for public ecclesiastical teaching. Since the *missio canonica* was not considered to be "fully equated with a true canonical mission," its deletion in the final version, and its replacement with *mandatum,* seems related to the association of *missio canonica* with jurisdiction and to yet unresolved questions concerning lay participation in the power of governance in the church.

In the preparation of the Second Vatican Council's Decree on the Apostolate of the Laity, the council fathers discussed the distinction between *mandatum* and *missio canonica.* In article 24 of the decree the Council set forth different grades or types of relationship between the lay apostolate and the hierarchy, beginning with the more remote relationships and moving to closer relationships in which the laity are fully subject to hierarchical direction. In so doing, the Council taught that there are certain forms of the apostolate of the laity that the hierarchy joins more closely to its own apostolic endeavors without, however, depriving the apostolate of the laity of its own nature, individuality, and initiative. This act of joining some forms of the apostolate of the laity to that of the hierarchy is called a *mandatum.*[13]

The same article then speaks of another form of cooperative relationship between laity and hierarchy in which the hierarchy "entrusts" to the laity some functions that are more closely connected with the pastoral duties of the hierarchy, such as the teaching of Christian doctrine, certain liturgical actions, and the care of souls.[14] The term *missio* is used here to describe those "entrusted" functions that are fully subject to hierarchical direction.

Father Provost noted that the distinction between *missio* and *mandatum* in article 24 has been used by some to explain canon 812. Although this distinction may provide some insight into the meaning of the *mandatum* of canon 812, the distinction is not all that clear. From the earliest discussions of the Preparatory Commission on the Apostolate of the Laity it was clear that no real clarity existed in regard to the notion of mandate. The concept was confused with both the notion of canonical mission and with other juridical meanings of *mandate.* Further attempts were made by the Conciliar Commission for the Apostolate of the Laity to clarify the distinction between canonical mission and mandate by appending lengthy explanatory notes to the 1963 schema.[15] One of the explanatory notes enumerated the areas of the apostolate requiring a *missio canonica* which included teaching Christian doctrine in a public manner.[16]

The Conciliar Commission prepared another draft of the text in 1964 which became the basis for discussion at the third session of the Council in October 1964. Criticism of the text was strong among the council fathers, although it came from differing viewpoints. The final text of the decree in September 1965 contained no changes in the distinction between *mandatum* and *missio.* Further clarity in the application of the two notions was lost as a result of the Commission's decision to delete the accompanying explanatory notes.

What does seem clear from the promulgated decree is that the Council considered mission and mandate to be two distinct concepts. Mission connotes entrusting to the laity certain tasks and certain offices that are considered to be proper to the hierarchy but which require neither the power of orders nor the power of jurisdiction for their lawful exercise. Mandate, on the other hand, refers to those apostolic activities that remain activities proper to the laity in virtue of baptism, but which, at times, are joined more closely to the apostolic responsibility of the bishop. When acting pursuant to a mandate, a lay person acts, it would seem, on his or her own and in communion with the bishop, but not in the name of the bishop or the church hierarchy.

The use of *mandatum* in canon 812 suggests that the teaching of theological disciplines differs from the teaching of Christian doctrine, by virtue of a less close relationship to the hierarchy. Unlike the teaching of Christian doctrine, which according to the conciliar decree requires a *missio,* the teaching of "theological disciplines" is not "entrusted" to the laity by the hierarchy, but is considered to be work appropriate to the laity (as well as to clergy), carried out in communion with the hierarchy, but not requiring the same degree of ecclesiastical recognition.

At the present time there does not seem to be a common interpretation of the distinction between *mandatum* and *missio canonica* nor is there a common understanding of the precise meaning of the mandate of canon 812. Some suggest the terms are interchangeable, while others note they are not equivalent. Some interpretations include understanding the *mandatum* as hierarchical deputation or agency,[17] a commission to teach,[18] a disciplinary matter,[19] and an expression of communion between theologian and hierarchy.[20] What is common to the various interpretations is that some ecclesiastical authorization is required for those who teach theological disciplines in Catholic colleges and universities. The implications of that authorization continue to be explored.

Procedures for Granting, Withdrawal, or Denial of the Mandate

Lack of a common interpretation of the mandate of canon 812 suggests a need for clarity on precisely what is required on the part of a Catholic theologian to receive a mandate from ecclesiastical authority and, at the same time, a determination of the conditions under which the mandate would be denied or withdrawn. This points to the necessity of establishing mutually acceptable standards and procedures for the granting, withdrawal, or denial of the mandate.

The proposed draft ordinances for the application of *Ex corde Ecclesiae* in the dioceses of the United States describe the mandate of article 4, section 3, as "recognition by competent ecclesiastical authority of a Catholic professor's suitability to teach theological disciplines." While this understanding of the mandate is certainly consistent with the meaning of canon 812, questions about its application may arise. For example, what determines one's suitability? Is it academic credentials, teaching experience, probity of life, orthodoxy of the theologian's writings, one's intention to teach in accord with the magisterium? All of the above? Moreover, on what basis can a Catholic theologian be denied the mandate? Under what conditions can it be withdrawn? Answers to questions such as these will be necessary if relations between bishops and theologians are to be "characterized by mutual trust, close and consistent cooperation and continuing dialogue" (n. 28).

What should be considered, from a canonical perspective, in developing standards and procedures to address the concerns reflected above? Canon 812 is a legal norm. It involves a right-and-duty situation,[21] namely, the granting, withdrawal, or denial of a mandate for teachers of theology. The requirement of a mandate is in the nature of a restriction on the rights of those engaged in sacred disciplines to freedom of inquiry and prudent expression, a right recognized in canon 218 of the 1983 code.[22]

In addition to canon 218, two other canons also affirm basic ecclesial rights of the Christian faithful. The first is canon 211 which affirms the duty and right of the faithful to participate in the spreading of the gospel;[23] the second is canon 216 which acknowledges the right of the faithful, in accord with each one's state and condition, to promote and support apostolic undertakings of their own initiative.[24]

As a restriction on the free exercise of rights, canon 812 is to be interpreted strictly, that is, as narrowly as is consistent with the ordinary meaning of the words (c. 18). Consequently, wherever canon 812 is susceptible to differing interpretations, the stricter or narrower interpretation should be given.

In addition to the canons that provide a frame of reference for *interpreting* canon 812, there are other relevant canons that afford an important framework for *applying* the canon. Canon 812, for example, also exists in the context of the basic human right to one's good reputation, a right recognized in canon 220 which states that one's reputation is not to be unlawfully damaged.[25] Any procedure for the application of canon 812, therefore, should be sensitive to foreseeable effects upon the reputation of those involved. Finally, canon 221 provides juridical protection of rights stating that the Christian faithful have a right to vindicate or defend their rights before a competent forum in the church.[26] Although canon 812 lays down no procedure for the granting, withdrawal, or denial of a mandate, canon law does afford recourse for wrongful, arbitrary action.

A sound understanding and interpretation of the meaning of the mandate should be made in light of such rights as are enumerated in these canons, and any application of the mandate should be careful not to ignore or infringe upon these same rights. Any procedure for the application of the mandate should respect the rights of both theologians and bishops. As teachers of the faith, bishops are to provide episcopal supervision over the transmission of the faith and to safeguard the integrity of Catholic teaching.[27] When the right of the bishop to protect the rights of the church and its members to receive the faith integrally and faithfully is in tension with the rights of the theologian enumerated above, mutual trust, cooperation, and dialogue are placed in jeopardy unless a just and equitable resolution is sought.

In this context, *Doctrinal Responsibilities,* a statement on the relationship between bishops and theologians,[28] provides an important framework for the implementation of the mandate of article 4, section 3, of the general norms of *Ex corde Ecclesiae.* The apostolic constitution ought not to "presuppose a situation of tension or envisage adversarial relations between bishops and theologians in the United States, as if the rights of one had to be protected against the other." Rather, it ought "to encourage increased communication and collaboration between bishops and theologians, to forestall disputes and if such disputes arise to promote their resolution for the good of the faithful."[29]

Should disputes arise concerning the granting, withdrawal, or denial of the mandate, it is important that agreed upon procedures be established for the resolution of such conflicts. Whether this procedure is based on the formal dialogue outlined in *Doctrinal Responsibilities* or the steps enumerated in *On Due Process*[30] for administrative matters or adapted from a procedure established in a particular diocese for dispute resolution, the manner in which it is carried out should respect the rights of all concerned—the bishop, the theologian, the college, or university, and the Christian faithful.

NOTES

1. Art. 4, sec. 3, speaks of "Catholic theologians, aware that they fulfill a mandate received from the Church, are to be faithful to the Magisterium of the Church as the authentic interpreter of Sacred Scripture and Sacred Tradition."

2. 1983 Code of Canon Law, c. 812: "It is necessary that those who teach theological disciplines in any institute of higher studies have a mandate from the competent ecclesiastical authority." All English translations of the 1983 code are taken from *The Code of Canon Law, Latin-English Edition* (Washington, D.C.: CLSA, 1983).

3. Pontificia Commissio Codici Iuris Canonici Recognoscendo, *Relatio* (Romae: Typis Polyglottis Vaticanis, 1981), p. 183. Text of the *Relatio* was reproduced in *Communicationes* 15 (1983): 57-109.

4. Ibid., p. 184: "opportunius visum est sermonem instituere de mandato, quam de missione canonica quae in hoc casu non plene aequaretur cum vera canonica missione."

5. "[q]ui vel prohibiti vel non missi, praeter auctoritatem ab Apostolica Sede vel episcopo loci susceptam publico vel privatim praedicare praesumpserint ... " C.9.X *de haeretics,* V.7.

6. See C.13.X *de haereticis,* V.7; Martinus V, *Inter cunctos,* 22 February 1418, art. 14; Concilio Tridentinum, sessio XXIII, *de ecclesiastica hierarchia et ordinatione,* c. 7.

7. 1917 code, c. 1328: "Nemini ministerium praedicationis licet exercere, nisi a legitimo Superiore missionem receperit, facultate peculiariter data, vel officio collato, cui ex sacris canonibus praedicandi munus inhaereat."

8. Title XX of the 1917 code was entitled, "de divina veri praedicatione." The title contained three chapters: "de catechetica institutione," "de sacris concionibus," and "de sacris missionibus." It would seem that the term "praedicatione" in the heading of title XX, which could be understood to connote preaching in the strict liturgical sense, should rather be understood in the broader sense of "teaching" so as to include each of the chapters of the title, namely catechetical instruction as well as "de sacris concionibus" which concerned preaching in the strict liturgical sense. For a similar opinion, see Heinrich Flatten, "Mission Canonica," in *Verkundigung und Glaube. Festschrift fur Franz X. Arnold,* ed. Theodor Filthaut and Josef A. Jungman (Freiburg-Br.: Herder, 1958), p. 134, note 36.

9. See, for example, E. F. Regatillo, *Institutiones Iuris Canonici* (1961), n. 178; F. X. Wernz and P. Vidal, *Ius Canonicum* 2 (1935), n. 48; A. Vermeersch and J. Creusen, *Epitome Iuris Canonici* 2 (1940), n. 656; P. M. Conte a Coronata, *Institutiones Iuris Canonici* 1 (1947), n. 168.

10. Pius XI, apostolic constitution *Deus scientiarum Dominus,* 24 May 1931: *AAS* 23 (1931): 251, art. 21, sec. 5.

11. Ibid., art. 22.

12. John Paul II, apostolic constitution *Sapientia christiana,* 15 April 1979: *AAS* 71 (1979): 469-99, art. 27, sec. 1.

13. *Apostolicam actuositatem,* 18 November 1965: *AAS* 58 (1966): 837-64, art. 24.

14. Ibid., p. 857.

15. Archivis Concilii Oecumenici Vaticani II, *Acta Synodalia Sacrosancti Concilii Oecumenici Vaticani II,* III/4 (Rome: Typis Polyglottis Vaticanis, 1974), pp. 677-78.

16. Ibid., p. 681.

17. John A. Alesandro, "The Rights and Responsibilities of Theologians: A Canonical Perspective," in *Cooperation Between Theologians and Ecclesiastical Magisterium,* ed. Leo J. O'Donovan, S.J. (Washington, D.C.: Canon Law Society of America, 1982), p. 107.

18. Ladislas Orsy, "The Mandate to Teach Theological Disciplines: On Canon 812 of the New Code," *Theological Studies* 44 (1983): 480-81.

19. James A. Coriden, "Book III: The Teaching Office of the Church" in *The Code of Canon Law: A Text and Commentary,* ed. James A. Coriden, et al. (Mahwah, N.J.: Paulist Press, 1985), p. 576.

20. John Strynkowski, "Theological Pluralism and Canonical Mandate," *The Jurist* 42 (1982): 532-33; Robert P. Deeley, "Canon 812: The Mandate for Those Who Teach Theology: An Interpretation," *Proceedings of the Canon Law Society of America* 50 (1989): 80.

21. Orsy, "Mandate to Teach Theological Disciplines," p. 480.

22. Canon 218: "Those who are engaged in the sacred disciplines enjoy a lawful freedom of inquiry and of prudently expressing their opinions on matters in which they have expertise, while observing a due respect for the magisterium of the church."

23. Canon 211: "All the Christian faithful have the duty and right to work so that the divine message of salvation may increasingly reach the whole of humankind in every age and in every land."

24. Canon 216: "All the Christian faithful, since they participate in the mission of the Church, have the right to promote or to sustain apostolic action by their own undertakings in accord with each one's state and condition; however, no undertaking shall assume the name Catholic unless the consent of competent ecclesiastical authority is given."

25. Canon 220: "No one is permitted to damage unlawfully the good reputation which another person enjoys nor to violate the right of another person to protect his or her own privacy."

26. Canon 221, sec. 1: "The Christian faithful can legitimately vindicate and defend the rights which they enjoy in the Church before a competent ecclesiastical court in accord with the norm of law."

27. Canon 753: "Although they do not enjoy infallible teaching authority, the bishops in communion with the head and members of the college, whether as individuals or gathered in conferences of bishops or in particular councils, are authentic teachers and instructors of the faith for the faithful entrusted to their care; the faithful must adhere to the authentic teaching of their own bishops with a sense of religious respect." See also art. 5, sec. 2, of *Ex corde Ecclesiae*.

28. National Conference of Catholic Bishops, *Doctrinal Responsibilities: Approaches to Promoting Cooperation and Resolving Misunderstandings between Bishops and Theologians* (Washington, D.C.: USCC Publications, 1989), p. 2.

29. Ibid., p. 2.

30. National Conference of Catholic Bishops, *On Due Process* (Washington, D.C.: USCC Publications, 1972).

COMMENT

REV. LADISLAS ORSY, S.J., *The Catholic University of America*

Once the portion of canon law that applies to Catholic institutions of higher education has been explained, it is legitimate to point out also the limits of the law. The awareness of such limits can be an important factor when the making of "ordinances" is considered by the competent authorities.

The spirit of a university ultimately exists in the minds and hearts of the people who every day re-create it. It follows, therefore, that if there is a need for the revitalization of Catholic universities, it can be done only by the awakening of the minds and hearts of those people who are the principal actors in its life, such as the members of the board, the faculty, and the officers of the administration.

If this principle is correct, as I believe it is, a question immediately emerges: *How far can canon law, in the form of ordinances, or in the form of other jurisdictional acts, be instrumental in the process of revitalization?*

The answer is complex: it shows the need for caution on five counts.

1. The point of departure for finding the correct answer is in acknowledging that legal norms by their very nature are external and do not have the capacity to transform the minds and hearts of persons. At best, they can serve as promptings; real energy and transformation can come from internal conviction and determination only.

A parallel case can be cited to illustrate the above statement. In the course of the history of the church, highly placed authorities had to face repeatedly the problem of religious orders losing their spirit and vitality and entering into a process of decline. Whenever councils, popes, and bishops attempted to remedy the situation and reverse the trend by legislation and other juridical commands, they had little success; the process continued. When, however, a reform movement sprang up inside an order, genuine renewal followed. The revitalization of monasticism by Cluny in the tenth century, its renewal by the Cistercians in the twelfth century, and the spirited reform of the Carmelites by Saint Teresa in the sixteenth century are perfect examples of how internal efforts have achieved what external norms could not do.

Laws and precepts can have an active role to play: they can provide an external framework for the internal spirit; they can never re-create the spirit.

2. Further, much caution and prudence is required in bringing into the orbit of canon law certain activities of Catholic universities. I explain.

Some of the Catholic universities have developed immensely powerful research facilities not only in humanities, but also in natural sciences, including medicine.

While we can speak of education as a significant task of the church and of universities as instrumental in fulfilling this mission, serious questions can arise concerning the relationship of spiritual church authorities to scientific research.

We know that the church has neither mandate nor capacity to pronounce on scientific questions; nor is the church able to judge the validity of scientific hypotheses. Had this principle been followed in the case of Galileo, much embarrassment could have been spared—as has been quite recently officially recognized. Nonetheless, it would be naive to think that because of that case (and other cases of more recent occurrence), the temptation for church authorities to watch empirical research and even to pronounce over some hypotheses "from a higher viewpoint" has entirely ceased.

No more needs to be said. It is obvious that much prudence, great caution, and self-restraint is necessary from the part of church authorities in approaching research facilities that are parts of Catholic universities.

3. The apostolic constitution states that the episcopal body, especially the local bishop, must not be considered extrinsic to the life of a Catholic university; that is, there is an intrinsic relationship between a Catholic institution and the hierarchy. This theoretical (should we call it ontological?) principle, so obviously true, does not determine, however, how in the practical order this relationship should be expressed.

As the constitution itself affirms, one of the principal tasks of the university is the integration of revealed truth with the knowledge that can be reached by human endeavor. This is a delicate task; it requires not only training in theology but also a high degree of competence in human and exact sciences.

To exercise episcopal jurisdiction over such activity is bound to be a delicate operation requiring more than sacramental ordination. We Catholics believe that the college of bishops is ultimately the authentic witness of the evangelical message, but clearly we must hold also that in matters of integrating faith and reason, a great deal of training and knowledge in matters that belong to reason is necessary. Aquinas compared the qualifications necessary for being an academic teacher (having a "magisterial cathedra") with those required for a bishop (in possession of a "pontifical cathedra"):

> . . . there is a threefold difference between the magisterial cathedra and the pontifical cathedra.
> The first is that the one who receives a magisterial cathedra does not receive any eminence that he has not had before; he receives only an opportunity, which he did not have, to communicate his learning . . . The one, however, who receives an episcopal cathedra, receives an eminence of power, which he did not have before; as regards power he was like all the others.
> The second difference is that the eminence of science, which is required for the magisterial cathedra is a perfection residing in the person; the eminence of power is attributed to a person only in relation to others.
> The third difference is that a person becomes qualified for a pontifical cathedra by being outstanding in charity; for a magisterial cathedra, however, a person becomes qualified through sufficient learning.[1]

It follows that special qualities, not given by ordination, are required in the bishops to offer competent help to universities. As a rule, bishops' conferences would be in better position than individual dioceses could ever be to designate competent persons to provide care and solicitude for universities. History again offers some lessons, one of which can be recalled, involving Aquinas himself. His great achievement, of course, was the integration of faith and reason: he used Aristotle's philosophy to bring about a better understanding of the Christian mysteries. This was, however, too much for Etienne Tempier, the bishop of Paris, where Aquinas was teaching. He could not understand the theologian and in 1277 condemned some fifteen propositions drawn from his writings. Two archbishops of Canterbury, Robert Kilwardby and John Peckham, showed no more appreciation and kept attacking Thomas's doctrine.

Modern examples of conflict between reflective theologians pioneering in knowledge and local ordinaries intent on preserving the Christian heritage are not missing.

The Holy See has not remained indifferent to this problem: since the medieval inception of universities, it often granted them (in one form or another) exemption from the jurisdiction of the local ordinary.

There is no other conclusion than that caution is necessary.

4. The warning, however, concerning the limits of the law should not be interpreted as an invitation to neglect a practical, or even institutional, approach to the "maintenance" of Catholic universities. Quite the opposite: without concerted and institutionalized practical actions from the part of the university,

it is virtually impossible to uphold its Catholic character. Such actions, however, must originate and be sustained within the university.

If there is a decline in the Catholic inspiration of universities, it is not for lack of discussions; it is for the lack of practical and institutionalized approach to the issue.

The approach, to be effective, must originate in, and be sustained by, the smallest cells of the university: on the academic level, the schools and departments; on the administrative level, the operational offices. Only when each unit raises the question for itself—"What can we do in the practical order to uphold and strengthen the Catholic orientation of the university?"—and finds a creatively wise answer for it (which must be a well-defined course of action) can the whole institution move forward in the intended direction.

Accountability in this operation is vital, hence it must be institutionalized and made permanent within the university; otherwise the process is likely to fail. Its basic pattern ought to be that of a dialogue, which can take many shapes and forms and must be carried on between different partners. Here is an example: the academic affairs committee of the board could meet regularly with representatives of schools, departments, and offices and ask the question (among many others): "What do you intend to do in the coming years to uphold and strengthen the Catholic character of the university?" The answer should go on record so that the next encounter a few years later could be a check as to what has been accomplished.

By and large too much time has been spent—and too much importance given—to so-called mission statements and too little effort has been expanded on prompting the constitutive units of the university to take practical action.

It stands repeating: such a practical and institutionalized approach can bring fruit only if it is wholeheartedly wanted by the units that participate in it. Imposition will not work, not even if it comes from internal university authorities. It remains always a matter of minds and hearts.

5. The question still remains as to what the relationship of a Catholic university to the hierarchy could be, and how should it be expressed.

As we have seen, both historical antecedents and theological reflections caution against overrating the capacity of canon law to uphold the Catholic character of the universities. A helpful approach is offered through the time-honored idea and practice of communion (hierarchical communion, as Vatican II has stated) between the bishops and the universities. Catholic universities need the bishops' witnessing of the faith, without them they are in danger of going astray. Catholic bishops need the university to help them to integrate the evangelical message with the culture in which they all are embedded and operating.

NOTE

1. Thomas Aquinas, *Quodlibet,* 3.9.c.

DISCUSSION

Discussion opened with several questions regarding canon 812, specifically regarding the applicability of the canonical mission and mandate to theologians. The panelists explained that the canonical mission is required for ecclesiastical faculties in seminaries; the mandate applies to all other Catholic institutions but not to non-Catholic faculty.

The practicalities of the mandate are of considerable complexity. First, there is the problem of conflicting expectations. Someone joins a Catholic university faculty and serves on that faculty for a number of years. Then the new mission is adopted, and expectations are fundamentally changed. Second, most local ordinaries will treat universities somewhat like health-care institutions; they won't want to interfere unless they are forced to. But the whole thrust of a document like *Ex corde Ecclesiae* encourages their involvement; the centralizing style of the Vatican is supportive; and the urgings of Cardinal Ratzinger are that bishops should be like the pope and engage in vigorous, "out front" determined leadership.

Although the language of the mandate in *Ex corde Ecclesiae* is personal, some people interpret that strictly while others consider the institution inevitably involved in the mandate.

Was the responsibility statement[1] drawn up in 1989 considered as a substitute for the idea of mandate? The question of the responsibility statement came up several times, but the bishops felt they could not substitute it for what *Ex corde Ecclesiae* requires. They have, however, agreed to cite the responsibility statement as a means of resolving problems.

Subsequent comments focused on the preferred reactions of the theological and academic communities to the apostolic constitution, with discussion participants differing over the degree to which it represented a "challenge" or a "threat." Several remarked on the need for greater accountability among theologians and within institutions.

Let us look at *Ex corde Ecclesiae* as a challenge, not a threat. Even where the threat is most obvious, the thrust of *Ex corde Ecclesiae* is to bureaucratize the settlement of the issue. Making everything depend on the mandate distracts attention from the primary responsibility of both the university and the ordinary to teach. Administrative measures are inevitably easier to design than are teaching measures and strategies.

In an institutional identity study conducted by a major Catholic university two or three years ago, administrators wanted no jurisdictional intervention in the university and also rejected any exercise of magisterial authority to identify departures from the faith.[2] It is not clear that the juridical approach, the bureaucratic response, by initiating the idea of "mandate" is any worse than the sacred cow of institutional autonomy, which is academic freedom in the tenuring process. Is not corruption of power through tenure also our concern? Does the Catholic college or university have *any* responsibility for the substantive issues of Catholic theology? In what ways do Catholic colleges take responsibility for the Catholic nature of their institutions, for orthodoxy in their teaching of theology?

Universities left to their own devices tend not to do a very good job of judging themselves. They are driven by market forces, by fearful faculty. The theological community is now a much more diverse body, and it is unclear where it fits in this schema. Theologians have tended to become self-protective about critiquing other theologians who have moved beyond the boundaries of orthodoxy.

This is something we have been reminded of for many years: Catholic theologians tend not to criticize other Catholic theologians. The reasons reflect both the bias of the academic community and the use and abuse of church authority with its hidden pressures.

How can the theological community be more self-critical? It could be, if more confidence were placed in it by church leadership. If the leadership of the church saw in the universities a desire to be more Catholic, it would be easier to think of *Ex corde Ecclesiae* as an inspirational document rather than a juridical benchmark.

The pressure on individual theologians is very much like the pressure in political parties. The pressure is to resign and not to say who is responsible for the resignation. It is very, very difficult to go public on these matters.

As long as the pressures on theologians occur secretly, we can never get out of the sinkhole. Theologians will never have enough self-confidence to criticize peers. Somehow criticisms need to be made public.

In response to questions, it was noted that only one university had requested the mandate, that the potential conflict between civil and canonical law raised difficult questions, and that a juridical attempt "to enforce discipline" within the episcopacy is problematic.

There is a clear limit to the effectiveness of a juridical approach to these issues. It is as if the church were to decree that all church art must be beautiful.

History shows us a distinct lack of success in using law to achieve certain ends, particularly law imposed from above.

It is appropriate to consider *Ex corde Ecclesiae* a challenge, but it would be foolhardy not to distinguish between part 1 of *Ex corde Ecclesiae* and part 2, the general norms. While part 1 is the basis for the norms, there is a distinct conflict in style and tone between parts 1 and 2. Institutions should face up to the challenge but put the juridical problem in its place: there is a very real threat here. There are liabilities involved, complexities of interpretation. *Ex corde Ecclesiae* is a much better document than it started out to be, but it started out very poorly.

While there is enormous diversity in the higher education community among universities and colleges, it may be that the degree of future diversity will emerge from varied levls of episcopal oversight applied to colleges in different jurisdictions.

NOTES

1. National Conference of Catholic Bishops, *Doctrinal Responsibilities: Approaches to Promoting Cooperation and Resolving Misunderstanding between Bishops & Theologians* (Washington, D.C.: USCC Publishers, 1989).

2. Responses to the statement: *"The residential bishop should not monitor what is taught at a Catholic university or college"*:

	AGREE	UNCERTAIN	DISAGREE
Bishops:	15.9%	2.6%	81.5%
Higher education:	69.5	7.6	22.9
All others:	48.5	6.7	44.8

Responses to the statement: *"The residential bishop should not express a judgment on what is taught at a Catholic university or college"*:

Bishops:	6.0%	10.6%	83.4%
Higher education:	38.1	16.2	45.7
All others:	29.1	12.7	58.2

Responses to the statement: *"The residential bishop should not control who is hired to teach theology at a Catholic university or college"*:

Bishops:	51.0%	11.3%	37.7%
Higher education:	92.4	1.0	14.9
All others:	79.9	12.7	14.9

Source: *The Future of Catholic Institutional Ministries: A Continuing Conversation* (New York: Third Age Center, Fordham University, 1992), pp. 52-53.

Philip Burling and Gregory T. Moffatt
Foley, Hoag & Eliot, Boston

Notes from the Other Side of the Wall:

A University Counsel's Reflections on Potential Interactions between the Civil Law and the Apostolic Constitution

This paper tries to provide an essentially pragmatic look at the potential interactions between the provisions of *Ex corde Ecclesiae*[1] and current state, federal, and municipal laws that a university counsel representing a Catholic university is likely to encounter. We begin from the church's historic recognition that it carries out its mission as a full participant in the life of the civil state,[2] pursuant to which it has determined to subject itself to the confines of the civil law, except where to do so would involve the church in a fundamental departure from its faith.[3] Our paper assumes that *Ex corde Ecclesiae* is intended to identify occasions in which the "except" clause in this statement of policy will come into play.

In keeping with its announced intent to focus on pragmatic issues, this paper will not attempt to provide an analysis of the constitutional framework of the relationship between church and state in this country (myriad works by scholars of the topic being readily available). Instead, the paper will proceed by hypothesizing some factual situations that might be likely to raise troublesome questions when ecclesiastical authorities, university administrators, faculty, students, alumni, the general public, and civil authorities seek to accommodate one another and work together in ensuring the fullest role possible for Catholic higher education in American society.[4]

THE "MANDATE" IN "EX CORDE ECCLESIAE" AND THE CIVIL LAW, AS ILLUSTRATED BY PRACTICAL SCENARIOS

A Scenario from the Hiring Season

The department of theology is looking for a professor to teach its upperlevel undergraduate course "Jesus in the Twentieth Century" as well as a section *153* in its fundamental course for freshmen. The professor will be expected to teach a third course each semester, filling a slot in an upperlevel lecture or seminar, as needs require. A candidate presents appropriate credentials in the form of a Ph.D. in theology from the University of Chicago. She is a systematic theologian with an expertise in Christology and has done substantial study in liberation theology. Her publications and teaching skills are exemplary.

The Chair of the Theology Department arrives in University Counsel's office with a copy of *Ex corde Ecclesiae* and asks if it has any bearing on the hiring season. University counsel will instantly recognize an apparent conflict stemming from the interaction between article 4, section 3, of the general norms and Title VII of the Civil Rights Act of 1964[5] (not to mention similar state and municipal antidiscrimination laws). The second sentence of article 4, section 3, of the general norms of *Ex corde Ecclesiae*, which is rooted in canon 812, requires Catholic professors of Catholic theology at a Catholic college or university to have a mandate to teach from the "competent ecclesiastical authority."[6] The apostolic constitution (art. 4, sec. 3) references the canon: "In particular, Catholic theologians, aware that they fulfill a mandate received from the Church, are to be faithful to the Magisterium of the Church as the authentic interpreter of Sacred Scripture and Sacred Tradition."[7] To a civil lawyer, the problem looks serious. While the college's mission statement will surely have set forth the college's Catholic identity, this hardly guarantees that everyone who applies for a position in theology will be a Catholic. What then is the obligation, if any, of the college to inquire whether or not the applicant is a Catholic who should be advised of the necessity of applying for the mandate?

If the department chair were required to determine whether the applicant requires the bishop's mandate, the candidate would have to be interviewed not only on her religious identity, but also on her understanding and willingness to teach in conformity with the church's magisterium. Title VII of the Civil Rights Act of 1964 prohibits discrimination in employment on the basis of religion, and the university will have announced its intention to comply therewith in many very public places. At the practical level, therefore, the conflict presented by the requirement of article 4, section 3 would be stark.

If the chair asks the candidate whether she is a Catholic, he risks an almost certain discrimination suit if she is a non-Catholic and is later turned down for the job. If he doesn't ask, is there some possibility that the bishop might take this as an indication of unwillingness on the part of the college to carry out the "spirit" of the apostolic constitution?

Happily, a closer analysis suggests that the situation is much less dire. To understand this aspect of *Ex corde Ecclesiae*, it is necessary to borrow from the learning of canon lawyers who have explicated the canons upon which *Ex corde Ecclesiae* relies. Those scholars have pointed out that canon 812 binds individual professors of theology rather than the universities in which they teach.[8]

To paraphrase this analysis: the Latin text of canon 812 uses the word *qui* (*those*) in describing the entities required to seek the mandate. Because *qui* can refer only to natural persons (and not institutions), the canon must be read to bind individual theologians, not the universities or colleges in which they seek to teach.[9] The force of this interpretation is enhanced by the fact that under canon law, whenever a law restricts the free exercise of a right, it is to be interpreted strictly;[10] the scope and force of its application "should be narrowed as much as it can be within the ordinary meaning of the terms."[11] In the context of canon 812 as carried out in *Ex corde Ecclesiae*, the language restricting the rights of the professor by requiring that she apply for the mandate cannot be read to place any obligation on the university.

It should also be noted that there is no apparent distinction drawn with regard to this mandate between "pontifical" or "ecclesiastical" universities with a specific canonical relationship to the church and those colleges and universities that have relationships principally through their sponsorship by religious orders of men or women, individual dioceses, or some more attenuated institutional affiliation.[12]

Further, should problems arise for colleges and universities as a result of the mandate requirement, they appear to be prospective. Thus, professors appointed to the theology faculty of a college or university prior to the effective date of *Ex corde Ecclesiae* have not been required to seek a mandate from the local ordinary.[13]

To reiterate, the canon and the apostolic constitution simply do not require action on the part of the university or college with regard to the matter of the mandate to teach Catholic theology, at least not in the absence of some existing controversy with regard to a faculty member's mandate. Thus, under the canon and the apostolic constitution, the university should neither be required to make inquiry of the professor's religious affiliation nor should it face difficulties with the local bishop in the event some subsequent controversy arises.

A word of caution is in order, however. A civil lawyer, whether serving as a judge or representing a plaintiff, would be hard put to work through the analysis described above in sources routinely used for civil-law research. As a result, he or she might well interpret *Ex corde Ecclesiae* on its face as requiring the institution to enforce the requirement of a mandate. Such a misunderstanding could be quite dangerous to a Catholic university trying to defend a baseless discrimination suit. For this reason, it would certainly be imprudent for an institution to go beyond the bishops' proposed ordinances and in some way adopt a screening requirement in aid of this provision of *Ex corde*.[14]

Less Clarity and More Concern: Article 4, Section 4

The requirement that Catholic theologians possess the mandate of the local bishop is presented relatively clearly in article 4, section 3, and simply resolved with the aid of canon law. The effect of the succeeding provision of the general norms is much less clear:

> Those university teachers and administrators who belong to other churches, religious communities, or religions as well as those who profess no religious belief, and also all students, are to recognize and respect the distinctive Catholic identity of the university. In order not to endanger the Catholic identity of the university or institute of higher studies, the number of non-Catholic teachers should not be allowed to constitute a majority within the institution, which is and must remain Catholic.

The first sentence of section 4 would appear to require that a university monitor the conduct and expressions of its non-Catholic members and act in some way to ensure that no disrespect of its Catholic identity occurs. And while the requirement of the second sentence seems straightforward—a majority of the faculty should always be Catholic—putting it into effect would surely provoke a clash with civil law. Again, resort to canon law suggests that these concerns do not arise for most Catholic institutions in the United States. As argued by Ladislas Orsy and construed by the proposed ordinances, most Catholic institutions are not obliged to comply with section 4. With the exception of the small number of institutions that are "juridical persons," Catholic colleges and universities in the United States are not "legal persons" in canon law and, therefore, are not intended to be bound by *Ex corde Ecclesiae*.[15] For those not bound, there is no obligation to confront the faculty with a need to change the terms and conditions of employment or risk the clashes with civil law which adoption would present.

However, because *Ex corde Ecclesiae* may be read as inviting institutions to adopt bylaw revisions to conform to its text, it seems worthwhile to identify the potential issues that could emerge if that course were chosen. From the perspective of the antidiscrimination laws, adoption of bylaws conforming to either of these sentences would present problems. For instance, good faith compliance with the first sentence would seem to require a university to be able to identify the non-Catholics among its employees and students; but it would be a mistake to maintain a record of the religious affiliation of all members of the community in their various personnel and student files. Antidiscrimination law, as it has developed since 1964, has created presumptions of bias when data resulting from forbidden inquiries is found in a defendant's records. Therefore, compliance, with section 4 if undertaken at all, should not involve prospective monitoring of the non-Catholic population of a university. Instead, we would suggest a purely post hoc compliance with the first sentence would be preferable. That is, the university should only *react* to a case of disrespect for its Catholic identity. There is no reason that it should not react with great firmness when there has been disrespect, but it will have taken that action without the need to rely on data that bear the stigma of religious discrimination.

The second sentence of article 4, section 4, also has the potential to implicate the university in discriminatory behaviors, if the attempted compliance is not discrete. First, there is the previously discussed problem of identifying the religious faith of the members of the faculty. Attempting to obtain this data through mandatory preemployment inquiries is flatly prohibited by most state and all federal antidiscrimination laws. It is possible to request voluntary submission of the data (as, for instance, data on race and gender are sometimes requested, "for applicant flow purposes"); but there is still a risk that a disappointed applicant will point to the collection of the data as evidence of discrimination. An institution willing to take a risk by complying with section 4 would be advised to use a postemployment request that faculty list their religious faith for purposes of identifying resources for the student body. Disclosure in this instance would be voluntary and for a permitted purpose. Then, by abstracting anonymous data on numbers of Catholics in the faculty, the school can begin to comply with section 4. Maintaining data on the religious demography of the university community is not illegal if the names of particular persons are not included, so the numerical basis for compliance with the second sentence can be obtained without difficulty, as long as a reasonable number of the faculty provide the data requested. Since only the number of Catholics is needed to determine a majority, and the Catholic faculty are more likely to be willing to identify themselves in a Catholic university, this approach offers some hope of a nondiscriminatory solution to the compliance dilemma.

But the second sentence of article 4, section 4, has another twist. It requires the university to ensure that the non-Catholic portion of the faculty never becomes a numerical majority. It seems clear that attempting to attain compliance with this requirement through the termination of non-Catholic faculty members (tenured or not) would involve civil lawsuits or de facto abandonment of secular status. Therefore, compliance can only be maintained (or, if necessary, attained) through attrition and/or hiring.

In addition to the legal difficulty of determining whether an applicant is Catholic,[16] reliance on hiring as a solution to the section 4 requirement raises the problem of making professed Catholicism a bona fide occupational qualification (BFOQ) in an avowedly nonsectarian institution.[17] We are aware of a single case holding that otherwise nonsectarian institutions founded by religious orders may treat membership in their founding order as a BFOQ;[18] but the authors are not aware of any successful effort to eliminate totally the distinction in Title VII between its general prohibitions on religious discrimination and the limited exemption provided to sectarian institutions to protect their religious beliefs.

As a result, an institution that wishes to obtain the benefits of nonsectarian status (i.e., state and federal funding) probably cannot claim that a particular religious belief is a BFOQ for general faculty hiring. The problem, then, is how it can prefer Catholics in the hiring process so as to attain and/or maintain a majority of co-religionists on its faculty.

It is worth remembering that selecting the most qualified applicant for a job is never discriminatory. As is the case with affirmative action, one way to find qualified candidates is to make sure that the pool of potential applicants is as wide as possible. It therefore behooves a Catholic university to look as far and as wide as it can in the hopes that a highly qualified candidate, who is also a Catholic, will turn up. This is a far safer strategy than trying to get away with using Catholicism as a BFOQ. However, Catholic universities that seek to attain major-league academic credentials, and their local bishops, need to be wary of conveying an "only Catholics need apply" message in the hiring market. It is to be hoped that there will be thought and reflection in the enforcement of the second sentence of article 4, section 4.[19]

As Charles Wilson has previously pointed out, there is a real concern that the provisions of canons 810 and 812 as imported into *Ex corde Ecclesiae* appear to require at least some colleges and universities to redraft their governing documents, and in turn faculty contracts and faculty handbooks in order to give notice of the canonical requirements to Catholic and non-Catholic employees.[20] Faculty members will almost certainly be resistant to such redrafting, on the grounds that it poses serious obstacles to hiring, retention, and tenure practices.[21] This fear should be taken seriously because federal labor relations laws could be invoked by faculty members resistant to the incorporation of *Ex corde Ecclesiae* into the terms and conditions of their employment.[22]

TO TERMINATE OR NOT: "EX CORDE ECCLESIAE" AND THE EMPLOYMENT STATUS OF EMPLOYEES: SOME TROUBLING SCENARIOS UNDER CANON 810

Application of the first sentence of article 4, section 3, of *Ex corde Ecclesiae*, which stems from canon 810, to continuing employment situations poses a far broader range of potential flashpoints likely to face Catholic colleges and universities. Because the range of situations requiring a university to consider the termination of an employee is very broad, the following scenarios have been chosen to cover as many as possible of those in which *Ex corde Ecclesiae* might conflict with state and federal employment laws. The problem must be considered even though some of the potential points of conflict appear remote, because the language of the apostolic constitution's general norms is quite broad, and it is unclear whether the language of the general norms, if adopted by a university, is meant to be understood as simply precatory or as a set of "rules of conduct and discipline the breach of which would lead to sanctions" which would require prior notice to faculty members of its application.[23]

A Nonissue: Retention of Tenure, Religious Obedience, and "Ex corde Ecclesiae"

We will begin with a scenario that presents a relatively easy case from the standpoint of civil law. It concerns the question of religious serving as tenured faculty at a Catholic college or university. In this scenario, a tenured professor at a Jesuit university holds a position in the history department. He is a Jesuit priest of a province other than that in which the university is located. He has an employment contract, including standard tenure provisions. What happens in the event that his provincial superior insists that he return to his local province, requiring him to abandon his tenured faculty position? Assuming the man is not a model of Jesuit "disinterestedness," what obligations if any does *Ex corde Ecclesiae* impose upon the administration of the university in seeing that the faculty member complies with his duty? The answer, it seems quite clear, is that the university as an institution of higher education has no obligation to act in this situation. The situation described is properly governed by the canons treating religious institutes, i.e., orders, rather than under either canon 810 or 812.

Perhaps the civil law could be implicated if the professor refuses to comply with the orders of his superior. We will assume that steadfast noncompliance with the order of a religious superior is grounds for dismissal from the order. Should that occur, could the university, acting through its Jesuit president, remove the professor from his tenured post? Canon 810 would appear to allow this on the grounds that the renegade professor has demonstrated a lack of "probity of life," as that rather vague term is used in the canon and adopted by reference in the general norms of *Ex corde Ecclesiae* (art. 4, sec. 1).[24] In fact, however, experience suggests that if there is no scandal to the university community, no such action would be taken absent extraordinary intervention by the local bishop.[25] Moreover, in the scenario as presented, there is little impetus for the bishop to attempt to intervene in a matter of governance within an exempt religious order. Presumably the bishop's hesitance to become involved would be further supported by the fact that the Jesuit university is most likely founded under the auspices of the Society of Jesus, and thus maintains its core identity through the order, rather than through a direct juridical bond with the church.[26]

Three Scenarios Involving Dismissal of Tenured Faculty

A Faculty-Student Affair

Another scenario that will likely turn out to be a nonissue with respect to *Ex corde Ecclesiae* could arise out of the discovery of an affair between a tenured Catholic member of the faculty and a student. Here, the probity of life language of canon 810, to which article 4, section 3, of the apostolic constitution refers, is available as a possible ground for disciplining or dismissing the faculty member. Basing disciplinary action exclusively on *Ex corde Ecclesiae*, however, would probably not be wise. To avoid the inevitable constitutional and contractual challenges to reliance on canon law, it is as well to base a termination on the "termination for cause" language found in most university statutes. Typically these provisions contain language that includes "conduct unbecoming" or "acts of moral turpitude" among the definitions of *cause*. More current statutes may even prohibit faculty-student affairs altogether. In short, this is a clear case where canon law, pursuant to canon 22, should cooperate with, if not defer to, the provisions of civil law, as these are likely to work to the same end result.

A More Troublesome Possibility: Divorced and Remarried Faculty

A more substantial issue could be raised under *Ex corde Ecclesiae* and canon 810 in the event that a Catholic faculty member, previously divorced, announced intention to remarry without having the previous marriage annulled. We raise the issue more because it illustrates the scope of the church's potential authority under the apostolic constitution and the canons than because we imagine that *Ex corde Ecclesiae* will be invoked with any frequency to seek removal of the professor.[27]

Without resorting to sociological data, the authors have assumed that a fair number of Catholic faculty members on Catholic university campuses have found themselves in this situation. Because divorced and remarried Catholics are in violation of the canonical impediment to marriage set forth in canon 1085,[28] and in some situations may be excommunicates in the eyes of canon law, the "probity of life" requirement of canon 810 would appear to require a compliant administration to terminate their employment. Just such a case arose in the mid-1980s at the Catholic University of Puerto Rico (CUPR), where a member of the English department was fired after marrying without an annulment of her prior marriage. She had been hired and subsequently given tenure after her first marriage ended in divorce. When she subsequently remarried and was fired, the CUPR argued that it was permitted to dismiss her for "professional or personal conduct which violates the moral and doctrinal principles of the Catholic Church." The dismissed professor sued and the American Association of University Professors (AAUP) considered sanctioning the CUPR, although the ultimate disposition of the civil case and the AAUP action, if any, were apparently not reported.[29]

As occurred in the CUPR case, such an action taken under *Ex corde Ecclesiae* would almost certainly prompt a resort to the civil court by the dismissed faculty member. Although the authors are not aware of any decided cases on this point, it is our belief that a civil court considering the officially nonsectarian nature of most Catholic universities would have difficulty in ruling in favor of the institution, unless the statutes or contract of employment had particular language requiring Catholics to comply with canon law.

Realistically, therefore, we would urge that, unless special factual circumstances attend, college administration or local ecclesiastical authorities ought not to seek termination in this type of situation. If the issue of the faculty member's impediment to receiving the sacraments is to be addressed, it should be in the context of pastoral care, rather than as a matter of employment discipline (see art. 6, sec. 1). In addition, the faculty member could be removed from any roles in the religious activities of the university community.

Withdrawal from Orders: An Even More Troublesome Scenario

A far more vexing problem would be posed in the situation of a priest-professor who abandoned his clerical vocation and married outside the church, without seeking (or waiting for) a removal of the impediment against marriage. This scenario would, in the eyes of many, clearly draw into play the "probity of life" language of canon 810, section 1. In contracting a marriage without dispensation, the priest-professor would suffer automatic suspension from his clerical office (c. 1394) and potential excommunication. Insofar as the man's history prior to his marriage has a public dimension, this scenario is far more likely to meet with some form of public disapproval or scandal within the university community and in the eyes of the local bishop than the remarriage of a divorced faculty member.

Let us assume, in such a case, that the local bishop determines that permitting the man to remain on the faculty under such circumstances runs counter to the university's Catholic identity and mission. We now have a serious potential for confrontation. Standard tenure provisions in faculty contracts define the award of tenure as "the right of an academic faculty member to hold his or her position and not to be removed therefrom except for just cause."[30] Unless Catholic universities place into the terms of their Catholic professors' contracts provisions that specifically state that they are subject to the strictures of canon law, the university will find it difficult to sustain its termination under a civil court's reading of employment law.[31] From the university's perspective, this scenario presents an opportunity for very thoughtful negotiations with its ordinary and the individual professor.

The authors recognize that this discussion of one of the thorniest problems in the sustenance of the identity of Catholic universities is likely to appear to be a cop-out. With typical legal facility, we have avoided the essential problem raised by the facts discussed: How is a university, which is nonsectarian in its relationships with civil governments, to sustain its commitment to those of the principles on which it was founded that *are* sectarian? Why is it not possible to provide contractual language that would give the university the right to protect itself and its traditions? It is beyond the scope of this paper to seek to resolve the issues of constitutional and antidiscrimination law that might be raised by a set of university statutes that explicitly provided that Catholic employees were required to abide by the requirements of canon law, while, by implication, non-Catholic employees were not. It must suffice to note down some of the possible problems and leave them for future resolution.

The first difficulty to be mentioned is the necessity of equivalency. Unless supported by a bona fide occupational qualification, an institution's conditions of employment may not discriminate either in favor of or against an individual on the basis of religion. Paradoxically, writing a provision into the university statutes that required Catholics to accept the strictures of canon law would constitute discrimination against Catholics in any instance in which adherence was more burdensome than the conditions imposed on other employees. The other side of the coin is, of course, the likelihood that, where such sectarian language is included in the conditions of employment, non-Catholic employees may see preferential terms and sue on that basis.

The "withdrawal from orders" scenario is a perfect exemplar of another predictable difficulty arising from the inclusion of sectarian conditions of employment in the statutes of an officially nonsectarian university. Even as conditions of employment, sectarian rules can be enforced only by the civil courts, which maintain an almost total aversion to "religious entanglements." Since the parties to a lawsuit do not, by definition, agree on the points raised in their suit, any case of termination for failure to adhere to a sectarian rule will force the civil court to become "entangled." To the extent that the dispute is exclusively factual, a court may be prepared to rule; but if there is a dispute on the interpretation of the sectarian rule, it is very unlikely that the court will agree to hear the case.[32] For this reason, the inclusion of sectarian rules in the conditions of employment at a Catholic university may not be as effective a way of sustaining a Catholic identity as the drafters of *Ex corde Ecclesiae* anticipated.

Finally, there is the convenience of a perpetually foggy demarcation between sectarian and nonsectarian so far as the federal government is concerned. Historically, few law makers have wished to render the line between what is sectarian and what is nonsectarian so clearly that it would disqualify religiously connected educational institutions altogether.[33] At the same time, Catholic colleges have become addicted to federal dollars. Like their sister institutions, most Catholic universities in America would be hit hard if they were disqualified from receiving federal and state funding. It is therefore worth considering the wisdom of complying with *Ex corde Ecclesiae* in such a way as to set up a legal conflict, the final resolution of which could produce a bright line test for what is nonsectarian.

STUDENT LIFE: RECOGNITION OF STUDENT GROUPS
AND REGULATION OF CAMPUS SPEECH

Although a series of hypotheticals has been promised, two of the best examples of the potential interactions between *Ex corde Ecclesiae* and student life on the campuses of Catholic universities can be taken from actual events at Georgetown. Each provides a useful vehicle through which to reflect on the complex, sometimes bristly relationship between the religion clauses of the First Amendment, civil rights law, concepts of academic freedom, and the university's role in defining itself, and the interplay of each of these with canon law.

Recognition of Student Groups

Typically, institutional "recognition" of a student group consists of two elements. Recognition permits the student group to identify itself with the university, i.e., the Rugby Club "of Saints College." It also qualifies the group to receive institutional support in the form of funds and the right to use facilities. Unfortunately, there has been some judicial confusion about these two, quite distinct, consequences of recognition.

The use of the words *of Saints College,* to identify a student group with a college is a form of speech and should be regulated as such. Therefore, an American court should have no power to compel a Catholic college to "speak" in favor of a student group that endorses a cause antithetical to the doctrines of the church by requiring the college to permit the group to use the college's name. Conversely, it is clearly a violation of federal law to discriminate among students in the provision of educational services on sectarian grounds.[34] On this analysis, a Catholic university ought to be successful in resisting a civil suit seeking recognition when its objection is to the association of its corporate names with that of the objectionable group, but it should not be successful when it refuses to provide educational services to student groups on doctrinal grounds. The cases do not often land conveniently at these declarative ends of our analytical spectrum, however. As we shall see in considering the Georgetown recognition case, in the real world it is very hard to respond as either the students or *Ex corde Ecclesiae* seem to expect.

In 1980, after almost four years of discussion with the university over their desire to receive official recognition and student activities funds, gay and lesbian groups on Georgetown's Main Campus and Law Center brought suit in the Superior Court of the District of Columbia. This case was brought under the District of Columbia's Human Rights Act, D.C. Code sec. 1-2520 (1981 ed.), which prohibits discrimination, *inter alia,* on the basis of sexual orientation. Georgetown defended on the grounds that the Human Rights Act did not apply to it and that, if it did, the Act violated the university's rights under the Free Exercise Clause of the First Amendment.

On appeal to the Court of Appeals of the District of Columbia, a nominal majority of that court, sitting *en banc,* held that the Human Rights Act did not require Georgetown to "recognize" or otherwise endorse student gay groups, but it held that the Act did require Georgetown to afford the groups equal access to university facilities and services.[35] Rather than seek review by the U. S. Supreme Court, Georgetown settled the case with the students on terms that both the university and the student groups accepted as essentially fair.[36] The case is studied principally as a piece of civil litigation, but it raises a number of intriguing questions with regard to the role of canon law including, now, *Ex corde Ecclesiae* in structuring a university's position in this type of litigation. Specifically, in laying out its free exercise defense, Georgetown relied on "the normative teachings of the Roman Catholic Church" with respect to sexuality, but did not specifically ground its defense in the requirements of canon law.[37] Instead, the university argued that university recognition could not be extended to any student group that fundamentally challenged Roman Catholic "moral norms."[38] In the terms employed by *Ex corde Ecclesiae* (art. 4, sec. 1), the university adopted the position that recognition of the groups would have ruptured the Catholic identity of Georgetown by forcing the university to express, at least tacitly, either neutrality toward or approval of a group that maintained a position in diametric opposition to Catholic doctrine.

It seems quite clear that under the Free Exercise and Free Speech Clauses[39] of the First Amendment, a university cannot be forced to identify itself with a group whose purpose is reasonably deemed to be fundamentally at odds with the religious doctrine of the university. The principal question raised by the outcome of the Georgetown litigation in light of *Ex corde Ecclesiae* is rather: What if ecclesiastical authorities are not satisfied that, so long as a Catholic university or college does not extend official or tacit recognition to student groups such as the gay and lesbian groups at Georgetown, it may continue to give them access to meeting space, university funding, and other "tangibles"[40] that the D.C. Court of Appeals was willing to distinguish from marks of official recognition? Does *Ex corde Ecclesiae* permit the university administrators or the local bishop to intervene and prohibit all such access to groups the goals of which constitute a fundamental challenge to "[t]he identity of a Catholic university" (art. 4, sec. 1; art. 5, sec. 2)? On the face of the apostolic constitution and canon 810, the answer is not clear and for this reason non-juridical institutions should probably not adopt the provisions of *Ex corde* without careful reflection on the risks involved.

Insofar as canon 810 is directed toward the appointment and retention of faculty, the canon does not address this question. Article 5, section 2, of the apostolic constitution, however, would permit the local ordinary to intervene whenever "problems should arise concerning [the university's] Catholic charac-ter."[41] This provision of the general norms would appear to give the local bishop, and ultimately the Holy See (see art. 1, sec. 1), authority to intervene in virtually all aspects of a covered university's life, in the event that the university's administration is unable or unwilling to take whatever measures are deemed necessary by the competent ecclesiastical authority.

Insofar as article 5, section 2, does empower ecclesiastical authorities to act so as to deny access otherwise protected under civil rights laws like the Human Rights Act, the legal implications for the university may be profound. At the extreme, the prospect of such intervention would present a covered university with two very unattractive alternatives. First, it could, through its board of directors, sever its institutional connection with the church in order to comply with the requirements of the civil law. Second, the university could comply with the ecclesiastical order to deny access to the challenged student group, but in doing so would face a variety of painful liabilities.[42]

Controlling Campus Speech

In February 1991, prior to the general application of *Ex corde Ecclesiae,* a group of students at Georgetown sought permission to form a group called G.U. Choice. The group was committed to discussing the prochoice position, but agreed not to advocate abortion or to make referrals to abortion clinics.[43] Georgetown found itself confronted by a group with a keen interest in addressing one of the key social and political issues of the day in accord with the academic freedom due students. University officials certainly recognized the enormous controversy that would be caused by permitting this group to meet on campus. After much discussion, the student group was permitted to meet. The decision was met with stern opposition from the archbishop of Washington, Cardinal Hickey, who stated that although he disapproved of the decision, he recognized that the school has principal responsibility for its own administration.[44]

Cardinal Hickey was then confronted with an extraordinary request when a law professor and a third-year law student filed a canon lawsuit on behalf of more than one thousand Georgetown alumni and students.[45] The petitioners asked Cardinal Hickey to strip Georgetown of its Catholic identity[46] unless G.U. Choice was banned.[47] Cardinal Hickey declined to intervene, taking the position that "It is not within my competency as a diocesan bishop to remove or negate a status which the Holy See has accorded Georgetown University . . . Only the Holy See can revoke what it has granted."[48] Ultimately, the group of alumni and students took their petition directly to the Vatican in March 1992, but any decision was mooted by Georgetown's decision to revoke funding for the group the following month.[49]

We can be sure that this was not the last time that a bishop will feel pressure to intervene to control student speech on campus. Indeed, one of the least noticed features of *Ex corde Ecclesiae* is its potential empowerment of factions within the greater Catholic community who are dissatisfied with events on the campuses of Catholic universities.[50] By its public statement of a bishop's obligation to intervene,[51] *Ex corde Ecclesiae* invites alumni and members of the surrounding community to put pressure on the ordinary, just as pressure was put on Cardinal Hickey. It will be a nice question whether those desirous of an end to some student activity or other will understand the careful regard for individual beliefs prescribed by the apostolic constitution or its distruction between covered and non-covered institutions.

We return to the question of free speech. Independent universities are a gem in America's constitutional crown, and Catholic universities are among the most sparkling. But there has lately been a considerable tension between the right of an independent institution to prevent its facilities from being a podium for ideas that it abhors and the absolute protection of free speech. It can be argued forcibly that the fundamental right of every independent person and entity ought to be the right to speak what he, she, or it believes to be the truth—and the equivalent right not to be compelled to speak an untruth. However, recent cases have rather surprisingly deprived universities of the right to exclude speakers from their campuses, even when the speech to be given endorsed ideas obviously abhorrent to the institution.[52]

This overly long paper would stretch beyond its readers' toleration if it undertook to discuss these and similar cases in full. It should be sufficient to say that civil law in the United States recognizes certain accretional rights to speak freely in certain traditional spaces, i.e., the Hyde Park Corner concept. Many Catholic university campuses have such locations. Under the current state of First Amendment law, it would be an exercise in futility to prohibit on-campus speeches even on matters such as birth control, when that speech is to occur at such judicially protected locations. But this is not the end of the matter.

While the role of university counsel is almost always to advise caution, it is hard to observe that restraint when considering the growing tension between an absolute interpretation of the right of freedom of speech and its application on the campuses of independent colleges and universities. Having advocated the need for moderation in applying *Ex corde Ecclesiae's* commitment to the maintenance of Catholic values on Catholic campuses, we also feel compelled to urge administrators to fight vigorously for their institution's own free speech rights. The eloquence of the proponents of absolute free speech does not absolve the guardians of religious freedom from the duty to struggle when these two constitutional principles clash. It is essential that there be tests of both principles to attain a working balance. Even so, head-on collisions may not be the best avenue of approach. Instead, tactical maneuver would appear more likely to be successful.

On the simplest level, this may well involve restructuring the process by which student groups are permitted to achieve some sort of official status. Done carefully, this process should protect the right of the university to deny the use of its name to groups that espouse ideas violative of its structure of beliefs while avoiding discrimination in the provision of educational services. Unfortunately, the use of facilities and the provision of funding are much more complex problems and may ultimately involve the choice between sectarian and nonsectarian status.

But the important thing is taking a stand on the fact that Catholic (indeed all private) universities are *not* governmental entities. As corporate citizens they have, and should demand, the constitutional right to uphold the principles of their faith. While the line between free speech and academic freedom on the one hand and institutional rejection of abhorrent ideas on the other is a very fine one, there is great danger in thinking that it is too difficult to perceive. Abandonment of all efforts to protect institutional autonomy will inevitably produce secularization. And while university counsel usually does everything in his or her power to avoid lawsuits, this is one area in which we would urge our clients to use the courts in furtherance of the mandate of *Ex corde Ecclesiae*.

CONCLUSION

Ex corde Ecclesiae did not shrink from the inherent conflict between church and state. The progress of its preliminary drafts reveals the effort that went into acclimatizing the final version to the varied academic and constitutional environments in which Catholic universities reside. Its genesis in a deep concern for the maintenance of the particular identity of Catholic higher education gives great power to the general norms that it expresses.

From the standpoint of a university counsel, *Ex corde Ecclesiae* will either be a source of great difficulty in the next decade or an exciting and centralizing focus in the representation of his or her client. To a great degree, the way in which the experience is perceived will depend upon the extent to which administrators at the institution and in the office of the local bishop understand how little clarity there is, still, in the law of church and state, and how risky absolute clarity could be.

POSTSCRIPT

We wish to add one additional note of caution occasioned by the publication of the proposed ordinances by the National Conference of Catholic Bishops Committee on Implementation of *Ex corde Ecclesiae*. Part 2, ordinance 3, as drafted, provides as follows:

> Periodically, and at least every ten years, each Catholic college and university is to undertake an internal review of the congruence of its research program ... , course of instruction ... , and service activity ... with the ideals and principles expressed in *Ex Corde Ecclesiae* [arts. 2 and 5].

For the reasons described in the body of the text with regard to redrafting internal governing documents and faculty contracts, faculty and professional associations can be expected to oppose the adoption of internal governance rules responding to such a mandated process of review. It will be argued that such a review is intended to expose a wide array of university programs to an essentially external examination of doctrinal content.

There is also a strong potential for difficulties under civil law, including the enhancement of arguments as to pervasive sectarianism affecting the availability of state and federal funding, and serious difficulties with accrediting agencies concerning academic freedom. The authors question whether the ordinance adds anything to the goals sought under the apostolic constitution and the proposed ordinances that would offset the substantial adverse implications flowing from permanent adoption of this element of the draft.

If some such review is to be part of the ordinances enforcing *Ex corde Ecclesiae*, it would be advisable not to include a specific requirement that such review be conducted on a regular basis. Colleges and universities, in the process of seeking renewal of their accreditation, already review all aspects of the institution's life. Presumably, at least on an internal basis, such review would include review of how the school has done in implementing the apostolic constitution and the ordinance as finally drafted. There is no reason to require such review by external church ordinance.

NOTES

1. *Ex corde Ecclesiae* was promulgated by Pope John Paul II as an apostolic constitution on 15 August 1990. The apostolic constitution was released generally on 25 September 1990.

2. Vatican Council II, *The Pastoral Constitution on the Church in the Modern World Gaudium et spes*, nn. 41, 76 (December 7, 1965); *Ex corde Ecclesiae*, art. 1, sec. 2.

3. Canon 22 states that the civil laws to which the law of the church defers should be observed in canon law with the same effects unless the civil law contradicts divine or ecclesiastical law. *The Code of Canon Law, Latin-English Edition* (Washington, D.C.: CLSA, 1983).

4. A particularly helpful overview of the civil law issues likely to arise out of *Ex corde Ecclesiae* is Charles H. Wilson, *"Ex corde Ecclesiae*: The New Apostolic Constitution for Catholic Universities," *The Catholic Lawyer* (1991): 17. The authors express their gratitude to Mr. Wilson for his illumination of several of the issues likely to be of relevance to Catholic colleges and universities as they strive to be faithful to the apostolic constitution while complying with the requirements of the civil law.

5. 42 U.S.C. sec. 2000e et seq. (Civil Rights Act of 1964, Pub. L. No. 88-352, title VII, secs. 701 et seq., 78 Stat. 253).

6. Canon 812. The canon does not describe what is meant by "competent ecclesiastical authority." Ladislas Orsy, S.J., recognizing that the locution is "puzzling,"

has stated that when read in context and barring the promulgation of authentic interpretation of the canon to the contrary, the first person who may be considered the "competent ecclesiastical authority" is the diocesan bishop in whose diocese the university is located. Ladislas Orsy, S.J., "The Mandate to Teach Theological Disciplines: On Canon 812 of the New Code," 44 *Theological Studies* (1983): 476, 483-85. The American bishops have tentatively recognized that normally the local "diocesan bishop or his delegate (cf. Canon 812)" is the "competent ecclesiastical authority." "Proposed Ordinances for Catholic Colleges and Universities in the United States," *Ex corde Ecclesiae* Implementation Committee, National Conference of Catholic Bishops, part 2, ord. 6 (May 4, 1993).

7. An accompanying endnote *Ex corde Ecclesiae* cites Vatican Council II, Dogmatic Constitution on the Church *Lumen gentium*, n. 25: AAS 57 (1965): 29; *Dei verbum*, nn. 8-10: AAS 58 (1966): 820-822; cf. c. 812.

8. Following the symposium at which this paper was presented, the *Ex corde Ecclesiae* Implementation Committee of the National Conference of Catholic Bishops issued a set of proposed ordinances through which the apostolic constitution will be implemented in the United States. The drafters of the proposed ordinances take the position that the process of seeking and obtaining the mandate involves the teacher and the appropriate bishops or their delegates. "Proposed Ordinances," part 2, ords. 5-6.

This view derives substantial support from Orsy, "Mandate to Teach Theological Disciplines," pp. 483-85.

9. See also Orsy, "Mandate to Teach Theological Disciplines," p. 479. As noted above, the American bishops recognize that this issue concerns the individual theologian and bishop rather than the university. "Proposed Ordinances," part 2, ord. 6. The same ordinance, however, as currently drafted, states that "Catholic professors of theological disciplines are to be advised by academic officials of the Church's expectation that they request the mandate from the competent ecclesiastical authority . . . " Thus, the college or university *could* be understood to be involved in the process at least in giving notice of the mandate requirement to prospective Catholic theology faculty members.

While the language of the canon, the apostolic constitution, and the proposed ordinances go a long way toward ensuring that the college or university will not become involved in an imbroglio in the event that a bishop is unwilling to extend the mandate to a given candidate, the relevant documents do not completely eradicate the possibility of the institution's amenability to suit in the event that a controversy arises over a candidate. While as a matter of canon law, the requirement does not appear to involve the university, there is of course no guarantee that a civil judge would find that the university was completely uninvolved in the event he is presented with a case in which a disappointed professor claims that the reason he or she was denied employment or promotion was due to a failure to obtain the mandate.

It may well be worth exploring whether the role of offering advice regarding the mandate might better be filled by one of the learned societies, for example, the Catholic Theological Society of America, than by individual colleges and universities.

10. Canon 18 provides: "Laws which establish a penalty or restrict the free exercise of rights or which contain an exception to the law are subject to a strict interpretation."

11. Orsy, "Mandate to Teach Theological Disciplines," p. 481.

12. There are a number of questions under canon law as to how broadly the scope of the relevant canons and the apostolic constitution should be interpreted. Those questions are beyond our competence to address. The proposed ordinances purport to cover all American "Catholic colleges and universities . . . which, through their governing boards freely commit themselves to the Christian message as it comes to us through the Catholic Church . . ." "Proposed Ordinances," part 2, ord. 1. The ordinances are accompanied by an appendix that lists five broad categories of such institutions. See idem., ord. 2 and appendix.

The apostolic constitution does not cover, and this presentation will not discuss, the special issues raised by the status accorded the "ecclesiastical" faculties of theology and philosophy in some Catholic universities and in seminaries. These faculties are governed, for purposes of canon law, under canons 815-821, and operate within the framework established in John Paul II, apostolic constitution *Sapientia christiana*, 15 April 1979: *AAS* 71 (1979): 469-99.

13. Orsy has previously pointed out that canon 812 (and by implication the text of *Ex corde Ecclesiae* that treats the mandate) is not retroactive, existing theology professors having "vested rights" that are not canceled out by the 1983 Code of Canon Law. Orsy, "Mandate to Teach Theological Disciplines," p. 483.

14. Because the interpretation of *Ex corde Ecclesiae* and the proposed ordinances requires reference to nuances of canon law, colleges and universities should be advised that even the chair of a theology department might, without proper instruction, interpret the apostolic constitution as requiring him or her to play an active role in facilitating the grant of a mandate for a prospective professor. Therefore, the lack of such requirement should be carefully explained to the appropriate administrators.

15. Orsy, "Mandate to Teach Theological Disciplines," p. 482.

16. The college may be able to argue successfully that it should be permitted to make such inquiry, at least with respect to the theology department, as the college is entitled to discriminate in hiring decisions related to its positions for Catholic theologians as a matter of free exercise, such positions being central to its religious mission. Compare *Maguire* v. *Marquette University,* 627 F. Supp. 1499, 1505 (E.D. Wisc. 1986) (Free Exercise and Establishment Clauses would be violated if a Catholic university were required to hire, pursuant to civil rights laws prohibiting sex discrimination, as a theology faculty member an applicant perceived hostile to the institutional church), *aff'd on other grounds,* 814 F.2d 1213 (7th Cir. 1987) with, e.g., *E.E.O.C.* v. *Southwestern Baptist Theological Seminary,* 651 F.2d 277 (5th Cir. 1981) (Free Exercise Clause does not permit discrimination on religious grounds for hiring support staff), *cert. denied,* 456 U.S. 905 (1982). See *"Curran* v. *Catholic University of America,"* Daily Washington Law Reporter 117, no. 62 (April 3, 1989): 653 (finding no breach of contract where member of ecclesiastical faculty at pontifical university subject to strictures of *Sapientia christiana* was removed following declaration by Sacred Congregation for the Doctrine of the Faith that he was not suitable to teach Catholic theology).

17. The statutory language relevant to the BFOQ is found at 42 U.S.C. sec. 2000e-2(e)(1) and (e)(2). Subsection (e)(1) permits an employer to employ an individual "on the basis of his religion, sex, or national origin in those certain instances where religion, sex, or national origin is a bona fide occupational qualification reasonably

necessary to the normal operation of the particular business or enterprise." Subsection (e)(2) permits an educational institution to employ persons of a particular religion if the institution is "in whole or in substantial part, owned, supported, controlled, or managed . . . by a particular religion or by a particular religious corporation, association, or society."

18. See *Pime* v. *Loyola University of Chicago,* 803 F.2d 351 (7th Cir. 1986) (recognizing membership in the Society of Jesus as a BFOQ with respect to the filling of three professorships in the department of philosophy at Loyola University).

19. The American bishops have thus far not addressed this particular aspect of art. 4, sec. 4, in their proposed ordinances.

20. See *Ex corde Ecclesiae,* art. 1, sec. 3. The incorporation of the general norms and their local and regional applications is mandatory for universities "established or approved by the Holy See, by an episcopal conference or other assembly of Catholic hierarchy, or by a diocesan bishop." Incorporation of the general norms and local or regional applications is recommended for all other Catholic universities (art. 1, sec. 3).

21. See Wilson, *"Ex corde Ecclesiae:* The New Apostolic Constitution," p. 26. Because the employment contracts offered by every college and university refer back to the institution's governing documents, the apostolic constitution virtually requires that covered colleges and universities amend their charters, bylaws, mission statements, and faculty handbooks to provide for the required notice provisions and other contractual provisions mandated. See *Ex corde Ecclesiae,* especially art. 1, sec. 3.

22. Labor unions are particularly alert to the opportunities presented when a university and its faculty members disagree on terms and conditions of employment.

23. See the comment on this paper by Charles H. Wilson.

24. We agree with Wilson's observation later in this volume that the language of canon 810 requiring the hiring and maintenance of professors who are "outstanding in their . . . probity of life" does not appear to restrict its admonition to the professor's professional behavior.

25. It is worthwhile to note, however, that courts might not give a college or university the same leeway to dismiss a tenured professor on these grounds that was accorded Catholic University in the *Curran* case. In *Curran,* the court ruled on quite narrow grounds that the action was appropriate given the ecclesiastic character of the department in which Father Curran was teaching and further given his prior experience as a seminary instructor, where he had been subject to a canonical mission requirement.

26. See David M. O'Connell, C.M., "An Analysis of Canon 810 of the 1983 Code of Canon Law and Its Application to Catholic Universities and Institutes of Higher Studies in the United States" (Doctoral diss., Catholic University of America, 1990), p. 180.

27. It is a favorite litigation and teaching technique of lawyers to raise the so-called "parade of horribles." The present scenario, at least in the eyes of the authors, fits into that category as well as any of the issues raised in this presentation. It provides, however, the opportunity to recognize that the civil law and the canon law operate with their focus on at least partly divergent goals. Ladislas Orsy, in cautioning on development of the proper framework for interpreting of canon law, has stated the distinction eloquently:

> The body of civil law ought to respond to the question: How to organize a community on the basis of justice? The body of canon law ought to respond

to the question: How to organize a community to receive the gift of redemption? Those two goals are so different that the rules they inspire and generate cannot be of the same nature even if they appear similar under many aspects.

The principal hermeneutical factor in interpreting canon law remains unique. It confronts the whole system as well as every part of it with the question: What is the redemptive value in this regulation?

Ladislas Orsy, S.J., "Models of Approaches to Canon Law and Their Impact on Interpretation," *The Jurist* 50 (1990): 83, 97. In examining the potential for conflict between the civil and canon law, and in thinking about methods for developing creative solutions, Orsy's illumination of the divergence of purpose between the two should not be far from our minds.

28. Canon 1085 provides that a person held to the bond of a prior marriage invalidly attempts marriage. The canon requires that a prior marriage, even if dissolved or thought invalid, must be "legitimately and certainly" recognized as null or dissolved by appropriate ecclesiastical authority, before (a subsequent valid) marriage can be contracted.

29. Michael A. Olivas, *The Law and Higher Education: Cases and Materials on Colleges in Court* (Durham, N.C.: Carolina Academic Press, 1989), p. 598.

30. See, e.g., Robert A. Bowser, ed., "Section 7," *Pennsylvania Higher Education: Laws, Regulations, Standards, Policies and Circular for State-Owned and State-Related Institutions* (Harrisburg: Pennsylvania Dept. of Education, 1980), p. 189.

31. In some instances, the legal protection available to the professor notwithstanding, a college might successfully dismiss such a professor, stating that his abandonment of orders and quick marriage outside the church are, in the context of the specific community of the college, "just cause." In fact, just such a situation arose at Loyola-Marymount in Los Angeles and resulted in the summary dismissal of the professor. Wilson, "*Ex corde Ecclesiae:* The New Apostolic Constitution," p. 32.

32. The courts will, in order to avoid excessive government entanglement in the sectarian affairs of churches or church-affiliated institutions, refuse to decide questions of religious doctrine or ecclesiastical law, deferring to the highest tribunal or other competent authority of the church organization. See, e.g., *Presbyterian Church* v. *Mary Elizabeth Blue Hull Memorial Presbyterian Church,* 393 U.S. 440 (1969) (where local dissenting church had subjected itself and its property to central church control, it could not appeal to civil courts for determination of whether central church had deviated from its doctrine, as such inquiry would constitute an impermissible inquiry into religious matters); *Serbian Eastern Orthodox Diocese* v. *Milivojevich,* 426 U.S. 696 (1976), *reh'g denied,* 429 U.S. 873 (1976) (any review of the jurisdiction of general church authorities or whether those authorities acted in conformity with church law would result in undue interference with the freedom of religion); see also *Maguire* v. *Marquette University,* 627 F. Supp. 1499, 1505 (E.D. Wisc. 1986). But see *Jones* v. *Wolf,* 443 U.S. 595 (1979) (inquiry by civil court is appropriate where court is asked to do no more than rely on neutral principles of applicable civil law in rendering its decision to resolve dispute between church groups).

33. The results of the two leading cases in the area, *Tilton* v. *Richardson,* 403 U.S. 672 (1971) (upholding federal grants made to church-affiliated colleges and universities

under the Higher Education Facilities Act, but overturning one section of the Act which would have provided a nonreturnable grant in perpetuity after twenty years, even if the college thereafter used the granted facility for sectarian purposes) and *Roemer* v. *Board of Public Works,* 426 U.S. 736 (1976) (upholding state grants for secular degree programs) demonstrate the willingness of the courts, and in particular the U.S. Supreme Court, to keep the lines between secular and sectarian obscure. In both cases, the justices wended their way in distinguishing the primarily secular mission of church-affiliated colleges and universities on the one hand and the primarily proselytizing mission of church-affiliated elementary schools and high schools on the other. In both *Tilton* and *Roemer,* the Court found that the colleges and universities operated on sufficiently secular principles to justify their receipt of government aid programs. *Tilton,* 403 U.S. at 687; *Roemer,* 426 U.S. at 765-66. It is questionable whether a court would find that a college or university that had fully incorporated the general norms of the apostolic constitution was sufficiently nondiscriminatory in general faculty hiring, particularly with regard to the mandate requirement for Catholic professors of theology and/or in its acceptance of nonsectarian principles of academic freedom to justify the availability of public funding if challenged.

34. Accord *Widmar* v. *Vincent,* 454 U.S. 263 (1981) (invalidating state university regulation which denied access to school facilities to religious student organizations as a violation of free speech; school had, with a secular purpose, created a limited open forum open to all forms of discourse, and could not thereby prohibit religious discourse).

35. *Gay Rights Coalition* v. *Georgetown University,* 536 A.2d 1, 16-17 (D.C. 1987) (*en banc*). Specifically, the Court of Appeals of the District of Columbia held in a divided opinion, that the Act did not require the university to give official recognition to the groups, but it distinguished an intangible endorsement from the provision of actual services. The court held that the university could not deny the groups tangible benefits in the form of student funding and meeting places on the basis of sexual orientation. The court accepted that the university's acceptance of federal funds did not waive its defense based on the constitutional right of free exercise of religion. Finally, although the court recognized that the Act burdened the university's free exercise right, it found that such burden was permissible in light of the District's compelling interest in eradicating discrimination on the basis of sexual orientation, which the court found outweighed the university's free exercise right. *Gay Rights Coalition,* 536 A.2d at 39.

36. The controversy spawned a second round of litigation between the United States and the City Council of the District of Columbia, following passage by the Congress of the Nation's Capital Religious Liberty and Academic Freedom Act, Pub. L. No. 100-462, sec. 145, 102 Stat. 2269-14 (1988) (popularly known as the Armstrong Amendment). The Armstrong Amendment conditioned federal appropriations to the District of Columbia on the city council's passage of specific legislation that would have amended the Human Rights Act to authorize religiously affiliated educational institutions to deny benefits or endorsements on the basis of sexual orientation. Rather than pass the legislation, the city council sued the United States and won a summary judgment finding the Armstrong Amendment an unconstitutional abridgement of the freedom of speech of the city council members. *Clarke* v. *United States,* 705 F. Supp.

605 (D.D.C. 1988), *aff'd*, 886 F.2d 404 (D.C. Cir. 1989). Georgetown did not participate in the second lawsuit.

37. *Gay Rights Coalition*, 536 A.2d at 17. At the time the suit was filed in 1980, the revised Code of Canon Law had not yet been promulgated.

38. Idem. at 19.

39. See *Miami Herald Publishing Co.* v. *Tornillo*, 418 U.S. 241, 258 (1974) (Free Speech Clause of First Amendment applies to corporations and other nonpersonal entities, and the freedom includes a freedom not to speak or to express a specific opinion).

40. *Gay Rights Coalition*, 536 A.2d at 20-21.

41. This clause does, however, have a direct link to the second section of canon 810, which provides that conferences of bishops and diocesan bishops have the duty and right of being vigilant that principles of Catholic doctrine are faithfully observed in Catholic universities.

42. In Georgetown's case, prior to the settlement of the *Gay Rights Coalition* action, the university was denied several million dollars in municipal bond funding over the course of years as the result of its decision not to grant recognition to the student groups.

43. "Abortion-Rights Club at G.U. Irks Hickey," *Washington Post*, 14 March 1991, p. C-5.

44. Ibid.

45. Student participation was apparently viewed as critical. A similar petition filed the year before against the University of San Francisco, also a Jesuit institution, was dismissed for lack of standing, since none of the petitioners was currently enrolled as a student.

46. Canon 808 provides as follows: "Even if it really be Catholic, no university may bear the title or name Catholic university without the consent of the competent ecclesiastical authority." The suit requesting that Georgetown be stripped of its Catholic identity was apparently predicated on the language of canon 808.

47. "Georgetown Pro-Lifers File Canon Lawsuit," *Washington Times*, 2 October 1991, p. B-3.

48. "Hickey Rules G.U. Catholicism Is Vatican's Issue," *Washington Times*, 4 January 1992, p. D-4.

49. "Georgetown University Pushes Abortion Rights Group Off Campus," *New York Times*, 25 April 1992, p. 9.

50. See also "Proposed Ordinances," part 2, ord. 7, which recognizes "individuals or groups within [Catholic colleges and universities]" as parties to potential disputes under the apostolic constitution.

51. The relevant wording within the apostolic constitution provides that "If problems should arise concerning this Catholic character, the local bishop *is to take* the initiatives necessary to resolve the matter, working with the competent university authorities in accordance with established procedures and, if necessary, with the help of the Holy See" (art. 5, sec. 2; italics added). This wording tracks the obligatory language of canon 810, which provides that "diocesan bishops concerned have *the duty and right* in being vigilant that in these universities the principles of Catholic doctrine are faithfully observed" (sec. 2).

52. See, e.g., *State* v. *Schmid,* 423 A.2d 615 (N.J. 1980) (Princeton University regulations which were devoid of reasonable standards designed to protect both private university and individual exercise of expressional freedom could not constitutionally be invoked to prohibit otherwise noninjurious and reasonable exercise of such freedom; private university violated state constitutional rights by evicting defendant and securing his arrest for leafletting on campus), *appeal dismissed sub nom Princeton University* v. *Schmid,* 455 U.S. 100 (1981); but see *Redgrave* v. *Boston Symphony Orchestra, Inc.,* 855 F.2d 888, 894-95 (1st Cir. 1988) (orchestra's cancellation of performance contract with controversial actress was not a form of symbolic speech, even though press reports indicated that cancellation was due to actress's publicly stated political views), *cert. denied,* 488 U.S. 1043 (1989). The combative relationship between Dartmouth College and the *Dartmouth Review,* as detailed in news accounts over the past several years, also highlights the tensions between the free speech rights of students and the quite limited ability of college administrators to take action against a group that stirs constant, even violent, controversy on campus.

COMMENT

CHARLES H. WILSON, *Attorney-at-Law*

AMERICAN CATHOLIC UNIVERSITIES AND "EX CORDE ECCLESIAE"—A MATTER OF CHOICE UNDER CIVIL LAW

The paper presented by Messrs. Burling and Moffatt provides a useful survey of some of the potential issues that will arise under civil law[1] if American Catholic colleges and universities adopt the apostolic constitution *Ex corde Ecclesiae*. The question the paper evokes is whether the clash it describes between ecclesiastical and civil law is inevitable. My thesis is that tensions will necessarily exist between an American Catholic university's civil law status and the obligations implicit in the apostolic constitution,[2] but that those who govern Catholic universities in this country can act to moderate those tensions.

As a Matter of Civil Law, Does "Ex corde Ecclesiae" Apply by Its Own Force to American Catholic Colleges and Universities?

The answer is no. Colleges and universities gain their standing as "legal persons" under civil law through the act of incorporation. By incorporating under the laws of the jurisdiction in which they are located, colleges and universities obtain all the rights, privileges, and obligations of all other "persons" under American civil law. One of those "rights" is the right to direct its own affairs, subject only to the laws of the jurisdiction of incorporation and the federal government that apply to all like "persons" in society.

Typically, the act of incorporation vests the governance of an institution of higher education in a board of trustees or a board of directors. That governing board alone establishes the rules of conduct by which the institution operates. Apart from applicable state and federal laws, only the rules and regulations promulgated by an institution's governing board bind the institution. Rules of conduct issued by an external entity, whether it be the Holy See or the American Association of University Professors (AAUP), cannot be applicable to a duly incorporated American college or university unless its governing board agrees to be bound by them. This fact of corporate existence under civil law establishes an institution's "legal autonomy."

This autonomy is not unbridled because, by incorporating under the laws of the jurisdiction in which it is located, an institution agrees to be bound by all state laws applicable to like entities. For example, a university's power to grant degrees, the core of the university enterprise, is conferred and regulated by state law. As an incorporated entity, the university is also subject to the full panoply of regulations that are the hallmark of the modern state, ranging from health and safety regulations, building and construction codes, zoning regulations, nondiscrimination obligations, restrictions on waste disposal, etc. The scheme of state regulation is overlaid by federal laws and obligations that result from a university's size[3] and participation in federally funded activities.[4] Some look at the growing scope of this regimen of state and federal regulation and consider the promise of autonomy that flows from incorporation illusory. Compliance with that regimen of regulation is, however, the necessary condition for obtaining the benefits that come with being a "legal person" in the eyes of the civil law.

The burden of complying with state and federal regulations aside, one of the benefits of the legal autonomy that comes with incorporation is the right of an institution to set its own course according to the vision and priorities of those who govern it. Pressures abound in the world surrounding the university for the university to conform to one emphasis or another: pressures from accrediting agencies to adopt their standards of quality, pressures from professional societies to accept their views of academic propriety, pressures from actual or potential benefactors to pursue one priority or another. In each of these instances, the university has a choice. It can choose to seek accreditation, knowing that the choice requires it to meet the quality standards established by the accrediting agency. It can choose to accept the AAUP's 1940 Statement on Academic Freedom, knowing that the choice means having the state of academic freedom on its campus measured by that statement and its subsequent adaptations. It can choose to accept a proffered gift, knowing that it must comply with the conditions the donor attaches to the gift.

So too with *Ex corde Ecclesiae*. It is true that a Catholic university some time in its history, most commonly at its founding, chose to identify itself as "Catholic." But, if the papers and discussion at this symposium establish anything, it is that there is no single definition or set of criteria that demarks an American "Catholic" university. Those who identified their universities as

"Catholic" in the near or distant past could not have anticipated the issuance of *Ex corde Ecclesiae* in 1990 and, as a matter of civil law, could not have agreed to be bound by it.

It must be remembered that American Catholic universities have been incorporated as "educational institutions" and not as "Catholic universities" as such. Once those institutions came into legal existence through incorporation, they had the same right as any other "legal person" to align themselves with any religious, social, or political movement. That a duly incorporated educational institution chooses to align itself with the Catholic church is, as it must be under the First Amendment, a matter of indifference to the state that permits the institution to incorporate.

As a matter of *civil law,* therefore, the Holy See is external to American Catholic universities,[5] and pronouncements of the Holy See, such as *Ex corde Ecclesiae,* have no binding effect on American Catholic universities unless their governing boards choose to adopt them and be bound by them.

Would Explicit Adoption of "Ex corde Ecclesiae" by an American Catholic University Affect Its Status under Civil Law?

Again, the answer is no. As noted, a university incorporates under civil law as an "educational institution." What *type* of educational institutional a particular college or university becomes is a matter of institutional choice. A wide variety of institutions—for-profit and not-for-profit, single-sex and coeducational, purely secular or intensely religious, strictly undergraduate or strictly graduate or some combination of the two—exists within the universe of postsecondary institutions. As long as the institution's bona fide reason for existence is to educate, it is entitled to incorporate as an educational institution and to attain the status of a "legal person" under civil law.

That an American Catholic university may become or be perceived as becoming more intensely, religiously oriented by explicitly adopting *Ex corde Ecclesiae* can have effects under civil law, an issue that will be discussed below. But the university's entitlement to the status of "legal person" under civil law and to the benefits and obligations that come with that status cannot be altered by its embrace of the apostolic constitution.

Does Civil Law Require an American Catholic University That Explicitly Adopts "Ex corde Ecclesiae" to Make Other Changes?

The answer is yes, if the institution has a concern about preventive law. As the Burling-Moffatt paper notes, the terms of the general norms of *Ex corde Ecclesiae* could affect in several ways the relationship between an American Catholic university and members of its faculty. The norms also contemplate a much greater oversight role by local bishops than the bishops have exercised over Catholic colleges and universities in the past. To the extent that the apostolic constitution alters or modifies existing internal or external relationships, an institution's documents that define those relationships must also be modified.

Under civil law, a private university's relationship with its faculty (and its students) is contractual in nature.[6] Under custom and usage in American higher education,[7] the terms of the contractual relationship between a university and its faculty members are contained not only in the formal contract document executed by the university and a professor but also in the faculty handbook.[8] To the extent that a Catholic university's adoption of *Ex corde Ecclesiae* alters the terms of its contractual relationships with its faculty, the institution's faculty handbook must be modified accordingly. It is not sufficient, for purposes of civil law, that the university publicizes the governing board's resolution adopting the apostolic constitution or incorporates the essential terms of that papal document into its mission statement. The contractual documents that set forth the terms of the rights and obligations of the institution's faculty members must be revised to reflect any changes in those rights and obligations brought about by the adoption of *Ex corde Ecclesiae*.

The mandate requirement imposed on Catholic theologians by *Ex corde Ecclesiae* (art. 4, sec. 3) and the Code of Canon Law (c. 812)[9] illustrates the point. I assume, as does the Burling-Moffatt paper, that the mandate requirement applies only to theologians who profess the Catholic faith and applies only prospectively. Following its adoption of *Ex corde Ecclesiae*, a university should amend its faculty handbook to state the mandate requirement for Catholic theologians, the effective date of the requirement, and the procedures by which a theologian obtains the mandate.

Other issues presented by *Ex corde Ecclesiae* are more problematic. For example, the importation of canon 810 into *Ex corde Ecclesiae* presumably obligates a Catholic university to assure that its Catholic faculty members are "outstanding in their integrity of doctrine and probity of life."[10] By its terms, canon 810 does not restrict its admonition to the conduct of professors in the classroom. Further, canon 810 also provides that "when those requisite qualities are lacking they [the teachers] are to be removed from the positions in accord with the procedure set forth in the [institution's] statutes." Given the range of conduct that could implicate a professor's "integrity of doctrine and probity of life," revising a faculty handbook to give faculty members adequate notice of the university's expectations in this regard will be a considerable challenge.

Different but equally complex issues surround the role of the local ordinary in the operations of Catholic universities that adopt *Ex corde Ecclesiae*. Article 5, section 2, of the general norms of the apostolic constitution provides:

> Each bishop has a responsibility to promote the welfare of the Catholic universities in his diocese and has the right and duty to watch over the

preservation and strengthening of their Catholic character. If problems should arise concerning this Catholic character, the local bishop is to take the initiatives necessary to resolve the matter, working with the competent university authorities in accordance with established procedures and, if necessary, with the help of the Holy See.

Section 2 of canon 810 has a somewhat similar provision.[11] The immediate problem posed by that provision is discerning the circumstances that would warrant episcopal intervention under *Ex corde Ecclesiae,* especially if that intervention affects the rights and obligations of faculty members. Is the faculty's maintenance of "integrity of doctrine" and "probity of life" to be equated with the institution's "Catholic character" for purposes of such intervention?

Broaching these issues raises a more fundamental question of the nature of the general norms of *Ex corde Ecclesiae:* Are those norms intended to be rules of conduct and discipline the breach of which would lead to sanctions? This is a central question for any fair assessment of the possible civil law impact of the apostolic constitution. Under traditional contract law, a party to a contract is entitled to adequate notice of the conduct that will be considered a breach on his or her part. If a Catholic university adopts *Ex corde Ecclesiae* with the intention, *inter alia,* of holding faculty members accountable for conduct that conflicts with its general norms, the institution must provide adequate notice by revising its faculty handbook accordingly. Otherwise, the university will be poorly positioned to defend a lawsuit that a faculty member files to challenge discipline imposed on the basis of the norms of *Ex corde Ecclesiae.*

By contrast, if the norms of the apostolic constitution are considered to be precatory or aspirational, such an editorial exercise with the faculty handbook would be unnecessary. Whether the norms of *Ex corde Ecclesiae* can fairly be construed to be precatory rather than disciplinary is beyond my competence, as a civil lawyer, to determine. The judgment of a canon lawyer is necessary to make that determination.

Will a Catholic University's Adoption of "Ex corde Ecclesiae" Affect Its Rights and Privileges under Civil Law?

The answer is perhaps. The most concrete context for examining this question is the continuing issue of the constitutional eligibility of church-affiliated educational institutions to participate in federal and state aid programs.

Catholic colleges and universities have consistently been successful in lawsuits challenging their eligibility under the Establishment Clause of the First Amendment[12] to participate in such aid programs. By contrast, Catholic parochial schools have lost most of the significant cases contesting their right and the right of their students to benefit from public aid programs. The different results stem directly from the courts' perceptions about how religion affects the academic programs at the college level, on the one hand, and at the elementary school level, on the other hand.

The most significant college-level cases are *Tilton* v. *Richardson*[13] and *Roemer* v. *Board of Public Works.*[14] Both decisions, by the narrowest of margins,[15] upheld the right of Catholic colleges to participate in the institutional aid programs challenged in those cases. In reaching those results, the Supreme Court emphasized certain characteristics of the defendant colleges that reflected the interaction of their church relationships with their academic programs. Those characteristics were as follows: (1) The colleges did not discriminate on religious grounds in faculty hiring and student admissions;[16] (2) although the colleges required their students to take courses in theology or religious studies, those courses were taught as academic disciplines and not to proselytize the Catholic faith;[17] (3) the colleges made no effort in any aspect of their curricula to proselytize religious doctrine; (4) the colleges did not compel their students to attend religious worship; and (5) the colleges adhered to accepted standards of academic freedom.

The Supreme Court also noted that the colleges in the two cases were operated by Catholic religious organizations and had faculties that were predominantly Catholic. But neither of those factors was constitutionally disabling. Rather, the Court in *Tilton* concluded that the Catholic colleges before it were "institutions with an admittedly religious function but whose predominant higher education mission is to provide their students with a secular education."[18]

The portrait of Catholic parochial schools that emerges from Supreme Court decisions is quite different. The Court has constructed a "profile" of pervasively sectarian schools to describe Catholic parochial schools. The seven to ten elements in that profile are the obverse of the *Tilton* and *Roemer* characteristics. Painting with a broad brush, the Court has described Catholic parochial schools as "schools in which education is an integral part of the dominant sectarian mission and in which an atmosphere dedicated to the advancement of religious belief is constantly maintained."[19] Based on these and similar descriptions, in case after case the Court has ruled that public aid programs that benefit Catholic parochial schools or their students impermissibly advanced religion or created the potential for excessive government entanglement with religion.[20]

For Catholic universities concerned about their continued eligibility for public aid programs, the issue presented by *Ex corde Ecclesiae* is whether institutions that adopt it will be perceived by the courts as having a more intense religious orientation than the colleges described in *Tilton-Roemer* and whether the perception of such an orientation will affect the eligibility determination. One difficulty in resolving that issue is that the Supreme Court has never considered an institutional aid program in a case in which the church-affiliated colleges have deviated from the *Tilton-Roemer* model. Only one court, a three-judge federal district court in Kansas, has examined colleges that deviated from the *Tilton-Roemer* model, and it ruled that a single deviation from that model, such as compulsory chapel attendance, was sufficient to render a college ineligible for public aid.[21] Because that case was not appealed, we do not know whether the Supreme Court would have agreed with the lower court's reasoning. Thus, attempting to project how a Catholic university's adoption of *Ex corde Ecclesiae* might affect a court's assessment of its eligibility for public aid is necessarily speculative.

Nevertheless, it is fair to examine how, under the *Tilton-Roemer* criteria, the provisions of *Ex corde Ecclesiae* might impact universities that adopt the apostolic constitution. In this regard, it is important to keep in mind that the concern is not so much with the language of the general norms of *Ex corde Ecclesiae* as with the document's explicit incorporation of those provisions of canon law that relate to Catholic universities. Canon 812 imposes the mandate requirement on Catholic theologians. A court could conclude that the mandate requirement arose from the church's concern for maintaining orthodoxy on the theological faculties of its universities and that the threat of withholding or withdrawing the mandate for not observing orthodoxy would inhibit the academic freedom of Catholic theologians. Courts that took such a view would be hard pressed to find that required theology courses at universities that adopt *Ex corde Ecclesiae* are taught as academic disciplines and not to indoctrinate or that the institutions are characterized by an atmosphere of academic freedom.

Comparable concerns arise from canon 810, which is also incorporated into *Ex corde Ecclesiae*. That canon would appear to require Catholic universities to remove from teaching positions Catholics who do not exhibit integrity of doctrine and probity of life. On its face, canon 810 applies to all Catholic faculty members, irrespective of their academic disciplines, and extends to how they conduct their personal lives. Thus, that canon could, at least in theory, lead to the discharge of a physics professor who is a Catholic and who divorces and remarries without obtaining an annulment of the first marriage. Many Catholic schools reserve in their contracts the right to discharge elementary school teachers for such conduct. Accordingly, a court considering the public aid eligibility of a Catholic university that adopts *Ex corde Ecclesiae* might consider such an institution closer to the parochial school model than to the *Tilton-Roemer* model.

Finally, article 5, section 2, of the general norms of *Ex corde Ecclesiae* combined with section 2 of canon 810, confers on local bishops broad powers of supervision over Catholic universities to assure that they remain faithful to their Catholic character. The Supreme Court in *Roemer* was not concerned that ordinaries and members of religious orders served on the governing boards of Catholic universities. But membership on governing boards makes bishops and religious internal to the institution and presumably subject to the same fiduciary obligations as other board members. Whether the Court would be as sanguine about the intervention in university affairs by religious authorities considered to be external to the institution is problematic.

This analysis notwithstanding, I would conclude that a Catholic university that adopts *Ex corde Ecclesiae* does not face a serious risk, from that act alone, of traditional litigation challenging its constitutional eligibility for public aid.[22] The last of the major institutional aid cases involving Catholic colleges was the *Roemer* case, which the Supreme Court decided seventeen years ago. I have always believed that the *Tilton* and *Roemer* decisions, which affirmed the general principle that church-affiliated colleges can constitutionally participate in public aid programs, have discouraged the organizations that traditionally challenge the participation of church schools in public aid programs from bringing further college-level challenges. The salutary message of *Tilton* and *Roemer* was that such challenges would have to brought on a college-by-college basis, an unappealing way to spend limited litigation resources.[23] I think it is fair to ask whether the mere adoption of the apostolic constitution, which is still of uncertain scope and applicability, by Catholic universities would be a sufficient impetus to prompt those organizations to get back into the quagmire of Establishment Clause litigation. That question should be examined in light of the fact that the emphasis in college-level public aid programs currently is on student aid, and the Supreme Court has twice ruled that students attending even pervasively sectarian colleges can constitutionally participate in student aid programs.[24]

A more likely source of litigation for Catholic universities will be faculty members. They have not hesitated to resort to the courts in the past when they believed their rights in the academy have been violated. If Catholic universities that adopt *Ex corde Ecclesiae* use that document to formulate rules of conduct and discipline for faculty members, at least some faculty members can be expected to seek vindication under the civil law if the application of those rules intrudes upon the bundle of rights that are loosely collected under the rubric of "academic freedom."

When *Ex corde Ecclesiae* was under consideration, those involved with and affected by the document anticipated that a three-stage process would precede its implementation. The first stage, accomplished on 15 August 1990, was the promulgation of the apostolic constitution by the Holy See after years of drafting and discussion. The second stage, which was in process at the time of the symposium, was the adoption of regulations by local episcopal conferences to adapt the general norms to local conditions. The third stage will be the submission of the regulations adopted by the episcopal conferences to the Holy See (art. 1, sec. 2), and specifically the Congregation for Catholic Education (art. 9), for "review."

Under American civil, however, a fourth stage will be necessary before *Ex corde Ecclesiae* can be given legal effect by an American Catholic university:

explicit adoption of the document and its episcopal regulations by the institution's governing board. Presumably, that final process will give the institution an opportunity to make further refinements to take account of its own particular circumstances.

NOTES

1. The term *civil law* means those legal standards and obligations that are imposed by legislatures and courts in the United States. American Catholic colleges also choose to comply with professional standards imposed and evaluated by accrediting agencies and professional societies. Consideration of the possible impact of *Ex corde Ecclesiae* on compliance with those professional standards is beyond the scope of this paper. For a discussion of some of the issues that *Ex corde Ecclesiae* could present in the accreditation process, see Charles H. Wilson, "Ex corde Ecclesiae: The New Apostolic Constitution for Catholic Universities," *The Catholic Lawyer* 34 (1991): 17, 27-29.

2. By the very terms of *Ex corde Ecclesiae,* its general norms are "to be applied concretely at the local and regional levels" (art. l, sec. 2). The apostolic constitution contemplates that episcopal conferences in various locales will engage in ecclesiastical rule-making to adapt the general norms to local conditions. The National Conference of Catholic Bishops in this country has begun that rule-making process, and it is impossible to know at this time whether that process will result in any significant modification of the general norms in the papal document. My necessary assumption, for purposes of this paper, is that the general norms will not be substantially modified when the American bishops complete their work, although the possible impact of the general norms on Catholic universities under American law should be one of the "local conditions" that the bishops will have to examine.

3. For example, colleges and universities must comply with the nondiscrimination provisions of Title VII of the Civil Rights Act of 1964, as amended (42 U.S.C. sec. 2000e), if they employ more than fifteen persons and their activities "affect" interstate commerce.

4. Each program that provides federal funds to independent colleges and universities carries its own set of rules and regulations with which recipients must comply. Invariably, participation in federally funded programs requires assurances of nondiscrimination. In addition, Title VI of the Civil Rights Act of 1964, as amended (42 U.S.C. sec. 2000d), prohibits discrimination on the basis of race, color, and national origin in any program or activity receiving federal financial assistance.

5. Whether the same is true as a matter of church law is beyond my competence, as a civil lawyer, to opine. Other participants in the symposium who have the necessary credentials have addressed that issue.

6. In this respect, private colleges and universities differ from their counterparts in the public sector. While faculty members at public universities who believe their rights have been infringed can claim breach of contract, they can also invoke the Due Process Clause of the Fourteenth Amendment if they believe the process by which their rights were infringed was irregular. Because the Fourteenth Amendment, by its own terms, applies only to governmental entities, no similar due process claim is

available to faculty members at private institutions. This distinction loses its significance when a professor claims his or her rights were violated because of lack of adequate notice. The legal analysis for contract and due process claims in such circumstances is quite similar.

7. In its analysis of the terms of the contractual relationship between a university and its faculty, an American court will examine the customs and practices of the university. See, for example, *Howard University* v. *Best,* 484 A.2d 958, 967 (D.C. 1984).

8. See, for example, *McConnell* v. *Howard University,* 818 F.2d 58, 62-63 (D.C. Cir. 1987).

9. Certain provisions of the Code of Canon Law are explicitly incorporated into *Ex corde Ecclesiae.* "These general norms are based on and are a further development of the Code of Canon Law" (art. 1, sec. 1). Note 42 at this point gives further detail: "Cf. in particular the Chapter of the Code: 'Catholic Universities and Other Institutes of Higher Studies' " (*CIC,* cann. 807-814)."

10. Because the Code of Canon Law imposes its obligations only on Catholics, faculty members of other religious faiths, or of none, would not be expected to meet this standard. However, *Ex corde Ecclesiae* provides that "Those university teachers and administrators who belong to other churches, religious communities, or religions as well as those who profess no religious belief ... are to recognize and respect the distinctive Catholic identity of the university" (art. 4, sec. 4). This provision raises the question whether the apostolic constitution anticipates that a standard of conduct similar to the "probity of life" requirement of canon 810 is to be applied to members of the university community who do not profess the Catholic faith.

11. Canon 810, sec. 2, provides: "The conference of bishops and the diocesan bishops concerned have the duty and right of being vigilant that in these universities the principles of Catholic doctrine are faithfully observed."

12. U.S. Constitution, Amend. 1: "Congress shall make no law respecting an establishment of religion ... "

13. 403 U.S. 672 (1971).

14. 426 U.S. 736 (1976).

15. In the *Tilton* case, the defendant Catholic colleges prevailed by a five to four vote in the Supreme Court. In *Roemer,* three justices joined the plurality decision, two justices concurred, and four justices dissented.

16. In this regard, I note that the general norms of *Ex corde Ecclesiae* state that, to avoid losing its Catholic identity, a Catholic university should not allow "the number of non-Catholic teachers ... to constitute a majority within the institution" (art. 4, sec. 4).

17. This criterion finds its source in *Tilton* alone. In *Roemer,* the trial court had been unable to conclude, based on the evidence presented, whether the theology courses were taught without the purpose of religious indoctrination. The Supreme Court ruled that gap in the trial court's findings was not inconsistent with its conclusion that the defendant Catholic colleges were not pervasively sectarian. 426 U.S. at 758 n.21.

18. 403 U.S. at 687.

19. *Meek* v. *Pittenger,* 421 U.S. 349, 371 (1975).

20. See idem.; see also *School District of Grand Rapids* v. *Ball,* 473 U.S. 373 (1985); *Aguilar* v. *Felton,* 473 U.S. 402 (1985); *Committee for Public Education* v. *Nyquist,* 413 U.S. 756 (1973); *Lemon* v. *Kurtzman,* 403 U.S. 602 (1971).

21. *Americans United* v. *Blanton,* 379 F. Supp. 872 (1974).

22. By "traditional" litigation, I mean the type of lawsuit that the Catholic colleges and universities faced in *Tilton* and *Roemer.* The nominal plaintiffs were taxpayers complaining that their tax funds were being expended in violation of constitutional limitations. But the real forces behind the cases were organizations, such as the American Jewish Congress and Americans United for Separation of Church and State, for which opposition to public aid to church-affiliated education is central to their agendas. While the interest of such organizations in college-level challenges waned after *Roemer,* there are other potential sources of eligibility challenges. For example, in the Georgetown gay rights case discussed by Messrs. Burling and Moffatt (*Gay Rights Coalition* v. *Georgetown University,* 536 A.2d 1 (D.C. 1987) (*en banc*), one of the claims made by the gay student organizations was that Georgetown University's reliance on the Free Exercise Clause of the First Amendment to justify its refusal to grant official recognition to those groups made the university constitutionally ineligible to receive further federal funds. The court gave virtually no consideration to that claim. However, faculty members who sue to challenge any discipline imposed on them as a result of a Catholic university's adoption of *Ex corde Ecclesiae* might make similar claims. For a case in which a faculty member made such a claim, see *Broderick* v. *Catholic University,* 530 F.2d 1035 (D.C. Cir. 1976).

23. The same organizations that have shied away from college-level challenges in recent years (see note 22, above), have continued to be quite active in mounting judicial challenges to aid programs that benefit Catholic elementary schools. See, for example, cases cited in note 20, above.

24. See *Witters* v. *Washington Dep't of Services to the Blind,* 474 U.S. 481 (1986); *Americans United* v. *Blanton,* 433 F. Supp. 97 (M.D. Tenn.), *aff'd,* 434 U.S. 803 (1977). The criteria of eligibility for public aid discussed in the text are those articulated by the Supreme Court in cases challenging aid programs under the Establishment Clause of the First Amendment. Many states have state constitutional provisions that are far more restrictive than the Establishment Clause on the issue of public aid to church-affiliated schools. A state aid program may pass constitutional muster under the Establishment Clause but be declared invalid under a state constitutional provision. Compare *Witters,* idem., 474 U.S. at 481-90, with *Witters* v. *State Comm'n for the Blind,* 112 Wash. 363, 363-66, 771 P.2d 1119, 1119-22, *cert. denied,* 110 S. Ct. 147 (1989). Thus, state constitutions must also be evaluated in any effort to determine how adoption of *Ex corde Ecclesiae* by a Catholic university may affect its eligibility for state aid programs.

COMMENT

DAVID THOMAS LINK, *University of Notre Dame*

A WALL THAT MAKES GOOD NEIGHBORS

On the subject of Catholic universities defining their "Catholic character," much of the discussion at this conference has centered around the question of whether the *Ex corde Ecclesiae* is a threat or an opportunity. A similar question is involved with the *Ex corde Ecclesiae* and civil law.

There are several areas where the language of *Ex corde Ecclesiae* may suggest the possibility of conflict between civil law and the apostolic constitution. However, as Philip Burling and Gregory Moffatt suggest, with proper application of the recommendations of *Ex corde Ecclesiae*, those conflicts can be kept to a minimum.

This paper explores a different tack: a theory suggesting that *Ex corde Ecclesiae* actually offers an opportunity to universities to clarify their status under civil law. Catholic and other religiously based universities, properly defining their multiple missions using documents such as the *Ex corde Ecclesiae* as guidelines, might be better able to walk the path of being "religiously affiliated" without being "pervasively sectarian."

First of all, there is great advantage in being a religious university with a clear religious mission added to but not interfering with the traditional educational missions of teaching, research, and service—those missions common to all universities and tertiary colleges. For example, many interpretations of civil law would indicate that a religiously affiliated university would qualify for the religious exemption to antidiscrimination laws and regulations (having to do with discrimination based on religious belief). Also, for such institutions, religious beliefs would qualify as a bona fide occupational qualification (BFOQ); termination connected with violations of moral codes would be in conformity *187* with the law, provided that proper procedures were followed, and institutions would not be required to recognize or support organizations that are contrary to the religious mission of the university. In other words, the troublesome legal problems analyzed by Burling and Moffatt may actually find some answers by virtue of universities properly relating their religious and educational missions using the guidance of *Ex corde Ecclesiae.*

This brief paper is not meant to be a complete legal analysis. There are myriad cases and interpretations of the Establishment Clause of the United States Constitution and other laws and regulations related to the problems discussed by Burling and Moffatt. A complete analysis would fill volumes. Further, there are divergent views as to where the law in this area is heading. Therefore, the ambition of this paper is to present an analysis of the above mentioned opportunity provided in *Ex corde Ecclesiae,* sufficient to stimulate further discussion among university administrators and counsel.

Consider at the outset that the Establishment Clause is a "two-edged sword" against both of the potentially negative aspects of the entanglement of church and state. That is, the Establishment Clause prohibits the state not only from "advancing" but also from "inhibiting" religion.

With regard to hiring questions and antidiscrimination laws, there are some obvious advantages to a university which qualifies as a religious organization. Consider the language of two exemptions to Title VII of the Federal Civil Rights Act of 1964. Section 702 of that act as amended in 1972 reads:

> This subchapter shall not apply to . . . a religious corporation, association, educational institution, or society with respect to employment of individuals of a particular religion to perform work connected with the carrying on by such corporation, association, educational institution, or society of its activities.[1]

Note that this allows a religious organization to base hiring preference on religious belief in all activities, not just religious activities.

The other relevant exemption, i.e., section 703 (e)(1) of Title VII, reads:

> It shall not be an unlawful employment practice for a school, college, university, or other educational institution or institution of learning to hire and employ employees of a particular religion if such school, college, university or other educational institution or institution of learning is, in whole or in substantial part, owned, supported, controlled, or managed by a particular religion or by a particular religious corporation, association or society, or if the curriculum of such school, college, university, or other educational institution or institution of learning is directed toward the propagation of a particular religion.[2]

Next, consider some of the many U.S. Supreme Court opinions interpreting Title VII. In *Corporation of the Presiding Bishop of the Church of Jesus Christ of Latter-Day Saints* v. *Amos,*[3] the Court found that the exemption under section 702, exempting religious organizations from Title VII's prohibition against religious discrimination in employment matters, does not violate either the Establishment Clause or the Equal Protection Clause. The *Amos* case involved an employee of a gymnasium owned by a church. This person had been working for sixteen years as a building engineer when he was discharged for failing to qualify for a temple recommend, that is, a certificate that he was a church member eligible to attend its temples. In deciding this case upholding the constitutionality of the religious exemption, the Court applied a three-part test set out in the case of *Lemon* v. *Kurtzman.*[4]

That "*Lemon* test" of constitutionality under the Establishment Clause requires first that a law being tested have a valid secular purpose. In this regard, the Court in *Amos* found that "it is a permissible legislative purpose to alleviate significant governmental interference with the ability of religious organizations to define and carry out their religious missions."[5] As to the other parts of the *Lemon* test, the Court found that section 702 of Title VII has "a principal or primary effect . . . that neither advances nor inhibits religion" and the exemption does not impermissibly entangle church and state but "effectuates a more complete separation of the two and avoids the kind of intrusive inquiry into religious belief. . . ."[6]

The critical factors in the *Amos* case are the religious mission of the institution and the resolve by the Court to allow religious organizations to define and carry out that mission free of governmental interference.

With regard to conduct cases, consider the U.S. Court of Appeals opinion in the case of *Little* v. *Wuerl.*[7] In that case a non-Catholic teacher brought a Title VII action against a Catholic school after it failed to renew her contract because of her remarriage. Specifically, the teacher was not rehired because she had not pursued "the proper canonical process available from the Roman Catholic Church to obtain validation of her second marriage."[8] Recognizing the religious exemption of sections 702 and 703(e)(1) of Title VII, the court found in favor of the archbishop and the school. While this is a school case and not one involving a university, the language of the opinion gives important insights:

> We recognize that Congress intended Title VII to free individual workers from religious prejudice. But we are also persuaded that Congress intended the explicit exemptions to Title VII to enable religious organizations to create and maintain communities composed solely of individuals faithful to their doctrinal practices, whether or not every individual plays a direct role in the organization's "religious activities". . . . We conclude that the permission to employ persons "of a particular religion" includes

permission to employ only persons whose beliefs *and conduct* are consistent with the *employer's religious precepts.*[9]

While the above cases and statutes are but a few of the precedents in this church-state legal discussion, and the analysis is therefore incomplete, the message is clear. If a university establishes itself as a religious institution performing some religious activity, civil law is not meant to be applied in such a way as to interfere with the religious mission and activities. That is very important to Catholic universities in hiring, dismissal, and many other related matters.

While universities have long recognized the advantages of being religious institutions, they have been reluctant to declare themselves as such for fear of losing qualification for certain state and federal funding or other benefits. It is in this regard that *Ex corde Ecclesiae* may be very helpful. There is a clear indication in civil law that it is not inconsistent to be a religious institution (with all of the protection of noninterference) and still meet the qualifications for *federal* funding. (Note that *state* funding questions would have to be considered on a state-by-state basis.)

It is important to note at this point that it is not necessary for an institution to qualify as nonsectarian to be eligible for federal funding and other benefits. While the Establishment Clause clearly proscribes the government from funding religious activities and from directly benefiting "pervasively sectarian" institutions, funding and benefits can be provided for secular activities of religious organizations as long as these benefits are also available to secular institutions.

The case of *Bowen* v. *Kendrick*[10] decided that the Adolescent Family Life Act (AFLA), which authorizes federal grants to public or nonprofit private organizations for services and research in the area of premarital adolescent sexual relations and pregnancy, does not, on its face, violate the Establishment Clause. In applying the *Lemon* test to AFLA, the Court provides a convenient review of the law regarding federal funding for religiously affiliated institutions:

> ... AFLA is similar to other statutes that this Court has upheld against Establishment Clause challenges in the past. In *Roemer* v. *Maryland Bd. of Public Works,* 426 U.S. 736 (1976), for example, we upheld a Maryland statute that provided annual subsidies directly to qualifying colleges and universities in the State, including religiously affiliated institutions. As the plurality stated, "religious institutions need not be quarantined from public benefits that are neutrally available to all." *Id.,* at 746 (discussing *Everson* v. *Board of Education,* 330 U.S. 1 (1947) (approving busing services equally available to both public and private school children), and *Board of Education* v. *Allen,* 392 U.S. 236 (1968) (upholding state provision of secular textbooks for both public and private school students)). Similarly, in *Tilton* v. *Richardson,* 403 U.S. 672 (1971), we approved the federal

Higher Educational Facilities Act, which was intended by Congress to provide construction grants to "all colleges and universities regardless of any affiliation with or sponsorship by a religious body." *Id.,* at 676. And in *Hunt* v. *McNair,* 413 U.S. 734 (1973), we rejected a challenge to a South Carolina statute that made certain benefits "available to all institutions of higher education in South Carolina, whether or not having a religious affiliation." *Id.* at 741. In other cases involving indirect grants of state aid to religious institutions, we have found it important that the aid is made available regardless of whether it will ultimately flow to a sectarian institution. See, e.g., *Witters* v. *Washington Dept. of Services for Blind,* 474 U.S. 481, 487 (1986); *Mueller* v. *Allen,* 463 U.S., at 398; *Everson* v. *Board of Education,* supra, at 17-18; *Walz* v. *Tax Comm'n,* 397 U.S., at 676. . . .

Only in the context of aid to "pervasively sectarian" institutions have we invalidated an aid program on the grounds that there was a "substantial" risk that aid to these religious institutions would, knowingly or unknowingly, result in religious indoctrination.[11]

Many recent cases make it clear that it is possible for a university to be a religious institution without being "pervasively sectarian." This is not some fine line that must be straddled, but, as indicated earlier, a relatively wide path, since case law indicates that only a small portion of religiously affiliated organizations could be considered to be "pervasively sectarian."

Ex corde Ecclesiae certainly assists the Catholic university in developing its Catholic mission. More important in connection with the theory of this paper, it also defines the nonsectarian responsibilities of the Catholic university:

"[A Catholic university] has always been recognized as an incomparable center of creativity and dissemination of knowledge for the good of humanity. By vocation, the *universitas magistorum et scholarium* is dedicated to research, to teaching and to the education of students who freely associate with their teachers in common love of knowledge. With *every other university* it shares that *gaudium de veritate,* so precious to St. Augustine, which is that joy of searching for, discovering and communicating truth in every field of knowledge."[12] (emphasis added)

Throughout the document, *Ex corde Ecclesiae* discusses the relationship between the religious and university missions, thus demonstrating that a Catholic university can be (and should be) a religious institution without being "pervasively sectarian." The Catholic university can be both truly Catholic and truly a university. This brings the double benefit of eligibility for such things as religious exemption, qualification of certain jobs for BFOQ status, and general protection against government interference with the institution's religious mission, without sacrificing eligibility for funding and benefits connected with the university's teaching, research, and service missions.

Conclusion

The thesis of this brief paper is quite simple and is a corollary to the position of "Notes from the Other Side of the Wall." Although everyone ought to recognize the importance of the separation of church and state, university administrators and their lawyers should not assume that such doctrine necessarily creates difficult or impossible conflicts between civil law and canon law or church documents such as *Ex corde Ecclesiae*. Universities should take advantage of the fact that the Establishment Clause not only prohibits the government from enhancing but also from inhibiting religion. *Ex corde Ecclesiae* provides Catholic universities the opportunity to define the relationship between their Catholic mission and their extensive secular mission.

This paper suggests that there is a Catholic style of being "not pervasively sectarian." Those Catholic universities that properly define the relationship between their Christian mission and their secular missions of teaching, research, and service will be rewarded by a government law and court system committed to not inhibiting the religious mission. Catholic universities should not fear the possible conflicts between *Ex corde Ecclesiae* and civil law. Instead, they should rejoice in the opportunity presented by the apostolic constitution.

NOTES

1. 42 U.S.C. 2000e-1.
2. 42 U.S.C. 2000e-2(e)(2).
3. *Corporation of Presiding Bishop of the Church of Latter-Day Saints v. Amos,* 483 U.S. 327, 107 S.Ct. 2862, 97 L.Ed.2d 273 (1987).
4. *Lemon et al.* v. *Kurtzman, Superintendent of Public Instruction of Pennsylvania, et al.,* 403 U.S. 602, 91 S.Ct. 2105, 29 L.Ed.2d 745 (1971).
5. See *Corporation of Presiding Bishop* v. *Amos,* 483 U.S. at 335, 107 S.Ct. at 2868.
6. See idem., 483 U.S. at 336 and 339, 107 S.Ct. at 2868, 2870.
7. *Susan Long Little* v. *Donald P. Wuerl, Bishop of Pittsburgh, as Trustee of St. Mary Magdalene School, and as Titular Head of the Catholic Diocese of Pittsburgh St. Mary Magdalene Parish,* 929 F.2d 944 (3rd Circuit) (1991).
8. Idem. at 946.
9. Idem. at 951; italics added.
10. *Bowen, Secretary of Health and Human Services* v. *Kendrick et. al.,* 487 U.S. 589, 108 S.Ct. 2562 (1988).
11. Idem., 487 U.S. at 608-609, 612.
12. *Ex corde Ecclesiae,* Apostolic Constitution on Catholic Universities, (August 15, 1990).

DISCUSSION

Discussion opened with references to court cases cited in one of the commentaries, focusing on the concept of sectarianism in a legal sense as applied to churches and schools.

There is a delicate line between an institution being "nonsectarian" and "pervasively sectarian." In the early 1970s lawsuits were filed to argue that some church-related institutions were "pervasively sectarian" and not eligible for direct federal aid. Parochial schools and seminaries are considered pervasively sectarian—not eligible for public aid and exempted from state and federal regulation. Universities generally are not pervasively sectarian; eligible for governmental funding but subject to subsequent regulation.

It is important to distinguish between the theological concepts of sectarian and nonsectarian and the purely legal construal of the terms by the Supreme Court. It is unclear exactly how the courts determine whether an institution is pervasively sectarian or not. It looks to the board of directors, to the extent of proselytizing, to a whole host of factors. Generally speaking, if universities, in cooperation with lawyers, are careful to define themselves properly, the courts will not get involved.

Several participants responded to the question: How far can you go to reestablish an institution's Catholic identity before it is labeled "pervasively sectarian"?

The courts in the early 1970s were result-oriented and had rather simplistic solutions. There was a presumption in favor of granting colleges public aid unless there were serious "red flags" such as a required faith statement. The question is whether the concepts of "probity of life" and "integrity of doctrine" under canon 812 would be new red flags. The *Tilton* case involved funding for a building program. The *Roemer* case involved noncategorical institutional aid. Usually student financial aid is not affected either way, because it goes to the *193* student not to the institution. If a school opted for sectarian status, it might be ineligible for a variety of federal research and grant contracts, even though some sectarian schools do get government contracts.

In the early 1970s many universities went around removing crucifixes from the walls in order to avoid risking the loss of federal financial aid. The pendulum has swung back to some extent and there is much less concern in this area. In the eyes of the Supreme Court, the absence of a catechetical approach is the important element in determining the "nonsectarian" quality of the university.

What if we added theologians to the biological sciences, the physical sciences and other departments in the university to explore the theological implications of Christianity in these disciplines? Some would argue that this makes for pervasive sectarianism. But it could be defended, depending on how it was handled—whether, for example, it was a seminar or a required course—and on how it was presented to faculty. University administrators should not be inhibited by the law from developing creative approaches.

If theology is an academic discipline, perhaps the very blandness of the mission statements of theology departments helps establish the fact that the institution is not "pervasively sectarian." It underscores the possibility of theology being "an academic discipline."

It's a mistake to devise academic policy on the basis of lawyers. It is true that somewhere along the spectrum a university could cross the line into "pervasive sectarianism." But there is considerable benefit in the foggy character of the federal policy articulated by the courts. The crucial thing is not to provoke creation of a "bright line."

It may be equally important not to create a bright line in internal university ecclesiastical issues, just as it is important not to create a bright line in the civil law sense.

Discussion returned to the apostolic constitution's effect on the relation of civil and canon law as well as to the implications of its implementation by universities.

Article 1 carefully crafts distinctions between those universities that must incorporate *Ex corde Ecclesiae* and those requested simply to internalize its goals and ideas. Are we being too hasty to talk about the dangers affecting universities required to incorporate *Ex corde Ecclesiae*? Canon law has no effect in the civil courts unless it is incorporated by the governing board of the institution and then brought into the institution's contracts with faculty. This means that boards should take their time deciding how to internalize the document's norms and ideas. And it also means that ordinaries should take their time.

It should be clear that canon law does not force governing boards of existing institutions to incorporate *Ex corde Ecclesiae;* it supports boards of trustees in their decisions. Of the classifications in article 1, the application of the tripartite classification (reserved for new institutions) to existing institutions is an inappropriate interpretation of *Ex corde Ecclesiae* and should be resisted vigorously by the universities.

Canon 810 is nothing new. Universities can continue to live with it.

In order to comply with *Ex corde Ecclesiae*, the universities must change their contracts with faculty. That will take a considerable amount of time.

If Catholic universities are not obliged to incorporate *Ex corde Ecclesiae*, why would they do so? It would depend on whether a university had an interest in terminating a faculty member for purely doctrinal reasons. It has an obligation to Catholic faculty members that if they are going to terminate them for reasons of orthodoxy, this has to become part of the faculty contract. And if it's going to be part of the faculty contract, the university probably has to change its basic governing statutes.

While some bishops might declare the university non-Catholic for refusal to consider incorporation, that is certainly not required by the text. And we cannot conclude that a university will be declared non-Catholic if it does not adopt *Ex corde Ecclesiae*.

We don't know the consequences of refusing to consider the development of Catholic identity by a board of trustees. We should think about this positively: there are some things that the university can do; some that it can't.

There may be many more positive ways to respond to *Ex corde Ecclesiae* than to adopt all of the norms.

Matters such as the dismissal or hiring of faculty raise serious discrimination problems. And there is always the risk of the institution losing federal and state funding, while it tries to maintain a sufficiently Catholic identity to invoke a real religious core. So for this reason, we have run through the list of horrors, from the perspective of civil law, if *Ex corde Ecclesiae* were implemented in a draconian or unthinking manner.

This may be the first time the representatives of Catholic universities have heard that they have some maneuvering room within the civil law—enough room to suggest that university administrators should be more courageous in pursuing the Catholic identity without fear of losing governmental funding. What is unclear is how to do this while avoiding trouble in the civil courts brought by disgruntled faculty members or trouble with an "impatient bishop."

Jaroslav Pelikan, *Yale University*

Ex corde Universitatis:
Reflections on the Significance of Newman's "Insisting Solely on Natural Theology"

The apostolic constitution *Ex corde Ecclesiae,* which is the basis for the explorations in this volume, states its purpose to be the definition of a Catholic university. Everyone would acknowledge, I suppose, the right of the teaching office of the church to set forth such a definition, as well as the inherent complexity of formulating it in relation to the pragmatic realities of the almost countless number of institutions around the globe laying claim in some sense to the title "Catholic university." Nevertheless, it is essential to the definition to point out that in the grammar of that title *Catholic* is the adjective and *university* the noun, as the apostolic constitution itself makes clear in its fundamental stipulation: "Every Catholic university, *as a university,* is an academic community" (n. 12). My particular assignment in this symposium is to reflect on the noun in the light of what can be broadly called its "spiritual meaning." It is an assignment I cordially welcome, for it permits me to chart some territory I was obliged to leave out of the cartography I explored in my recent book, which had to deal with the church and with theology only *en passant.*[1]

Most of the works quoted in the text and cited in the endnotes of *Ex corde Ecclesiae* have come, as has the apostolic constitution itself, from the official magisterium of the Roman Catholic church. Almost certainly, the most important exception to this is John Henry Newman's *The Idea of a University.*[2] Near the beginning (n. 4), the constitution quotes from—and slightly adapts, by making the church rather than the pope the subject of the sentence— Newman's words in the preface to *The Idea of a University:* "He [the pope] rejoices in the widest and most philosophical systems of intellectual education, from an intimate conviction that Truth is his real ally, as it is his profession; and that Knowledge and Reason are sure ministers to Faith."[3] But it is essential to recognize that although Newman was celebrated as, in the words of Nathan

Söderblom, Lutheran archbishop of Uppsala, "England's outstanding theologian and Catholicism's—at least besides Leo XIII—most significant personality in the last century,"[4] and although he did not stop being a Roman Catholic theologian when he became the founding rector of the Catholic University of Ireland, he was not speaking explicitly in that role in *The Idea of a University*. "I have been insisting solely on Natural Theology":[5] with this formula at the conclusion of discourse III, Newman identified the theological venue of these discourses. Or, as he had warned at the very beginning,

> Let it be observed, then, that the principles on which I would conduct the inquiry are attainable, as I have already implied, by the mere experience of life. They do not come simply of theology; they imply no supernatural discernment; they have no special connexion with Revelation ... It is natural to expect this from the very circumstance that the philosophy of Education is founded on truths in the natural order.[6]

The relation between his "insisting solely on Natural Theology" in the discourses of 1852 and his submission to the authority of the Holy See seven years earlier is a complex one, both psychologically and theologically. Leaving (happily) the psychological examination to some other scholar, I have been impressed by the complexity of the relation between university and church within the total context of Cardinal Newman's thought. In his exhaustive biography, written for the centenary of Newman's death in 1990, Ian Ker comments on Newman's development of "his own Catholic ecclesiology" and observes: "What is so striking is the resemblance between his idea of the Church and his earlier idea of the university, a similarity which suggests if not influence at least a common source in a unified vision."[7] Already in his critical edition of *The Idea of a University* for Clarendon Press, published fourteen years earlier, Ker had summarized the counterpoint of that resemblance, with apposite quotations from *The Idea of a University* and others of Newman's writings:

> Newman's idea of the Church is couched in terms noticeably similar in some respects to his idea of the university. The former is "the representative of the religious principle," the latter "the representative of the intellect." The "University is an intellectual power ... just as the Church is a religious power." The Church "is imperial, that is, One and Catholic," while the university is "an empire ... in the sphere of philosophy and research." The Church is the "guardian" of the "circle of ... dogmatic truths," the university "the high protecting power" of "the whole circle of ... knowledge." If "among the objects of human enterprise ... none higher or nobler can be named than that which is contemplated in the erection of a University," the Church in her turn is "a supereminent prodigious power sent upon earth to encounter and master a giant evil."[8]

Combining such statements with the explanation that Newman was "insisting solely on Natural Theology," we are, I believe, justified in claiming his authority for the endeavor to speak about the university *ex corde universitatis,* in some similarly complex dialectic with speaking about it *ex corde ecclesiae* as the apostolic constitution has done.

In that endeavor, having originally borrowed these categories from Newman in order to make them the three major divisions of my book *The Idea of the University—A Reexamination,* I feel authorized now to borrow them from myself and to address my present assignment under those three headings: (1) Pushing Things Up to Their First Principles; (2) The Business of a University; and (3) Duties to Society. In each category I want to look at the concept chiefly as it comes *ex corde universitatis,* that is, its significance within what Newman calls "natural theology," but then also—though more briefly, because that is the theme of other papers—as its definition proceeds *ex corde ecclesiae* as well.

PUSHING THINGS UP TO THEIR FIRST PRINCIPLES

The Latin for "first principle" is, of course, *principium* and the Greek is *arche* [ἀρχή], which is not only the first noun in the Vulgate and Septuagint versions of the Bible but also the title of the first great monument in the history of Christian scholarship, the *Peri archon* [Περὶ ᾿Αρχῶν] or *De principiis* of Origen of Alexandria, written between 220 and 230.[9] The reception of that work during Origen's own lifetime and during the centuries that followed may likewise be taken as the first important case study in the set of problems with which we are concerned here: How much "elbow-room, not indeed in the domain of faith, but of thought," to use Newman's phrase,[10] is the institutional church prepared to grant to a scholar who is, in the beautiful title that Henri de Lubac found in Origen and then applied to him, "homme d'église,"[11] but who takes up the task of exploring questions on which, as Origen said in the preface to *De principiis,* the church and the apostles have not definitively spoken?[12] Although, out of deference to the venue of this apostolic constitution and of this symposium, I shall be concentrating on Roman Catholicism and the university, this is, as many of us have ample reason to know, a set of problems not confined to any one church: to paraphrase Patrick Henry's famous speech of 29 May 1765, Roman Catholicism had its Galileo, American Protestantism its Scopes trial, and the other churches—may profit by their example!

From the very "beginning"—which is how the word *arche* [ἀρχή] or *principium* is most often translated—Christian thought has had a vital interest in, to quote from Newman as he quotes from Sydney Smith in the *Edinburgh Review,* "pushing things up to their first principles."[13] When it has been truest to itself, moreover, Christian thought has been concerned not only that theology should do so, but that each intellectual discipline should faithfully carry out that task in relation to its own special genius and distinctive vocation. Such locutions as "when it has been truest to itself" and "its own special genius and distinctive vocation" are, of course, weasel phrases. For in the concrete, the "warfare" of which Andrew Dickson White, founding president of Cornell, spoke in the title of his best-known work[14] is the narrative of the continuous attempts by Christian theology, regardless of denomination, to override that "special genius and distinctive vocation" and to dictate to science and scholarship what their conclusions ought to be. Particularly in more recent times, it is also the narrative of the frequent attempts—to which White, characteristically, paid far less attention—by a reductionistic science to reciprocate by denying the legitimacy of the theological enterprise altogether. As in its relation to the state, the church (and again regardless of denomination, or almost so) has repeatedly been tempted not to acknowledge the technical autonomy of the created political order and instead to claim that it could derive political principles from the authority of divine revelation, so an intellectual and scientific form of "theocracy" has repeatedly been tempted to identify revelation with a particular cosmology or biology, denying to human reason and research the independence to investigate such topics on their own. But such intellectual "theocracy" has been a violation of the first principles both of those sciences and of the science of Christian theology, a violation that the consideration of the university also within the church must strive to avoid.

Is it possible to infer any such "first principles" about the university from the history and the practice of the university as a cultural institution? I believe that it is. And I believe that the church does have the right and the duty to insist that those who speak for the university search out those first principles and articulate them. I believe, moreover, that when the church does so, it is, in Cardinal Newman's phrase, "insisting solely on Natural Theology" and is not imposing the authority of its own supernatural revelation on the university. For in its divine vocation as a defender of nature and reason, the church is obliged to warn against any effort to undermine nature and reason. That danger has perhaps never been described more chillingly than by Goethe's Mephistopheles, appropriately disguised at the time in the academic cap and gown of a "Doktorschmaus":

Verachte nur Vernunft und Wissenschaft,
Des Menschen allerhöchste Kraft,
Laß nur in Blend- und Zauberwerken
Dich von dem Lügengeist bestärken,
So hab' ich dich schon unbedingt[15]

—except that nowadays the "Blend- und Zauberwerke" usually consist in the disparagement of "Vernunft und Wissenschaft" in the name of some trendy ideology or of a naturalistic irrationality, rather than in the name of the supernatural and magical. In each generation, even and especially in this generation, those who live within the university have the responsibility of speaking *ex corde universitatis* about the fundamental presuppositions by which the university is shaped and defined.

If it is a duty as well as a right to assert such first principles on behalf of the university, their integrity as such deserves the same respect from the church as does that of the other dimensions of *natura* with which the *gratia* of Christian revelation has to deal; for the first principle that obtains here is one that was formulated, with a simplicity that can easily be deceptive, by Saint Thomas Aquinas in the very first question of the *Summa Theologiae:* "*Gratia non tollit naturam sed perficit.*"[16] The simplicity can be so deceptive because, in the intellectual milieu and the university politics of thirteenth-century Europe, that first principle had been contested and was still being contested in the name of what presented itself, in an oversimplified party label, as "Augustinianism."[17] Yet Thomas—who, it may be said, was speaking here *ex corde universitatis*—was confident that he was speaking *ex corde ecclesiae* as well; and in the event he was vindicated, though with the ironic outcome that an oversimplified party label of "Thomism" has sometimes gone on to behave in much the same way that so-called Augustinianism behaved then. The most severe test for the first principle that grace does not do away with nature was, within the system of Saint Thomas himself, the doctrine of creation.[18] For Aristotle, whose thought was the prime instance of *natura* at work in the realm of human reason, had provided, in his theories of motion and of causality, the requisite tools for demonstrating on the basis of reason the doctrine of creation and the doctrine of a Creator; but he had also, by his theory of the eternity of matter, negated the definition of creation as a *creatio ex nihilo.* The Thomistic formulation of the doctrine of creation in questions 44 through 49 of the Prima Pars of the *Summa* is a discriminating act of surgical metaphysics: *natura* was competent to prove creation, and *gratia* did not revoke that competence; but *creatio ex nihilo* belonged to the realm of grace and of revelation, just as did the doctrine of the Trinity in relation to the monotheism with which nature and reason were likewise equipped to deal. The stunning opening sentence of the *Metaphysics* of Aristotle, "All human beings by nature want to know *pantes phusei oregontai tou eidenai* [Πάντες ἄνθρωποι τοῦ εἰδέναι ὀρέγονται φύσει]"[19] (which, as I like to say, teachers of university undergraduates repeatedly have occasion to question), is, I would argue, the same kind of first principle, and one that is not abolished by grace and revelation. It is, indeed, the first of first principles for the university, which is why Newman made it (by way of its adaptation in Cicero) the basis for his foundational discourse V, "Knowledge Its Own End";[20] and it is not abolished by the teaching of the church, although it is "perfected" by the theological and Augustinian recognition that the evil in human life is a consequence of a defect of will rather than only of a defect of knowledge.

THE BUSINESS OF A UNIVERSITY

I want to stay with Aristotle a moment longer, to suggest an additional implication, this time for what Newman calls "the business of a university."[21] The most faithful disciples of Aristotle—and, for that matter, of Thomas Aquinas—in the seventeenth and eighteenth centuries proved to be not those in the Inquisition who took Aristotle as a final authority, but those like Galileo who followed his methods of observation and experimentation even when those methods led to conclusions that turned out to be divergent from his.[22]

So it is, I would argue, with Cardinal Newman's definition of the business of a university in the preface to *The Idea of a University:* "That it is a place of *teaching* universal *knowledge,* [which] implies that its object is, on the one hand, intellectual, not moral; and, on the other, that it is the diffusion and extension of knowledge rather than the advancement."[23] I would contend that we are being the most faithful to that definition when we now nevertheless include in it the "advancement" of knowledge, not only its "diffusion and extension," therefore, in our current vocabulary, "research" and not only "teaching." As has been pointed out in his defense, Newman did place considerable emphasis on research in his university.[24] It would even be possible to use the serio-comic story of Newman's relation with Archbishop Paul Cullen of Armagh (later of Dublin), as a cautionary tale also in this respect.[25] For by seeming to subordinate the research function so completely to the teaching function in his definition, Newman can be said to have been unwittingly reinforcing the short-sighted view of the mission of the university to which representatives of the church, including Archbishop Cullen but also including many of the laity, have all too often been prone. From the insistence of the New Testament on the imperative of "teaching," which is explicitly embodied even within the "great commission" of Christ, "Go therefore and make disciples of all nations . . . *teaching* them" (Matt. 28:19-20 NRSV; italics added), the primacy of instruction in the mission of any school of the church may easily be inferred. It is a far more subtle assignment to find grounding within the New Testament for the research mission. Ultimately, I suppose, that grounding would have to be sought in a passage that has repeatedly served as the charter for any Christian humanism: "Finally, beloved, whatever is true, whatever is honorable, whatever is just, whatever is pure, whatever is pleasing, whatever is commendable, if there is any excellence and if there is anything worthy of praise, *think about these things*" (Phil. 4:8 NRSV; italics added). For its admonition to "think about" these ideas of the Good, the Beautiful, and the True, and its inclusion of one of the very few New Testament references to the archetypical Greek concept of *areté* [ἀρετή], in which, as Werner Jaeger has said at the very beginning of his magisterial work, "we can find a . . . clue to the history of Greek culture,"[26] seem to require investigation, analysis, reflection, and speculation—in a word, "research" and not merely "teaching."

But in fact, as the classical provenance of the concept of *areté* [ἀρετή] also indicates, the definition of research as essential to the business of a university must be derived chiefly from *natura* rather than from *gratia,* whereas a strong case can be made for teaching on the basis of *gratia* as well as on the basis of *natura.* Moreover, in the evolution of the modern research university, which can be said to have begun with the creation of the University of Berlin in 1810[27] and to have continued in the United States with the opening of Johns Hopkins and of the University of Chicago in 1876 and 1892 respectively, the church and its tradition cannot claim to have played anything resembling the role they played in the evolution of the teaching university from the Middle Ages to the modern era.[28] And this holds despite the valid though subtle point Newman makes about the problems of "a University more emphatically Catholic" in the Middle Ages.[29] That dependence of research on *natura* becomes evident also from the experience of universities tied to the church when they made research more central to the definition of themselves as institutions and to the job descriptions and standards of appointment and promotion for their faculty members, with what social scientists call a paradigm shift, all of which has taken place for most of them within living memory.

To be sure, many critics of the university contend that the shift has gone too far, but in carrying it out Catholic universities have, in the first instance, been guided by the definition of *university* rather than by the definition of *Catholic;* as Newman says, somewhat defensively, at the beginning of his preface, "Some persons may be tempted to complain, that I have servilely followed the English idea of a University."[30] At the same time it must be stressed that precisely by their development as research institutions, the church's universities have acquired the ability to provide for the church a resource that it has not been able to provide for itself, that it indeed has often not even recognized to be needed and has often not wanted to hear. When *Ex corde Ecclesiae* states that "If need be, a Catholic university must have the courage to speak uncomfortable truths which do not please public opinion, but which are necessary to safeguard the authentic good of society" (n. 32), this ought to be seen as including the "public opinion" and the "authentic good" of the institutional church.

What Newman, near the end of the last of his discourses, said of the university, that "It is not a Convent, it is not a Seminary,"[31] applies here as well: despite the tragic separation of seminary from university—which was at least in part the result of the legislation of the Council of Trent in its twenty-third session, 15 July 1563[32]—the *re-sourcement* that the church in the period between the First and the Second Vatican Councils needed from Scripture, the Fathers, and the liturgy, and the deepening that its concept of tradition acquired through scholarly investigation into the historical development of doctrine—when, as Père Congar has said, "the idea of development became an inner dimension of that of tradition"[33]—were the fruits of research carried on chiefly in the university rather than in the seminary.

At least one of the reasons for this is the demand and expectation usually laid upon seminary professors, which has left little time for scholarly research: when Newman says that "he, too, who spends his day in dispensing his existing knowledge to all comers is unlikely to have either leisure or energy to acquire new,"[34] he could have been thinking, though apparently he was not, of a professor in a typical diocesan seminary.

Because of the almost endemic tendency of the institutional church to look upon scholarly research and Newman's ideal of "Knowledge Its Own End" as a frill, it has had to be the Catholic university—backed up by the pressure of the "secular" demand for research as a condition of appointment and promotion—rather than the Catholic seminary that has supplied the research. That situation has begun to change, but once again much of the pressure has not come *ex corde ecclesiae* but *ex corde universitatis,* or at any rate from surveys and other activities by associations of theological schools with significant ties to the university and its ethos.[35]

Newman's formulation of the proper business of a university, as contained in his preface and as quoted earlier, includes the further stipulation "that its object is . . . intellectual, not moral."[36] Even longtime students of *The Idea of a University* are sometimes taken aback by this statement and find it surprising that it should have come from, of all people, Cardinal Newman. At least in part, his intent would seem to have been apologetic: Believing as he did so deeply that what was authentically "moral" in the full sense of the word was ultimately dependent on grace and not simply on nature, he went on in the discourses to speak of "the danger which awaits a civilized age" and of "the ordinary sin of the Intellect" when "conscience tends to become what is called a moral sense; the command of duty is a sort of taste; sin is not an offence against God, but against human nature."[37] This makes it, as A. Dwight Culler has said, "ironic" that "Newman's celebrated portrait of the 'gentleman' should so often be taken as a serious expression of Newman's positive ideal," when he intended it to be a polemic against that very "danger."[38] Nevertheless, Newman's portrait is, as a careful student of the period has said, "a superb, searching definition, feeling its way, as no other definition of the period does, into the nuances of the gentlemanly character."[39] In our own day as in his, there are many—some of them Christians and some of them not—who continue to have fundamental doubts about the capacity of the university, functioning within its own methodologies of the natural sciences, the humanities, and the social sciences, to work out a comprehensive moral system, as distinguished from a system of professional, scholarly, and scientific ethics, that can lay claim to broad assent even from its own community; that has become evident again, for example, from the response of various college and university administrators to the AIDS crisis.

Philosophically and theologically, this is, of course, the question traditionally considered in the debates about "natural law" and "natural morality." Not because that is not a supremely important question but because it is not my direct assignment here, I would want to concentrate instead on the more narrow implication of Newman's disjunction "that its object is . . . intellectual, not moral." For there is also a profound sense in which, for the definition of the business of a university, that disjunction is fatally flawed: the "intellectual" *is* the "moral," and it remains valid to speak, once again with the acknowledgment of a debt to Aristotle, about "intellectual virtues." I am, I fear, probably not the only one to have had the experience, in a confrontation with a freshman over plagiarism, of being informed, "No one ever told me it was wrong," and of being overtaken by the haunting fear that, after twelve years of American schooling, maybe no one had! But it remains a significant challenge for "natural morality," and for the teaching of the church in support of *natura,* to develop ways, at all levels of education, to formulate and cultivate these "intellectual virtues."

DUTIES TO SOCIETY

In attending to the intellectual virtues, the university, including the Catholic university, is carrying out a responsibility succinctly formulated by Cardinal Newman: "That training of the intellect, which is best for the individual himself, best enables him to discharge his duties to society."[40] In this paper, however, my emphasis is not directly on the personal "duties to society" that such an individual is enabled to discharge by virtue of the "training of the intellect," but on the more technically "social" and in that sense "professional" training carried out by the university, as well as on the function of the university as a public forum for the analysis of society. The total context of the negative definition of the university I quoted earlier from Newman, "It is not a Convent, it is not a Seminary," is the positive definition that "it is a place to fit men of the world for the world."[41]

To a degree that Newman did not envision—indeed to a degree that I for one do not applaud—that fitting of "men [and women] of the world for the world" takes place not only through the professional schools of the university, but also through the professional and quasiprofessional programs that are lodged, more or less comfortably, within the arts and sciences; these latter would include the large and growing number of programs of vocational training within the undergraduate colleges of the university.

While I must restrain myself at this time from entering upon an extended discussion of these programs and of the relation between vocationalism and the liberal arts, I do want to turn specifically to the professional schools as a primary vehicle through which the university discharges its duties to society. I do so also out of a deepening conviction that a review and clarification of the mission of its professional and vocational faculties must occupy a prominent place on the agenda of the university, including the Catholic university, as it moves into the twenty-first century.

Let me therefore set down—"up front," as the almost unavoidable current buzz word has it—a first principle about the ambiguous but decisive positioning of the professional school between the university, in its dedication to research and teaching, and the society as represented by the professional constituency of that school. That first principle has been formulated by an American educator who is uniquely qualified to make such a judgment by his distinguished career as a legal philosopher and scholar, as a law school dean, as a university president, and as a member of the federal cabinet at the head of the U.S. Department of Justice in one of the most critical periods of its history, Edward H. Levi: "The professional school which sets its course by the current practice of the profession is, in an important sense, a failure."[42] And I would have to add that the failure is compounded if (as has been known to happen) such a professional school is part of an institution identifying itself as a "Catholic university."

Believing as I fervently do in the authority of the several faculties of the university to dispose over their own curricula and programs, I believe no less fervently in the responsibility of the university as a corporate entity, through its faculties or their designated representatives, to exercise continuing vigilance also in relation to the curricula and programs of its professional schools. For what Levi calls "the current practice of the profession" reflects not only the state of the profession as a craft guild, but also the society it serves and the expectations of that society for the profession and for the university. If the professional school is not to "set its course by the current practice of the profession," the questions necessarily arise: What does society have the right to expect of the professional school, and where else except in the current practice of the profession is the professional school to look for illumination about its academic course and thus its "duties to society"? The answer to that question, especially in the total setting of the modern university, is complex; but at least two of the potential sources of such illumination deserve to be examined here, distinctly if all too briefly.

In addition to (or in inseparable connection with) its courses of training in the *techne* [τέχνη] and skill of the profession—surgery or torts or homiletics or marketing—every professional curriculum must contain large chunks of scholarly and scientific material that it shares with one or more departments of the arts and sciences. It is a grave impoverishment of the research and teaching in the arts and sciences concerned with these fields to be deprived of the insight that could come from the scholarship of professional colleagues. But the converse would also hold, that the scholarly and scientific content of the professional curriculum needs to be in an ongoing—and a structured—dialogue with its counterparts elsewhere within the university. Neuroscience and comparative jurisprudence are two examples among many of fields with far-reaching social implications whose intellectual content has proved to be so interdisciplinary that neither the professional faculties within which they originally arose nor the departments of the arts and sciences in which they are occupying an increasingly important place can afford to handle them alone. As *Ex corde Ecclesiae* points out (nn. 15-16), it is difficult to imagine that this intellectual interdependence—and therefore the need for academic integration—will not increase exponentially in the twenty-first century.

Without expatiating for the moment on the distinction I have proposed elsewhere between those professional schools that are *of* a university and those that are only *at* it, I would urge that one duty that the university owes to society in its professional programs is that of encouraging more dialogue among the several professional schools themselves. To the insider, each of the professions and each of the professional schools must seem unique, while to the outsider the analogies between them must seem obvious; both judgments are superficial, but both have some contribution to make. The analogies and the conflicts between the professions themselves are properly a major object of concern within the society, as the current debates over professional malpractice make clear. Where else except within the walls of the university can we ever hope to get a rational examination of the interrelations between two or more professions—in this case, to begin with, law and medicine—as they affect society as a whole but also as they affect the training of future professionals?

Both of these sources of illumination, considered here *ex corde universitatis,* would appear to bear a special relevance if considered as well *ex corde ecclesiae.* For the professional schools and programs of the university are also the logical staging area for the university to contribute to the ongoing dialogues not only within society, but also within the church. This question of the university and the public forum is an issue deserving of special and detailed attention on its own, which I have tried to give it elsewhere; but for the moment I want to pay particular attention to its function as such a forum for the church. For in its address to the universities of the church, the apostolic constitution *Ex corde Ecclesiae* seems to be expressing the church's need for the kind of forum that only the university can provide. When I said earlier that "every professional curriculum must contain large chunks of scholarly and scientific material that it shares with one or more departments of the arts and sciences," I was not excluding theology; nor was I exempting the official pronouncements of the church, both dogmatic and moral, from the obligation to take seriously those implications of university research that impinge directly on them. As, in quite different ways, the experience of the thirteenth century and the experience of the sixteenth century made clear, the church cannot afford to formulate such pronouncements without the benefit of the *disputatio* which is the peculiar contribution of the university, and when it has failed to recognize this the results have often been disastrous. Above all in moral theology, the church needs to take more seriously than it often does the findings of empirical research primarily in the social sciences but also in the natural sciences, and it would be difficult to invent any better venue for *disputatio* about the relation of moral theology and empirical research than the university. Through such *disputatio* (to stick with the categories of this paper) what comes *ex corde universitatis* can make a contribution to what comes *ex corde ecclesiae*; and I make bold to hope that this may be true to some extent even of what has come *ex corde universitatis* in this paper as a contribution to what has come *ex corde ecclesiae* in the apostolic constitution of that name.

NOTES

1. It also gives me an opportunity to acknowledge, within the vast secondary literature, two works that, by their titles, manifest a kinship with mine: James M. Cameron, *On the Idea of a University* (Toronto: University of Toronto Press, 1978), with many of whose judgments I find myself in agreement; and J. M. Roberts, "The Idea of a University Revisited" in *Newman after a Hundred Years,* ed. Ian Ker and Alan G. Hill (Oxford: Clarendon Press, 1990), pp. 193-222, with many of whose judgments I find myself in disagreement.

2. In citing this work, I shall follow my earlier practice of referring to the two parts by uppercase Roman numerals, to the individual discourses by lowercase Roman numerals, and to the sections of those discourses by Arabic numerals, all on the basis of the first truly critical edition: John Henry Newman, *The Idea of a University Defined and Illustrated,* ed. I. T. Ker (Oxford: Clarendon Press, 1976); page references are to this edition.

3. Newman, *Idea of a University,* Preface, p. 6.

4. Nathan Söderblom, *Religionsproblemet inom katolicism och protestantism,* 2 vols. (Stockholm: Hugo Gebers Fourlag, 1910), 1:35; Söderblom's entire chapter, pp. 33-75, concentrates on Newman's *Essay on the Development of Christian Doctrine* of 1845, but in so doing illumines the qualities of mind and spirit that also make themselves evident in Newman's *Idea of a University.*

5. Newman, *Idea of a University,* I.iii.10, p. 71.

6. Ibid., I.i.2, p. 22.

7. Ian Ker, *John Henry Newman: A Biography* (Oxford: Oxford University Press, 1990), p. 396.

8. Newman, *Idea of a University,* "Editor's Introduction," p. lxxv, with the sources of the quotations labeled.

9. Johannes Quasten, *Patrology,* 4 vols. (Westminster, Md.: Newman Press and Christian Classics, 1951-86), 2:57-62.

10. Newman, *Idea of a University,* II.viii.7, p. 383.

11. Henri de Lubac, *Histoire et esprit* (Paris: Aubier, 1950), pp. 47-91.

12. "That alone is to be accepted as truth which differs in no respect from ecclesiastical and apostolic tradition . . . On some subjects they merely stated the fact that things were so, keeping silence as to the manner of the origin of their existence, clearly in order that the more zealous of their successors, who should be lovers of wisdom might have a subject of exercise on which to display the fruit of their talents." Origen, *De principiis,* preface, 2-3 (Rufinus).

13. Newman, *Idea of a University,* I.vii.4, pp. 142-43.

14. Andrew Dickson White, *A History of the Warfare of Science with Theology in Christendom* (New York: D. Appleton and Company, 1896); the book has been reprinted several times.

15. Johann Wolfgang von Goethe, *Faust,* 1851-55. Barker Fairley translates: "Keep it up. Go on despising reason and learning, man's greatest asset. Let me entangle you in my deceits and magic shows and I'll get you for sure." *Faust,* tr. Barker Fairley (Toronto: University of Toronto Press, 1970), p. 27.

16. Thomas Aquinas, *Summa Theologiae,* I.1.8.

17. Jaroslav Pelikan, *The Christian Tradition: A History of the Development of Doctrine,* 5 vols. (Chicago: University of Chicago Press, 1971-89), 3:270-84.

18. Richard P. McKeon, "Aristotelianism in Western Christianity," in *Environmental Factors in Christian History,* ed. J. T. McNeill et al. (Chicago: University of Chicago Press, 1939), pp. 206-31.

19. Aristotle, *Metaphysics* 980a22.

20. Newman, *Idea of the University,* I.v, pp. 94-112.

21. Newman, *Idea of a University,* I.vii.1, p. 135.

22. William A. Wallace, ed., *Reinterpreting Galileo* (Washington, D.C.: Catholic University of America Press, 1986).

23. Newman, *Idea of a University,* preface, p. 5; italics in the original.

24. A. Dwight Culler, *The Imperial Intellect: A Study of Newman's Educational Ideal* (New Haven: Yale University Press, 1955), p. 311, n. 37.

25. Newman, *Idea of a University,* "Editor's Introduction," pp. xviii-xxi, xxxi.

26. Werner Jaeger, *Paideia: The Ideals of Greek Culture,* 2nd German ed., tr. Gilbert Highet, 3 vols. (New York: Oxford University Press, 1939, 1945), 1:5.

27. Friedrich Wilhelm Schelling, Johann Gottlieb Fichte, Friedrich Schleiermacher, Henrik Steffens, and Wilhelm von Humboldt, *Die Idee der deutschen Universität: Die fünf Grundschriften aus der Zeit ihrer Neubegründung durch klassischen Idealismus und romantischen Realismus* (Darmstadt: H. Gentner, 1956); this remarkable collection would bear translation into English.

28. It should, however, be added that it was, arguably, more of a factor in the founding vision of William Rainey Harper at Chicago than in that of Daniel Coit Gilman at Johns Hopkins. See James P. Wind, *The Bible and the University: The Messianic Vision of William Rainey Harper* (Atlanta: Scholar's Press, 1987).

29. Newman, *Idea of a University,* II.v.1-2, pp. 310-12.

30. Ibid., Preface, p. 5.

31. Ibid., I.ix.8, p. 197.

32. "Directions for Establishing Seminaries for Clerics," *Canons and Decrees of the Council of Trent,* ed. H. J. Schroeder (St. Louis: B. Herder, 1955), pp. 175-79.

33. Yves M.-J. Congar, *Tradition and Traditions,* tr. Michael Naseby and Thomas Rainborough (New York: Macmillan, 1967), p. 211.

34. Newman, *Idea of a University,* Preface, p. 8.

35. H. Richard Niebuhr, Daniel Day Williams, and James M. Gustafson, *The Advancement of Theological Education* (New York: Harper and Brothers, 1957).

36. Newman, *Idea of a University,* Preface, p. 5.

37. Ibid., I.viii.5, p. 165.

38. Culler, *Imperial Intellect,* p. 238.

39. Robin Gilmour, *The Idea of the Gentleman in the Victorian Novel* (London: Allen and Unwin, 1981), p. 91.

40. Newman, *Idea of a University,* I.vii.10, p. 154.

41. Ibid., I.ix.8, p. 197.

42. Edward H. Levi, *Point of View: Talks on Education* (Chicago: University of Chicago Press, 1969), pp. 38-39.

COMMENT

ELIZABETH TOPHAM KENNAN, *Mount Holyoke College*

Professor Pelikan's characteristically penetrating paper takes us with scholarly precision to a mapping of first principles for universities that are avowedly Catholic and then, with a practicality that recalls his years as a dean, takes us to the business of those universities. Rather than expand upon his cogent analysis of Cardinal Newman's insistence that natural theology, rather than revelation, be the frame for teaching and learning in a Catholic university, I should like to take up his call to consider the business of the university, what it chooses to teach and to provide for purposes of research. Thus we can touch upon another aspect of the question of what makes a university distinctively "Catholic," that is, in the terms of the apostolic constitution *Ex corde Ecclesiae*, what is "its way of serving at one and the same time both the dignity of man and the good of the Church" (n. 4).

A number of sets of disciplines that have been taught at Catholic universities through the centuries, including the twentieth, have prominent place here because they pertain to the understanding of what it means to be Catholic. Over the years, the persistence of these disciplines, the skilled interpretation brought to them by faculty, and the libraries made accessible for their support have been key to the maintenance of coherent Catholicism in this country. At the same time they have been seen to be crucial to the larger society in understanding its own foundations. Scriptural and patristic studies, history of philosophy and theology, ancient languages including Coptic as well as the lesser known Semitic groups, paleography, diplomatic, medieval, Byzantine, and early Christian studies are necessary to open for new generations knowledge of the cultures that shaped Christianity, and understanding of the human issues that have colored theological debate. They are less and less available in any depth and coherence in secular universities, which have often sacrificed them to free funds in support of other, more topical, subjects. The church in America has a high stake in seeing to it that they continue to be taught at Catholic universities, or, at least, at certain of the Catholic universities (where they should be strongly supported), lest divisions among the faithful become divisions based simply upon ignorance rather than conviction.

Catholic universities and scholars should be able to look to the bishops for support of libraries and the scholarship pertaining to these fields. They will also find support for them in the society at large. The Program in Early Christian Studies at the Catholic University of America, the Ambrosiana project at Notre Dame, the Hill Monastic Microfilm Library at Saint John's College, and even the Cistercian Publications series, a distinctly Catholic enterprise embedded for a significant period of its history in a secular setting at Western Michigan University, have all been able, over many decades, to draw support from individuals and foundations outside the church. It would be a tragic and wasteful mistake to forget that many of the pillars of the Catholic faith rest upon understanding of a very complex past, and that Catholic universities themselves are responsible for providing that understanding to future generations.

To maintain the quality of Catholic scholarship in these areas is not a trivial matter. It requires the maintenance of faculty positions, the continued expansion of library collections in these fields, and the preservation of library and archival materials, some of which are now in a serious state of decay. Continued, and in some cases, expanded allocation of resources to these fields will be necessary if Catholic universities are to serve the good of the church. And, in so far as so much of the history of the pain and the dignity of man in the West is embedded in the history of the church, the second goal of serving human dignity set out in the introduction to *Ex corde Ecclesiae* will also rest upon such allocations.

No one would argue that the role of the Catholic university is simply historical. Indeed, the anxiety built into questions of allocating resources comes directly from the countervailing pull of expanding disciplines affected by today's agendas in the arts and sciences, in the professions, and in the interwoven borders between social science and social service. These fields call for commitment from Catholic universities in terms that are insistent. David Hollenbach, in a paper that appears elsewhere in this volume, has described eloquently the imperative for a social humanism in our universities that comprehends the range of human experience in the world today and the profundity of human suffering that exists. Catholic universities are particularly pressed to address such issues because the experience of their best students often entails travel and study in afflicted regions and the questions they bring back to their own church are insistent. There is a research agenda embedded in this confrontation with the evils that plague today's world, an agenda that responds exactly to the papal call of "proclaiming the meaning of truth, that fundamental value without which freedom, justice and human dignity are extinguished" (n. 4). Centers for Latin American studies, for peace and justice, for study of conditions of poverty, all address these issues, and all have found places in American Catholic universities, helping to shape their distinctive service to truth.

But there is arguably a call to consideration in Catholic universities beyond the formation of special centers or the development of particular concerns in curriculum. Professor Pelikan locates that call explicitly in Philippians 4:8: "Finally, beloved, whatever is true, whatever is honorable, whatever is just, whatever is pure . . . think about these things." Professor Pelikan argues from this passage, correctly, I think, that the function of the modern Catholic university goes beyond teaching to embrace research. I should add to his conclusion another intellectual territory, neither teaching nor research *in se,* but pertinent to them both, that is, *reflection.* It is the characteristic of intellectual endeavor in secular society that it drives constantly toward the ever more particular, each discovery leading to the refinement of a more precise—and smaller—question.

These are conditions that do not normally welcome synthesis of results among cognate findings nor intuition of connection among fields nor even the posing of overarching questions of value or behavior. Such reflections, pertinent to the dignity of humanity and the relation of man and woman to God, are characteristic of Catholic higher education and are explicitly invoked in the introduction that frames *Ex corde Ecclesiae.* Catholic universities can offer a unique and crucial service to our distracted and fragmented society: they can offer territory for the articulation and testing of understanding that goes beyond mere knowledge, a territory in which one dares to state meaning and in which calls for debate upon the ends of our actions are honored.

Nowhere is that territory more precious to contemporary society than in the professions, and it is in its professional schools that Professor Pelikan locates the Catholic university's central role of service to society. Highly visible and valuable adjuncts to Catholic universities, the medical, law, and business schools are capable of generating enormous centrifugal forces. Faculty and students are often focused on their profession to the virtual exclusion of the university that contains them. It is sometimes difficult even to maintain a sustained curricular commitment to biomedical ethics or Christian jurisprudence, for example, and reflection upon the implications of knowledge and the ends of our activities can be as alien to the normal habits of faculty here as in any state university.

And yet these are the areas in which Catholic universities have, *in potentia,* some of the most profound opportunities for service. If faculty debate on broadening curricula to permit a formal framework for such reflection would be sterile (and it probably would), then the opportunity still exists for convocations, seminars, and publications that will invite those who seek a wider reflection to find it in a Catholic professional setting. Wise stewardship of such opportunities, careful editing of resulting publications, and attention on campus to discussions that ensue from them can and will enhance the understanding of all and will enable the church to embody in its universities a kind of social humanism, both practical and profound, that would be a gift to the twenty-first century.

COMMENT

MICHAEL J. LACEY, *Woodrow Wilson International Center for Scholars, Smithsonian Institution*

THE CHURCH AND ITS DUTY TO THE PROGRESS OF KNOWLEDGE

Teaching and learning are interdependent, and in the ongoing life of the post-Vatican II church, those countless acts of understanding and judgment that flow into the interpretation of documents issued by the magisterium are no less important than those that flow into their composition. In the introduction to *Ex corde Ecclesiae,* the Holy Father expresses the hope that this new document will serve as "a sort of 'magna carta' " for Catholic universities, helping perhaps to open up within them the promise of "future achievements that will require courageous creativity and rigorous fidelity" (n. 8) if we are to experience "a new flowering of Christian culture in the rich and varied context of our changing times" (n. 2).

I share the pontiff's hopes for the future and his estimate of the foundational importance of *Ex corde Ecclesiae* itself. For just as Magna Carta signaled the emergence of a new sense of the rule of law that determined relations among all those responsible for preserving the good of order in England of the high middle ages, so *Ex corde Ecclesiae* begins to determine relations among those who will be broadly responsible for developing the life of the mind within the world's Catholic community of the twenty-first century. I say "begins" because in any living tradition the interplay of composition and interpretation never ends. Magna Carta initiated and secured a developing tradition of governance; it did not render the need for development unnecessary. As it was elaborated in the United States via continuing reinterpretation of the Constitution and the Bill of Rights, the most important feature of the process that began with

Magna Carta has been the modern development of the jurisprudence of due process, which plays so central a part in American thought and culture.[1]

Like Magna Carta, *Ex corde Ecclesiae* provides a framework for collaborative creativity by establishing some of the juridical and institutional elements necessary to collaboration. It does not obviate the need for creativity. The document helps to bring into focus what John Courtney Murray would have called "the growing end" of our history, that delicate point at which "there is always the possibility and need of progress in the consensus that sustains its life, as there is likewise the possibility and the danger of decadence."[2] This observation applies to relations between the magisterium and the whole people of God as well as it does to any other set of institutional arrangements preserved and operated by human beings.

The documents produced by the magisterium are meant to be read, and in the modern church we understand that each and all who combine to make up the "people of God" have some degree of responsibility to participate in the work of interpretation. Without the participation of the taught, it makes little sense to speak of the teaching office of the church, or to imagine that anything resembling authentic learning actually goes on in the course of ecclesiastical history. So far as *Ex corde Ecclesiae* is concerned, the responsibilities of interpretation are especially acute for the bishops, who are here given important new duties, and for the scholars, administrators, and trustees of Catholic universities as well. To all those involved in the work of interpretation, Professor Pelikan has contributed an important set of insights that surely will be of long-term use.

His overriding concern is with the centrality of scholarship as the heart of the university enterprise. As Professor Pelikan has argued forcefully elsewhere, today's university is distinguished from its historical forerunners by the strict primacy accorded to the requirements of scholarly and scientific research above all the other just claims registered by the many constituencies of higher education. Scholarly research "defines the nature of the university"; it is of the *essence* of the university, not simply incidental to the other activities that are always underway on its premises. Good teaching aims to communicate insight into the process of scholarly research as well as its results, and to inculcate a sense of respect for the value of scholarly integrity.[3]

But it comes as no surprise that the primacy of free inquiry and research, which defines the nature of the university *qua* university, often conflicts with other legitimate needs of society and culture, particularly those of religion. That potential for conflict is what makes the relationship between the university and the church interesting and important. There are a number of possible ways in which the rationale for a proper working relationship between church and university might be conceived. *Ex corde Ecclesiae* contains traces of a number of them, although for the most part emphasis is given to the grounding in Scripture for the commitment of the church to scholarship: "thanks to her

Catholic universities . . . the church, expert in humanity, . . . explores the mysteries of humanity and of the world, clarifying them in light of Revelation" (n. 3). Quoting Pope Paul VI, "The intelligence is never diminished, rather, it is stimulated and reinforced by that interior fount of deep understanding that is the Word of God, and by the hierarchy of values that results from it" (n. 46), *Ex corde Ecclesiae* makes clear the reasons why "The Christian researcher should demonstrate the way in which human intelligence is enriched by the higher truth that comes from the Gospel" (n. 46).

Though himself a preeminent student of the tradition of Western reflection upon the higher truth that comes from the gospel, Dr. Pelikan suggests the wisdom of an alternative way of construing the relationship between church and university. His contribution is to draw our attention to the existence of complementary grounds lying deep within the Catholic tradition that do *not* rely upon revelation for their authority in orienting the church to the university. He points to the possibilities inherent in Cardinal Newman's insistence "solely on Natural Theology" in grounding the duties of the church toward the development of knowledge.

In working up this theme he draws out the importance of Saint Thomas's assertion that grace does not do away with nature, the point being that the natural order itself provides sufficient reasons for protecting the integrity of the scholarly life whenever it is necessary to do so. Dr. Pelikan shows the importance of not subordinating research to teaching, an especially powerful temptation within the Catholic university, and refutes the notion that Newman advised this subordination. He reminds us of the importance of Newman's claim that the proper business of the university is "intellectual, not moral" and makes clear the truth that the achievement of scholarly integrity has a demanding ethic of its own, indicating the sense in which the intellectual *is* the moral.

The thrust of his paper, therefore, is to deepen and reinforce the reasons for protecting academic freedom and the autonomy of the university as these are set out in *Ex corde Ecclesiae*. Given the history of continuous attempts of Christian theology, "regardless of denomination," as he points out, "to dictate to science and scholarship what their conclusions ought to be" (and certainly Marxism, dogmatic naturalism, various types of unreflective liberalism, and a host of other secular ideologies of the day have incessantly endeavored—and continue to endeavor—to do the same thing), it is helpful to be reminded that there are good reasons—theologically relevant ones that flow from the *natural desire* to see God—steadfastly to provide scholars with the "elbow room" they need to do their work. For those in the future who may have to make case by case decisions on whether the writings of theologians at Catholic universities are in compliance with the requirements of *Ex corde Ecclesiae,* Dr. Pelikan has identified some specific components of the Catholic tradition that might usefully be factored into the flow of their juridical reasoning. Surely it will continue to be worth recalling that two of the greatest Catholic thinkers in the past have emphasized the importance of reasoning independently of revelation when thinking about the university.

History of the Church-University Relationship

Nor is his paper confined to theological matters, but it has something to say about history as well. While acknowledging the accomplishments of the medieval church vis à vis the development of knowledge, Professor Pelikan gently reminds us that in the evolution of the modern research university, "the church and its tradition cannot claim to have played anything resembling the role they played in the evolution of the teaching university from the Middle Ages to the modern era." He does not go into the reasons why this was so, but it may be useful here briefly to recall the major one, because any repetition in the future would surely jeopardize the good of order in relations between the church and her universities. It had to do mainly with the suspicion of the Vatican that scholarly and religious integrity were somehow necessarily in conflict, a view that Dr. Pelikan has demonstrated to have had no place in the thinking of Newman or Aquinas.

Bernard Lonergan has pointed out that "from the schools of Alexandria and Antioch, through the medieval university, to *Pascendi* and *Humani Generis,* Catholic intellectuals have been discounted as a doubtful blessing."[4] Doubtful and discounted indeed! The condemnations and denunciations issuing from the Americanist controversy and the modernist crisis within Roman Catholicism had a profoundly harmful effect on the spirit of scholarship dwelling precariously within Catholic colleges and universities, as a mounting body of scholarship is demonstrating in depth.[5]

Have the proper lessons been learned from this historical experience? For more than anything else the memory of it accounts for the wariness with which scholars approach *Ex corde Ecclesiae,* a point that its nonscholarly interpreters ought to bear in mind if they would understand the hesitancy to offer a warm embrace. A great many Catholic thinkers have been the victims of friendly fire, to resort to a military metaphor, in their struggle to seek the truth and instruct the ignorant. Father Komonchak, in his symposium paper, points out that the list of Catholic thinkers who at one time or another fell under Roman suspicion and suffered various degrees of ecclesial disability included Montalembert, Newman, Rosmini, Lagrange, Duchesne, Blondel, Rousselot, Batiffol, Bardy, Bonsirven, Maritain, Teilhard, Chenu, Congar, de Lubac, Bouillard, Rahner, and John Courtney Murray. Lonergan is not on such a list, as a friend once remarked, only because reading him can be such hard going: it is unlikely that many in the curia made the effort. The infliction of disabilities on scholars such as these is plainly not the stuff of which a distinguished tradition of cooperative university governance is likely to arise.

Since the work of those who were disciplined did not scandalize the faithful but rather—as we now see—contributed disproportionately to the intellectual integrity and vitality of modern Catholicism, it is clear that a more fruitful relationship between the hierarchy and the community of Catholic scholars must be developed if the life of the mind is to flourish within world Catholicism in the future. It is their work—varied and diverse in its range and emphasis—that contemporary scholars feel called upon to recover as the evidence for a continuing, creative engagement of Catholic intellects with the problems of modernity.

Perhaps *Ex corde Ecclesiae* marks a profound historic turning point with respect to relations between the Vatican and the church's universities, given the many reassuring statements it contains with regard to academic freedom and university autonomy. But as Father Komonchak indicates (and the point is confirmed in Father Provost's symposium paper), there is in this new magna carta what *could* become—unless remedied in evolving interpretation and practice—a disturbing institutional and juridical imbalance. It provides no procedural or institutional safeguards against the abuse of ecclesiastical authority.

Because the abuse of ecclesiastical authority has unquestionably been an impediment to the good of order in the past, this matter requires some attention by those who must implement the apostolic constitution and adapt it to local conditions. It would be well, it seems, for all involved to ask themselves the question: Had *Ex corde Ecclesiae* existed when any of those scholars mentioned above came into his time of need, would its provisions and norms have made any difference? If not, what has been achieved, and what might be done to improve the situation in the future, given the need of the church for a vigorous and committed scholarly community? Is the development within the canon law tradition of something like the due process jurisprudence of the civil law tradition a real possibility?

Scholarly Research within the Catholic System

There is another matter bearing on the problems of research in the Catholic university system that bears mention for the benefit of those who will be responsible for weaving the provisions of *Ex corde Ecclesiae* into the life of the system in the future. It is the pressing need to upgrade the research capacity of the system as a whole. The many encouraging statements, all rooted in tradition, about the importance of research and all that goes with it which appear throughout the text of the apostolic constitution may leave the impression that the Catholic colleges and universities must be in fact paragons of scholarly productivity and academic leadership. The impression would be mistaken, and holding to it would likely lead to irresponsible neglect of the serious, long-term needs of the system on the part of those who are newly encouraged to take a more active part in its life. Ever since 1955 when Monsignor John Tracy Ellis set out the problem in his famous article on American Catholics and the intellectual life, concerns over the shortcomings of Catholic scholarship have been repeatedly expressed.[6]

As far as the bishops are concerned, and the point applies to members of the boards of trustees and top administrators as well, it should be clear that fitful concern with the occasional problems of orthodoxy that come up from time to time will not suffice to achieve the long-term hopes for a renewal of Christian intellectual life as called for in *Ex corde Ecclesiae*. Leadership carries with it a responsibility to provide for the conditions of creativity, and at least in America the needs of high scholarship and research within the system of Catholic higher education have been virtually ignored from the beginning.

While much important scholarship is being produced by the core research universities of the Catholic system—and increasingly so in recent decades—the fact remains that in comparison to the broader national system that surrounds it, the Catholic system does not perform very impressively. Since promising young Catholic scholars are welcomed in prestigious non-Catholic universities to the degree that their research and writing are of high caliber, something like a "brain drain" situation encouraging migration away from the Catholic campus is at work. Catholic universities produce only a small fraction of the annual research output of American universities, and their university presses contribute only a small part annually to the nation's scholarly literature.

In the most comprehensive and scientifically sophisticated evaluation yet published regarding the quality and prestige of American scholarship and science in all fields (excepting theology) in all universities, public and private, the Catholic universities did not do well. With one exception, and that of minor importance, Catholic departments did not rank in the top twenty in any field of study. The Catholic University of America, which played such an important historic role in the attempts to upgrade higher education within the community, ranked in the lowest one-sixth of universities involved in doctoral education. Faculty members at Catholic colleges and universities routinely have fared poorly in competition for fellowships and grants provided by government and the major foundations.

As Andrew Greeley, who since the 1960s has paid close attention as an empirically oriented researcher to the problems involved, puts the matter in a nutshell, the Catholic universities are "thus far failures as research institutions" and have not "on the average even begun to approach what would be considered presentable mediocrity in the American academic marketplace."[7] Father Lonergan once remarked, apropos of the need to upgrade the research capacities and improve the research environment for faculty within the system, that no one can "suppose that a second rate Catholic university is any more acceptable to God in the New Law than was in the Old Law the sacrifice of maimed or diseased beasts."[8] Professor Pelikan notes that it is only within living memory that a noticeable "paradigm shift" toward the primacy of research has taken place on Catholic university campuses, and he points out that the slowly growing capacity of the Catholic system to generate high-level scholarship represents "the ability to provide for the church a resource that it has not been able to provide for itself," an observation that underscores why it is important to do better.

Looking to the Future

In closing it is important to note how strongly *Ex corde Ecclesiae* calls upon everyone to do better with respect to the vocation of scholarship in its Catholic context. Specific encouragement for a new, cooperative style of improvement is offered:

> In order better to confront the complex problems facing modern society, and in order to strengthen the Catholic identity of the institutions, regional, national, and international cooperation is to be promoted in research, teaching, and other university activities among all Catholic universities, including ecclesiastical universities and faculties. Such cooperation is also to be promoted between Catholic universities and other universities, and with other research and educational institutions, both private and governmental. (art. 7, sec. 1)

This article (7) can be seen as an important building block for the needed institutional development of the future. From the standpoint of governance, given the need to make the principle of subsidiarity actually work as far as relations between the church and its universities are concerned, this "future oriented" encouragement ought to be singled out for special attention on the part of all—bishops, trustees, administrators, and faculty—who have a stake in the evolution of arrangements.

Surely in America there is no need for the founding of any new Catholic universities. There is a pervasive need for upgrading the conditions for and commitments to scholarly research within the existing system, however, and this need is related strategically to the troubling problem of the adequacy of supply, now and in the future, of committed and productive Catholic scholars to staff the faculties of the system. The problems facing the many scholars who are actually trying to do the sort of scholarship that the apostolic constitution hopes to invigorate need to be examined and addressed.

With these points in mind, it would seem advisable, as part of the preparations for sensibly operating the new rules of governance within the Catholic system, for all those with leadership responsibilities to equip themselves with an empirically rich, in-depth knowledge of the actual circumstances of scholarship and its needs within the system. We need to know who our scholars are and what might be done to ease their lot and increase their number if we are to begin to realize the possibilities of *Ex corde Ecclesiae*. Perhaps a commission of inquiry into the needs and opportunities for scholarship inherent in the existing system ought to be established to gather the necessary information. As I have suggested elsewhere (and others have made the same suggestion), perhaps we ought to think about establishing some kind of institute for advanced study to be devoted to the needs of Catholic scholars in all of the humanities and social sciences.[9] Such an institute—open to laymen and women as well as clergy, foreign scholars as well as those from America—might help to provide the fiscal and institutional structure through which the ideals expressed in *Ex corde Ecclesiae* could be advanced and a new type of Catholic intellectual community slowly brought into being.

NOTES

1. For scholarship that reassesses in light of recent research the place of Magna Carta and the ancient constitution in forming the fabric of law and government from the thirteenth century onward, see Ellis Sandoz, ed., *The Roots of Liberty: Magna Carta, Ancient Constitution, and the Anglo-American Tradition of Rule of Law* (Columbia: University of Missouri Press, 1993).

2. John Courtney Murray, *We Hold These Truths: Catholic Reflections on the American Proposition* (Kansas City: Sheed and Ward, 1960), p. 99.

3. Jaroslav Pelikan, *Scholarship and Its Survival: Questions on the Idea of Graduate Education* (Princeton, N.J.: Carnegie Foundation for the Advancement of Teaching, 1983), p. 5.

4. Bernard Lonergan, "The Role of the Catholic University in the Modern World," in *Collection*, Volume 4, *Collected Works of Bernard Lonergan*, ed. Frederick E. Crowe and Robert M. Doran (Toronto: University of Toronto Press, 1988), p. 112.

5. For insight into the history of the antimodernist project, see Lester R. Kurtz, *The Politics of Heresy: The Modernist Crisis in Roman Catholicism* (Berkeley: University of California Press, 1986), and Bernard M. G. Reardon, ed., *Roman Catholic Modernism* (Stanford, Calif.: Stanford University Press, 1970). Gabriel Daly's *Transcendence and Immanence: A Study in Catholic Modernism and Integralism* (Oxford: Clarendon Press, 1980) is a cogent discussion of the episode and its retardant effects on the development of Catholic religious thought. Gerald P. Fogarty's *American Catholic Biblical Scholarship: A History from the Early Republic to Vatican II* (San Francisco: Harper & Row, 1989) examines the damage that was wrought with regard to the progress of Catholic studies of Scripture.

6. For a discussion of the emergence of the so-called "Catholic intellectualism" debate in the 1950s as "the central issue in American Catholic life," see Philip Gleason, "Immigrant Assimilation and the Crisis of Americanization," in *Keeping the Faith: American Catholicism Past and Present* (Notre Dame, Ind.: University of Notre Dame Press, 1987). The late Monsignor Ellis revisited the problem from time to time, most recently in 1984, when he found that "the progress of Catholic institutions in regard to

excellence in the humanities and the liberal arts has been anything but notable, to put it mildly." John Tracy Ellis, "Catholic Intellectual Life: 1984," *America*, 6 October 1984, p. 180.

7. Data gleaned from Conference Board of Associated Research Councils, *An Assessment of Research Doctorate Programs in the United States*, 5 vols. (Washington, D.C.: National Academy Press, 1982). The exception of minor importance I had in mind was the University of Notre Dame, which ranked twentieth in philosophy and would no doubt rank higher at the moment. In his *Adapting to America: Catholics, Jesuits, and Higher Education in the Twentieth Century* (Washington, D.C.: Georgetown University Press, 1991), William P. Leahy points out (p. 136) that in 1983 only 21 of 716 Fulbright scholarships went to the faculty of Catholic institutions. The same year just 4 of 439 fellowship awards from the National Endowment for the Humanities went to faculty at Catholic institutions, and the following year just 2 of 283 Guggenheim fellowships. The faculty at any one of the top non-Catholic research universities may do better along these lines in a given year than the combined faculties of the entire Catholic higher educational system with its 230 colleges and universities. Andrew Greeley, *American Catholics since the Council: An Unauthorized Report* (Chicago: Thomas More Press, 1985), p. 146.

8. Lonergan, "The Role of the Catholic University in the Modern World," p. 111.

9. Michael J. Lacey, "The Backwardness of American Catholicism," *CTSA Proceedings* 46 (1991): 1-15.

DISCUSSION

Most discussion participants explored the academy's dual emphasis on teaching and research, with opinion differing widely concerning current conditions in higher education. Among the recurring themes were the particular importance of the first years of undergraduate education, particularly at Catholic institutions, and the difficulty of giving parallel prominence simultaneously to both teaching and research.

Kennan's picture of the positive role of Catholic universities in research might once have been true, but it is certainly less true today.

Article 7 of *Ex corde Ecclesiae* is correct in suggesting eliminating needless duplication in the research functions of Catholic universities. This may well be possible with the communication resources of the day. We need to be less jealous about our institutional autonomy.

There is an analogy applicable to the traditional research-versus-teaching dichotomy in higher education. Research functions are concentrated outside the university in the academy of sciences in Eastern Europe. To some extent, in medieval Europe the religious orders represented independent research centers. If we are not careful in this country, the "goose" (the federal government) that is laying the golden egg of overhead will go other places for research. This is a genuine problem facing American universities.

Some of the great French Jesuits in the early twentieth century were teachers in Jesuit schools closed at the end of the nineteenth century. This led a generation of scholars to do extended research because they were denied their schools for teaching.

The celebrated "exiles" cited by Lacey all retained their loyalty to the church at a time when they were under constraint by the church. It should be pointed out to the hierarchy that they cannot count on that same loyalty in the final decade of the twentieth century; there are too many places for these people to go.

What about the undergraduate college? Wasn't Newman's basic point that teaching was a pastoral function? This is slipping away from places where research becomes prominent. Teaching always goes first. This is a vast question. A college has its own finality that is distinct from the other aspects of higher   *223* education. There should be a hiring and governance that is responsive to this. Otherwise the core curriculum will become the province of adjuncts. Promotion requirements should concentrate on teaching and should weigh teaching heavily.

Perhaps we should hire people under different rubrics, some emphasizing teaching in a college and others emphasizing research in a university, not exclusively so, but giving emphasis. That system might work well for hiring within, but it is hard to apply with appointments from without, namely lateral hires.

Some institutions have tried the "lead scholar" and "lead teacher" categories. This is a fine concept but it is hard to translate into practice, especially in promotion and tenure policies.

Ex corde Ecclesiae doesn't really address the teaching of undergraduates.

Peer review is much easier for research than it is for teaching.

It is always difficult to get consensus on teaching quality.

Surely undergraduate education is the heart of Catholic higher education. It is also the core of responsible democracy.

There is nothing in Europe like the American college, where the first two years provide a "rounded education," but very different from Newman's concept of a liberal education. It is an education more like training in social democracy. Then students move to a major, to a department where there is specialized research, a very strange thing in European eyes.

Catholic universities should not be squeamish about the need to hire people who can teach undergrad courses in those first two years, for all four undergraduate years, and at the graduate level. Teaching and research are not intractable opposites.

The distinctive function of the university is research, which means the graduate school. And the issue we should be addressing is duplication in graduate schools.

We need to connect undergraduate education with social humanism. After all, a very important function of Catholic universities is to educate minority students who are largely unprepared and require a great deal of time, energy, and attention. When we connect this with the ambitions for research, we generate real problems.

It is not at all clear that Catholic universities are doing a very good job at the moment in producing a rounded education in the first two undergraduate years. Indeed there is cause for pessimism that the cycle of producing first-rate scholars has been broken. The ship is foundering and needs repair.

On the contrary, the first two years are a cause of optimism, at least at some institutions. It is self-destructive to identify scholarship in the humanities with the pattern that is dominant in the natural sciences. The great scholars of the past had a large comprehensive grasp of the world and were able to assimilate culture; they did not have this narrow specialization stemming from the pressures of the natural sciences.

It is good to move from our fears about *Ex corde Ecclesiae* to the challenges. We need to think of creative ways to embody the vision of Catholic higher education, to avoid the pitfalls of either excessive control or the loss of identity.

GENERAL WRAP-UP DISCUSSION

Participants were invited both to make concluding comments about the topics discussed throughout the symposium and to identify additional issues for subsequent consideration. It was noted that parents and alumni and faculty from the social and natural sciences could offer potentially valuable perspectives. Several participants emphasized the need for ongoing dialogue about "Ex corde Ecclesiae," particularly its implementation, and about the challenges facing all committed to Catholic higher education.

We have talked about faculty and students and boards of directors and bishops and alumni, but not one word about administration, the group that leads the enterprise. We need in the administration of American universities people who can fashion a vision, commend the vision relentlessly to the faculty and community, and set priorities and allocate resources—material, social, and academic—on the basis of their beliefs. We have not focused on the crucial role of leadership.

Also unresolved is the contribution of the university to Catholic intellectual life in the United States. American Catholic universities don't seem to be generating broad scholarship. There is no sustained research agenda, as a result of the pressures of the various individual disciplines. There is no intellectual outline, or there is a lack of self-confidence on how to pursue such an outline. Therefore the dichotomy between teaching and research generates more acute tensions in the Catholic university.

We need to talk candidly about the decline in the numbers of religious, who after all lead most Catholic universities. Lay faculty still associate the presence of religious with the symbolism of the whole institution. How can we share responsibility with the lay people? How can we talk more candidly about it? We are avoiding this issue.

Another issue of concern is how few junior faculty care about the Catholic nature of the institution. It is increasingly hard to find younger Catholics to hire at Catholic institutions. *Ex corde Ecclesiae* generates great resistance and fear among younger faculty. It would have been helpful had younger faculty members been able to attend this symposium, because they would come to appreciate the history of the problem and the nature of some of the changes.

They would be amazed that senior people in American higher education are worried about *Ex corde Ecclesiae.*

There are also serious generational questions. Many of us were raised in the pre-Vatican II church where there was a certain solidity, perhaps even suffocation and perhaps even triumphalism. We felt liberated by Vatican II. Young people today don't seem rooted in anything. The university must face the question of how we are passing on what we are passing on. This is a real-world problem: we don't really know this most basic question of what we are actually achieving.

It may be difficult to discuss the Catholic nature of the university without being defensive. The risk of outside prohibitions generates negative reactions among faculty. But there does seem to be a real interest among younger faculty in moving beyond specialization. And therefore the excitement is to translate the challenge of *Ex corde Ecclesiae* into intelligible language for faculty who have some interest in an integrating vision. This might touch their own experience and generate a sense of a valuable conversation across the disciplines.

Keep in mind that just having this discussion shows that value-oriented education is still alive in Catholic education. We needn't be fearful of being politically incorrect because we are talking about values.

There is much too much party labeling in these discussions. It is important to have a free, earnest, serious criticism within the fraternity. Perhaps authorities would be less eager to step in if there were a fuller, franker internal dialogue about these issues. It may be in the self-interest of universities to summon up the courage for more internal criticism.

What's gone on in this symposium is a rather uncontentious discussion. We have some areas of disagreement, but generally we have been quite agreeable. We all agree that *Ex corde Ecclesiae* represents both a challenge and a threat. The challenge is to affirm the Catholic identity and character of our universities; everyone in the group agrees with *Ex corde Ecclesiae* on this point. There is also some reason to view with alarm the atrophy of religion in American Catholic universities. There was no discussion of the criteria for assessing Catholic identity or for identifying the various signs of religious and intellectual vitality, but we all recognize there is a precarious balance between the impulses to be both more Catholic and to deal with secularization. There is some real concern over those who point to and are distressed by what they see as countersigns that show a lack of Catholic identity. Everybody seems to prefer a nonjuridical approach that would emphasize something like exemplary projects, new ideas and approaches toward which we could be moving.

Perhaps the threat of *Ex corde Ecclesiae* is not so pressing as we had thought, but much depends on how the norms are applied in specific terms.

It was healthy to talk about the challenge of *Ex corde Ecclesiae*, which we were able to do because some felt the external threat was not as serious as they initially had thought. But the threat is not just from the right. The threat comes from a public vision of the Catholic church in which Catholic approaches to social issues are lumped with fundamentalists such as Falwell. We don't have appropriate public representation of the classic Catholic way of approaching public issues.

When we ask ourselves "where is the Catholic difference?" we tend to talk about values or ethics or practice being open to the world, but there is more to religion than this. There is the vision of the universe of God and the human community.

The notion of integration or synthesis is an uphill battle with respect to governance or curriculum revision or faculty recruitment. There perhaps is much less room for optimism than is represented by the discussion we had here.

One goal of this symposium was to establish that *Ex corde Ecclesiae* deserves our respect and our study. One hopes the volume that comes out of this symposium will represent a lasting contribution to that study and a better understanding of the document. While the context of the implementation and the reception of the document still remain unclear, we surely cannot be self-satisfied about the Catholic college or university.

Appendix A:

APOSTOLIC CONSTITUTION, Ex corde Ecclesiae,
OF THE SUPREME PONTIFF, JOHN PAUL II,
ON CATHOLIC UNIVERSITIES

CONTENTS

INTRODUCTION   *231*

Part I: *IDENTITY AND MISSION*   *234*
     A. *THE IDENTITY OF A CATHOLIC UNIVERSITY*   *234*
         1. *Nature and Objectives*   *234*
         2. *The University Community*   *236*
         3. *The Catholic University in the Church*   *238*
     B. *THE MISSION OF SERVICE OF A CATHOLIC UNIVERSITY*   *239*
         1. *Service to Church and Society*   *239*
         2. *Pastoral Ministry*   *241*
         3. *Cultural Dialogue*   *242*
         4. *Evangelization*   *244*

Part II: *GENERAL NORMS*   *244*

TRANSITIONAL NORMS   *248*

CONCLUSION   *249*

NOTES   *250*

INTRODUCTION

1. Born from the heart of the Church, a Catholic university is located in that course of tradition which may be traced back to the very origin of the university as an institution. It has always been recognized as an incomparable center of creativity and dissemination of knowledge for the good of humanity. By vocation, the *universitas magistrorum et scholarium* is dedicated to research, to teaching and to the education of students who freely associate with their teachers in a common love of knowledge.[1] With every other university it shares that *gaudium de veritate*, so precious to St. Augustine, which is that joy of searching for, discovering and communicating truth[2] in every field of knowledge. A Catholic university's privileged task is "to unite existentially by intellectual effort two orders of reality that too frequently tend to be placed in opposition as though they were antithetical: the search for truth, and the certainty of already knowing the fount of truth."[3]

2. For many years I myself was deeply enriched by the beneficial experience of university life: the ardent search for truth and its unselfish transmission to youth and to all those learning to think rigorously, so as to act and to serve humanity better.

Therefore, I desire to share with everyone my profound respect for Catholic universities and to express my great appreciation for the work that is being done in them in the various spheres of knowledge. In a particular way, I wish to manifest my joy at the numerous meetings which the Lord has permitted me to have in the course of my apostolic journeys with the Catholic university communities of various continents. They are for me a lively and promising sign of the fecundity of the Christian mind in the heart of every culture. They give me a well-founded hope for a new flowering of Christian culture in the rich and varied context of our changing times, which certainly face serious challenges but which also bear so much promise under the action of the Spirit of truth and of love.

It is also my desire to express my pleasure and gratitude to the very many Catholic scholars engaged in teaching and research in non-Catholic universities. Their task as academics and scientists, lived out in the light of the Christian faith, is to be considered precious for the good of the universities in which they teach. Their presence, in fact, is a continuous stimulus to the selfless search for truth and for the wisdom that comes from above.

3. Since the beginning of this pontificate, I have shared these ideas and sentiments with my closest collaborators, the cardinals, with the Congregation for Catholic Education, and with men and women of culture throughout the world. In fact, the dialogue of the Church with the cultures of our times is that vital area where "the future of the Church and of the world is being played out as we conclude the 20th century."[4]

There is only one culture: that of man, by man and for man.[5] And thanks to her Catholic universities and their humanistic and scientific inheritance, the Church, expert in humanity, as my predecessor, Paul VI, expressed it at the United Nations,[6] explores the mysteries of humanity and of the world, clarifying them in the light of Revelation.

4. It is the honor and responsibility of a Catholic university to consecrate itself without reserve to *the cause of truth*. This is its way of serving at one and the same time both the dignity of man and the good of the Church, which has "an intimate conviction that truth is [its] real ally ... and that knowledge and reason are sure ministers to faith."[7] Without in any way neglecting the acquisition of useful knowledge, a Catholic university is distinguished by its free search for the whole truth about nature, man and God. The present age is in urgent need of this kind of disinterested service, namely of *proclaiming the meaning of truth*, that fundamental value without which freedom, justice and human dignity are extinguished. By means of a kind of universal humanism a Catholic university is completely dedicated to the research of all aspects of truth in their essential connection with the supreme Truth, who is God. It does this without fear but rather with enthusiasm, dedicating itself to every path of knowledge, aware of being preceded by him who is "the Way, the Truth, and the Life,[8] the *Logos*, whose Spirit of intelligence and love enables the human person with his or her own intelligence to find the ultimate reality of which he is the source and end and who alone is capable of giving fully that Wisdom without which the future of the world would be in danger.

5. It is in the context of the impartial search for truth that the relationship between faith and reason is brought to light and meaning. The invitation of St. Augustine, "*Intellege ut credas; crede ut intellegas*,"[9] is relevant to Catholic universities that are called to explore courageously the riches of Revelation and of nature so that the united endeavor of intelligence and faith will enable people to come to the full measure of their humanity, created in the image and likeness of God, renewed even more marvelously after sin, in Christ, and called to shine forth in the light of the Spirit.

6. Through the encounter which it establishes between the unfathomable richness of the salvific message of the Gospel and the variety and immensity of the fields of knowledge in which that richness is incarnated by it, a Catholic university enables the Church to institute an incomparably fertile dialogue with people of every culture. Man's life is given dignity by culture, and, while he finds his fullness in Christ, there can be no doubt that the Gospel, which reaches and renews him in every dimension, is also fruitful for the culture in which he lives.

7. In the world today, characterized by such rapid developments in science and technology, the tasks of a Catholic university assume an ever greater importance and urgency. Scientific and technological discoveries create an enormous economic and industrial growth, but they also inescapably require the correspondingly necessary *search for meaning* in order to guarantee that the new discoveries be used for the authentic good of individuals and of human society as a whole. If it is the responsibility of every university to search for such meaning, a Catholic university is called in a particular way to respond to this need: Its Christian inspiration enables it to include the moral, spiritual and religious dimension in its research, and to evaluate the attainments of science and technology in the perspective of the totality of the human person.

In this context Catholic universities are called to a continuous renewal, both as "universities" and as "Catholic." For "what is at stake is the *very meaning of scientific and technological research, of social life and of culture*, but, on an even more profound level, what is at stake is the *very meaning of the human person*."[10] Such renewal requires a clear awareness that, by its Catholic character, a university is made more capable of conducting an *impartial* search for truth, a search that is neither subordinated to nor conditioned by particular interests of any kind.

8. Having already dedicated the Apostolic Constitution *Sapientia Christiana* to ecclesiastical faculties and universities,[11] I then felt obliged to propose an analogous document for Catholic universities as a sort of "magna carta," enriched by the long and fruitful experience of the Church in the realm of universities and open to the promise of future achievements that will require courageous creativity and rigorous fidelity.

9. The present document is addressed especially to those who conduct Catholic universities, to the respective academic communities, to all those who have an interest in them, particularly the bishops, religious congregations and ecclesial *institutions*, and to the numerous laity who are committed to the great mission of higher education. Its purpose is that "the Christian mind may achieve, as it were, a public, persistent and universal presence in the whole enterprise of advancing higher culture and that the students of these institutions become people outstanding in learning, ready to shoulder society's heavier burdens and to witness the faith to the world."[12]

10. In addition to Catholic universities, I also turn to the many Catholic institutions of higher education. According to their nature and proper objectives, they share some or all of the characteristics of a university and they offer their own contribution to the Church and to society, whether through research, education or professional training. While this document specifically concerns Catholic universities, it is also meant to include all Catholic institutions of higher education engaged in instilling the Gospel message of Christ in souls and cultures.

Therefore, it is with great trust and hope that I invite all Catholic universities to pursue their irreplaceable task. Their mission appears increasingly necessary for the encounter of the Church with the development of the sciences and with the cultures of our age.

Together with all my brother bishops who share pastoral responsibility with me, I would like to manifest my deep conviction that a Catholic university is without any doubt one of the best instruments that the Church offers to our age, which is searching for certainty and wisdom. Having the mission of bringing the Good News to everyone, the Church should never fail to interest herself in this institution. By research and teaching, Catholic universities assist the Church in the manner most appropriate to modern times to find cultural treasures both old and new, "*nova et vetera*" according to the words of Jesus.[13]

11. Finally, I turn to the whole Church, convinced that Catholic universities are essential to her growth and to the development of Christian culture and human progress. For this reason, the entire ecclesial community is invited to give its support to Catholic institutions of higher education and to assist them in their process of development and renewal. It is invited in a special way to guard the rights and freedom of these institutions in civil society, and to offer them economic aid, especially in those countries where they have more urgent need of it, and to furnish assistance in founding new Catholic universities wherever this might be necessary.

My hope is that these prescriptions, based on the teaching of Vatican Council II and the directives of the Code of Canon Law, will enable Catholic universities and other institutes of higher studies to fulfill their indispensable mission in the new advent of grace that is opening up to the new millennium.

Part 1: IDENTITY AND MISSION

A. The Identity of a Catholic University

1. Nature and Objectives

12. Every Catholic university, *as a university*, is an academic community which, in a rigorous and critical fashion, assists in the protection and advancement of human dignity and of a cultural heritage through research, teaching and various services offered to the local, national and international communities.[14] It possesses that institutional autonomy necessary to perform its functions effectively and guarantees its members academic freedom, so long as the rights of the individual person and of the community are preserved within the confines of the truth and the common good.[15]

13. Since the objective of a Catholic university is to assure in an institutional manner a Christian presence in the university world confronting the great problems of society and culture,[16] every Catholic university, as *Catholic*, must have the following *essential characteristics*:

"1. A Christian inspiration not only of individuals but of the university community as such;

"2. A continuing reflection in the light of the Catholic faith upon the growing treasury of human knowledge, to which it seeks to contribute by its own research;

"3. Fidelity to the Christian message as it comes to us through the Church;

"4. An institutional commitment to the service of the people of God and of the human family in their pilgrimage to the transcendent goal which gives meaning to life."[17]

14. "In the light of these four characteristics, it is evident that besides the teaching, research and services common to all universities, a Catholic university, *by institutional commitment*, brings to its task the inspiration and light of the *Christian message*. In a Catholic university, therefore, Catholic ideals, attitudes and principles penetrate and inform university activities in accordance with the proper nature and autonomy of these activities. In a word, being both a university and Catholic, it must be both a community of scholars representing various branches of human knowledge, and an academic institution in which Catholicism is vitally present and operative."[18]

15. A Catholic university, therefore, is a place of research, where scholars *scrutinize reality* with the methods proper to each academic discipline, and so contribute to the treasury of human knowledge. Each individual discipline is studied in a systematic manner; moreover, the various disciplines are brought into dialogue for their mutual enhancement.

In addition to assisting men and women in their continuing quest for the truth, this research provides an effective witness, especially necessary today, to the Church's belief in the intrinsic value of knowledge and research.

In a Catholic university, research necessarily includes (a) the search for an *integration of knowledge*, (b) a *dialogue between faith and reason*, (c) an *ethical concern*, and (d) a *theological perspective*.

16. *Integration of knowledge* is a process, one which will always remain incomplete; moreover, the explosion of knowledge in recent decades, together with the rigid compartmentalization of knowledge within individual academic disciplines, makes the task increasingly difficult. But a university, and especially a Catholic university, "*has to be a 'living union' of individual organisms* dedicated to the search for truth. . . . It is necessary *to work toward a higher synthesis* of knowledge, in which alone lies the possibility of satisfying that thirst for truth which is profoundly inscribed on the heart of the human person."[19] Aided by the specific contributions of philosophy and theology, university scholars will be engaged in a constant effort to determine the relative place and meaning of each of the various disciplines within the context of a vision of the human person and the world that is enlightened by the Gospel, and therefore by a faith in Christ, the *Logos*, as the center of creation and of human history.

17. In promoting this integration of knowledge, a specific part of a Catholic university's task is to promote *dialogue between faith and reason*, so that it can be seen more profoundly how faith and reason bear harmonious witness to the unity of all truth. While each academic discipline retains its own integrity and has its own methods, this dialogue demonstrates that "methodical research within every branch of learning, when carried out in a truly scientific manner and in accord with moral norms, can never truly conflict with faith. For the things of the earth and the concerns of faith derive from the same God." [20] A vital interaction of two distinct levels of coming to know the one truth leads to a greater love for truth itself, and contributes to a more comprehensive understanding of the meaning of human life and of the purpose of God's creation.

18. Because knowledge is meant to serve the human person, research in a Catholic university is always carried out with a concern for the *ethical* and *moral* implications both of its methods and of its discoveries. This concern, while it must be present in all research, is particularly important in the areas of science and technology. "It is essential that we be convinced of the priority of the ethical over the technical, of the primacy of the person over things, of the superiority of the spirit over matter. The cause of the human person will only be served if knowledge is joined to conscience. Men and women of science will truly aid humanity only if they preserve 'the sense of the transcendence of the human person over the world and of God over the human person.' "[21]

19. *Theology* plays a particularly important role in the search for a synthesis of knowledge as well as in the dialogue between faith and reason. It serves all other disciplines in their search for meaning, not only by helping them to investigate how their discoveries will affect individuals and society but also by bringing a perspective and an orientation not contained within their own methodologies. In turn, interaction with these other disciplines and their discoveries enriches theology, offering it a better understanding of the world today, and making theological research more relevant to current needs. Because of its specific importance among the academic disciplines, every Catholic university should have a faculty, or at least a chair, of theology.[22]

20. Given the close connection between research and teaching, the research qualities indicated above will have their influence on all teaching. While each discipline is taught systematically and according to its own methods, *interdisciplinary studies*, assisted by a careful and thorough study of philosophy and theology, enable students to acquire an organic vision of reality and to develop a continuing desire for intellectual progress. In the communication of knowledge, emphasis is then placed on *how human reason in its reflection* opens to increasingly broader questions and how the complete answer to them can only come from above through faith. Furthermore, the *moral implications* that are present in each discipline are examined as an integral part of the teaching of that discipline so that the entire educative process be directed toward the whole development of the person. Finally, Catholic theology, taught in a manner faithful to Scripture, Tradition and the Church's Magisterium, provides an awareness of the Gospel principles which will enrich the meaning of human life and give it a new dignity.

Through research and teaching the students are educated in the various disciplines so as to become truly competent in the specific sectors in which they will devote themselves to the service of society and of the Church, but at the same time prepared to give the witness of their faith to the world.

2. The University Community

21. A Catholic university pursues its objectives through its formation of an authentic human community animated by the spirit of Christ. The source of its unity springs from a common dedication to the truth, a common vision of the dignity of the human person and, ultimately, the person and message of Christ, which gives the institution its distinctive character. As a result of this inspiration, the community is animated by a spirit of freedom and charity; it is characterized by mutual respect, sincere dialogue, and protection of the rights of individuals. It assists each of its members to achieve wholeness as human persons; in turn, everyone in the community helps in promoting unity, and each one, according to his or her role and capacity, contributes toward decisions which affect the community and also toward maintaining and strengthening the distinctive Catholic character of the institution.

22. *University teachers* should seek to improve their competence and endeavor to set the content, objectives, methods and results of research in an individual discipline within the framework of a coherent world vision. Christians among the teachers are called to be witnesses and educators of authentic Christian life, which evidences an attained integration between faith and life, and between professional competence and Christian wisdom. All teachers are to be inspired by academic ideals and by the principles of an authentically human life.

23. *Students* are challenged to pursue an education that combines excellence in humanistic and cultural development with specialized professional training. Most especially, they are challenged to continue the search for truth and for meaning throughout their lives, since "the human spirit must be cultivated in such a way that there results a growth in its ability to wonder, to understand, to contemplate, to make personal judgments, and to develop a religious, moral and social sense".[22] This enables them to acquire or, if they have already done so, to deepen a Christian way of life that is authentic. They should realize the responsibility of their professional life, the enthusiasm of being the trained "leaders" of tomorrow, of being witnesses to Christ in whatever place they may exercise their profession.

24. *Directors and administrators* in a Catholic university promote the constant growth of the university and its community through a leadership of service; the dedication and witness of the *non-academic staff* are vital for the identity and life of the university.

25. Many Catholic universities were founded by religious congregations, and continue to depend on their support; those religious congregations dedicated to the apostolate of higher education are urged to assist these institutions in the renewal of their commitment and to continue to prepare religious men and women who can positively contribute to the mission of a Catholic university.

Lay people have found in university activities a means by which they too could exercise an important apostolic role in the Church, and, in most Catholic universities today the academic community is largely composed of laity; in increasing numbers, lay men and women are assuming important functions and responsibilities for the direction of these institutions. These lay Catholics are responding to the Church's call "to be present, as signs of courage and intellectual creativity, in the privileged places of culture, that is, the world of education—school and university."[24] The future of Catholic universities depends to a great extent on the competent and dedicated service of lay Catholics. The Church sees their developing presence in these institutions both as a sign of hope and as a confirmation of the irreplaceable lay vocation in the Church and in the world, confident that lay people will, in the exercise of their own distinctive role, "illumine and organize these [temporal] affairs in such a way that they always start out, develop, and continue according to Christ's mind, to the praise of the Creator and the Redeemer."[25]

26. The university community of many Catholic institutions includes members of other churches, ecclesial communities and religions, and also those who profess no religious belief. These men and women offer their training and experience in furthering the various academic disciplines or other university tasks.

3. The Catholic University in the Church

27. Every Catholic university, without ceasing to be a university, has a relationship to the Church that is essential to its institutional identity. As such, it participates most directly in the life of the local Church in which it is situated; at the same time, because it is an academic institution and therefore a part of the international community of scholarship and inquiry, each institution participates in and contributes to the life and the mission of the universal Church, assuming consequently a special bond with the Holy See by reason of the service to unity which it is called to render to the whole Church. One consequence of its essential relationship to the Church is that the *institutional* fidelity of the university to the Christian message includes a recognition of and adherence to the teaching authority of the Church in matters of faith and morals. Catholic members of the university community are also called to a personal fidelity to the Church with all that this implies. Non-Catholic members are required to respect the Catholic character of the university, while the university in turn respects their religious liberty.[26]

28. Bishops have a particular responsibility to promote Catholic universities, and especially to promote and assist in the preservation and strengthening of their Catholic identity, including the protection of their Catholic identity in relation to civil authorities. This will be achieved more effectively if close personal and pastoral relationships exist between university and Church authorities characterized by mutual trust, close and consistent cooperation and continuing dialogue. Even when they do not enter directly into the internal governance of the university, bishops "should be seen not as external agents but as participants in the life of the Catholic university."[27]

29. The Church, accepting "the legitimate autonomy of human culture and especially of the sciences", recognizes the academic freedom of scholars in each discipline in accordance with its own principles and proper methods, and within the confines of the truth and the common good.

Theology has its legitimate place in the university alongside other disciplines. It has proper principles and methods which define it as a branch of knowledge. Theologians enjoy this same freedom so long as they are faithful to these principles and methods.

Bishops should encourage the creative work of theologians. They serve the Church through research done in a way that respects theological method. They seek to understand better, further develop and more effectively communicate the meaning of Christian Revelation as transmitted in Scripture and Tradition and in the Church's Magisterium. They also investigate the ways in which theology can shed light on specific questions raised by contemporary culture. At the same time, since theology seeks an understanding of revealed truth whose authentic interpretation is entrusted to the bishops of the Church,[29] it is intrinsic to the principles and methods of their research and teaching in their academic discipline that theologians respect the authority of the bishops, and assent to Catholic doctrine according to the degree of authority with which it is taught.[30] Because of their interrelated roles, dialogue between bishops and theologians is essential; this is especially true today, when the results of research are so quickly and so widely communicated through the media.

B. The Mission of Service of a Catholic University

30. The basic mission of a university is a continuous quest for truth through its research, and the preservation and communication of knowledge for the good of society. A Catholic university participates in this mission with its own specific characteristics and purposes.

1. Service to Church and Society

31. Through teaching and research, a Catholic university offers an indispensable contribution to the Church. In fact, it prepares men and women who, inspired by Christian principles and helped to live their Christian vocation in a mature and responsible manner, will be able to assume positions of responsibility in the Church. Moreover, by offering the results of its scientific research, a Catholic university will be able to help the Church respond to the problems and needs of this age.

32. A Catholic university, as any university, is immersed in human society; as an extension of its service to the Church and always within its proper competence, it is called on to become an ever more effective instrument of cultural progress for individuals as well as for society. Included among its research activities, therefore, will be a study of *serious contemporary problems* in areas such as the dignity of human life, the promotion of justice for all, the quality of personal and family life, the protection of nature, the search for peace and political stability, a more just sharing in the world's resources, and a new economic and political order that will better serve the human community at a national and international level. University research will seek to discover the roots and causes of the serious problems of our time, paying special attention to their ethical and religious dimensions.

If need be, a Catholic university must have the courage to speak uncomfortable truths which do not please public opinion, but which are necessary to safeguard the authentic good of society.

33. A specific priority is the need to examine and evaluate the predominant values and norms of modern society and culture in a Christian perspective, and the responsibility to try to communicate to society those *ethical and religious principles which give full meaning to human life*. In this way a university can contribute further to the development of a true Christian anthropology, founded on the person of Christ, which will bring the dynamism of the creation and redemption to bear on reality and on the correct solution to the problems of life.

34. The Christian spirit of service to others for the *promotion of social justice* is of particular importance for each Catholic university, to be shared by its teachers and developed in its students. The Church is firmly committed to the integral growth of all men and women.[32] The Gospel, interpreted in the social teachings of the Church, is an urgent call to promote "the development of those peoples who are striving to escape from hunger, misery, endemic diseases and ignorance; of those who are looking for a wider share in the benefits of civilization and a more active improvement of their human qualities; of those who are aiming purposefully at their complete fulfillment."[33] Every Catholic university feels responsible to contribute concretely to the progress of the society within which it works: For example, it will be capable for ways to make university education accessible to all those who are able to benefit from it, especially the poor or members of minority groups who customarily have been deprived of it. A Catholic university also has the responsibility, to the degree that it is able, to help to promote the development of the emerging nations.

35. In its attempts to resolve these complex issues that touch on so many different dimensions of human life and of society, a Catholic university will insist on cooperation among the different academic disciplines, each offering its distinct contribution in the search for solutions; moreover, since the economic and personal resources of a single institution are limited, cooperation in *common research projects* among Catholic universities, as well as with other private and governmental institutions, is imperative. In this regard, and also in what pertains to the other fields of the specific activity of a Catholic university, the role played by various national and international associations of Catholic universities is to be emphasized. Among these associations the mission of the *International Federation of Catholic Universities*, founded by the Holy See,[34] is particularly to be remembered. The Holy See anticipates further fruitful collaboration with this federation.

36. Through programs of continuing education offered to the wider community, by making its scholars available for consulting services, by taking advantage of modern means of communication, and in a variety of other ways, a Catholic university can assist in making the growing body of human knowledge and a developing understanding of the faith available to a wider public, thus expanding university services beyond its own academic community.

37. In its service to society, a Catholic university *will relate especially to the academic, cultural and scientific world* of the region in which it is located. Original forms of dialogue and collaboration are to be encouraged between the Catholic universities and the other universities of a nation on behalf of development, of understanding between cultures and of the defense of nature in accordance with an awareness of the international ecological situation.

Catholic universities join other private and public institutions in serving the public interest through higher education and research; they are one among the variety of different types of institutions that are necessary for the free expression of cultural diversity, and they are committed to the promotion of solidarity and its meaning in society and in the world. Therefore they have the full right to expect that civil society and public authorities will recognize and defend their institutional autonomy and academic freedom; moreover, they have the right to the financial support that is necessary for their continued existence and development.

2. Pastoral Ministry

38. Pastoral ministry is that activity of the university which offers the members of the university community an opportunity to integrate religious and moral principles with their academic study and non-academic activities, thus *integrating faith with life*. It is part of the mission of the Church within the university, and is also a constitutive element of a Catholic university itself, both in its structure and in its life. A university community concerned with promoting the institution's Catholic character will be conscious of this pastoral dimension and sensitive to the ways in which it can have an influence on all university activities.

39. As a natural expression of the Catholic identity of the university, the university community *should give a practical demonstration of its faith in its daily activity*, with important moments of reflection and of prayer. Catholic members of this community will be offered opportunities to assimilate Catholic teaching and practice into their lives and will be encouraged to participate in the celebration of the sacraments, especially the Eucharist as the most perfect act of community worship. When the academic community includes members of other churches, ecclesial communities or religions, their initiatives for reflection and prayer in accordance with their own beliefs are to be respected.

40. Those involved in pastoral ministry will encourage teachers and students to become more aware of their responsibility toward those who are suffering physically or spiritually. Following the example of Christ, they will be particularly attentive to the poorest and to those who suffer economic, social, cultural or religious injustice. This responsibility begins within the academic community, but it also finds application beyond it.

41. Pastoral ministry is an indispensable means by which Catholic students can, in fulfillment of their Baptism, *be prepared for active participation in the life of the Church*; it can assist in developing and nurturing the value of marriage and family life, fostering vocations to the priesthood and religious life, stimulating the Christian commitment of the laity and imbuing every activity with the spirit of the Gospel. Close cooperation between pastoral ministry in a Catholic university and the other activities within the local Church, under the guidance or with the approval of the diocesan bishop, will contribute to their mutual growth.

42. Various associations or movements of spiritual and apostolic life, especially those developed specifically for students, can be of great assistance in developing the pastoral aspects of university life.

3. Cultural Dialogue

43. By its very nature, a university develops culture through its research, helps to transmit the local culture to each succeeding generation through its teaching, and assists cultural activities through its educational services. It is open to all human experience and is ready to dialogue with and learn from any culture. A Catholic university shares in this, offering the rich experience of the Church's own culture. In addition, a Catholic university, aware that human culture is open to Revelation and transcendence, is also a primary and privileged place for a *fruitful dialogue between the Gospel and culture*.

44. Through this dialogue a Catholic university assists the Church, enabling it to come to a better knowledge of diverse cultures, discern their positive and negative aspects, to receive their authentically human contributions, and to develop means by which it can make the faith better understood by the men and women of a particular culture.[36] While it is true that the Gospel cannot be identified with any particular culture and transcends all cultures, it is also true that "the kingdom which the Gospel proclaims is lived by men and women who are profoundly linked to a culture, and the building up of the kingdom cannot avoid borrowing the elements of human culture or cultures."[37] "A faith that places itself on the margin of what is human, of what is therefore culture, would be a faith unfaithful to the fullness of what the Word of God manifests and reveals, a decapitated faith, worse still, a faith in the process of self-annihilation."[38]

45. A Catholic university must become more attentive to *the cultures of the world of today*, and to the *various cultural traditions existing within the Church* in a way that will promote a continuous and profitable dialogue between the Gospel and modern society. Among the criteria that characterize the values of a culture are, above all, the *meaning of the human person*, his or her liberty, dignity, *sense of responsibility*, and openness to the transcendent. To a respect for persons is joined *the preeminent value of the family*, the primary unit of every human culture.

Catholic universities will seek to discern and evaluate both the aspirations and the contradictions of modern culture, in order to make it more suited to the total development of individuals and peoples. In particular, it is recommended that by means of appropriate studies, the impact of modern technology and especially of the mass media on persons, the family, and the institutions and whole of modern culture be studied deeply. Traditional cultures are to be defended in their identity, helping them to receive modern values without sacrificing their own heritage, which is a wealth for the whole of the human family. Universities, situated within the ambience of these cultures, will seek to harmonize local cultures with the positive contributions of modern cultures.

46. An area that particularly interests a Catholic university is the *dialogue between Christian thought and the modern sciences*. This task requires persons particularly well versed in the individual disciplines and who are at the same time adequately prepared theologically, and who are capable of confronting epistemological questions at the level of the relationship between faith and reason. Such dialogue concerns the natural sciences as much as the human sciences which posit new and complex philosophical and ethical problems. The Christian researcher should demonstrate the way in which human intelligence is enriched by the higher truth that comes from the Gospel: "The intelligence is never diminished, rather, it is stimulated and reinforced by that interior fount of deep understanding that is the Word of God, and by the hierarchy of values that results from it. . . . In its unique manner, the Catholic university helps to manifest the superiority of the spirit, that can never, without the risk of losing its very self, be placed at the service of something other than the search for truth."[39]

47. Besides cultural dialogue, a Catholic university, in accordance with its specific ends, and keeping in mind the various religious-cultural contexts, following the directives promulgated by competent ecclesiastical authority, can offer a contribution to ecumenical dialogue. It does so to further the search for unity among all Christians. In interreligious dialogue it will assist in discerning the spiritual values that are present in the different religions.

4. Evangelization

48. The primary mission of the Church is to preach the Gospel in such a way that a relationship between faith and life is established in each individual and in the sociocultural context in which individuals live and act and communicate with one another. Evangelization means "bringing the Good News into all the strata of humanity, and through its influence transforming humanity from within and making it new. . . . It is a question not only of preaching the Gospel in ever wider geographic areas or to ever greater numbers of people, but also of affecting and, as it were, upsetting, through the power of the Gospel, humanity's criteria of judgment, determining values, points of interest, lines of thought, sources of inspiration and models of life, which are in contrast with the Word of God and the plan of salvation."[40]

49. By its very nature, each Catholic university makes an important contribution to the Church's work of evangelization. It is a living *institutional* witness to Christ and his message, so vitally important in cultures marked by secularism, or where Christ and his message are still virtually unknown. Moreover, all the basic academic activities of a Catholic university are connected with and in harmony with the evangelizing mission of the Church: research carried out in the light of the Christian message which puts new human discoveries at the service of individuals and society; education offered in a faith-context that forms men and women capable of rational and critical judgment and conscious of the transcendent dignity of the human person; professional training that incorporates ethical values and a sense of service to individuals and to society; the dialogue with culture that makes the faith better understood, and the theological research that translates the faith into contemporary language. "Precisely because it is more and more conscious of its salvific mission in this world, the Church wants to have these centers closely connected with it; it wants to have them present and operative in spreading the authentic message of Christ."[41]

Part II: GENERAL NORMS

Article 1. The Nature of These General Norms

§1. These general norms are based on, and are a further development of, the Code of Canon Law[42] and the complementary Church legislation, without prejudice to the right of the Holy See to intervene should this become necessary. They are valid for all Catholic universities and other Catholic institutes of higher studies throughout the world.

§2. The general norms are to be applied concretely at the local and regional levels by episcopal conferences and other assemblies of Catholic hierarchy[43] in conformity with the Code of Canon Law and complementary Church legislation, taking into account the statutes of each university or institute and, as far as possible and appropriate, civil law. After review by the Holy See,[44] these local or regional "ordinances" will be valid for all Catholic universities and other Catholic institutes of higher studies in the region, except for ecclesiastical universities and faculties. These latter institutions, including ecclesiastical faculties which are part of a Catholic university, are governed by the norms of the apostolic constitution *Sapientia Christiana*.[45]

§3. A university established or approved by the Holy See, by an episcopal conference or another assembly of Catholic hierarchy, or by a diocesan bishop is to incorporate these general norms and their local and regional applications into its governing documents and conform its existing statutes both to the general norms and to their applications and submit them for approval to the competent ecclesiastical authority. It is contemplated that other Catholic universities, that is, those not established or approved in any of the above ways, with the agreement of the local ecclesiastical authority, will make their own the general norms and their local and regional applications, internalizing them into their governing documents, and, as far as possible, will conform their existing statutes both to these general norms and to their applications.

Article 2. The Nature of a Catholic University

§1. A Catholic university, like every university, is a community of scholars representing various branches of human knowledge. It is dedicated to research, to teaching, and to various kinds of service in accordance with its cultural mission.

§2. A Catholic university, as Catholic, informs and carries out its research, teaching and all other activities with Catholic ideals, principles and attitudes. It is linked with the Church either by a formal, constitutive and statutory bond or by reason of an institutional commitment made by those responsible for it.

§3. Every Catholic university is to make known its Catholic identity, either in a mission statement or in some other appropriate public document, unless authorized otherwise by the competent ecclesiastical authority. The university, particularly through its structure and its regulations, is to provide means which will guarantee the expression and the preservation of this identity in a manner consistent with Section 2.

§4. Catholic teaching and discipline are to influence all university activities, while the freedom of conscience of each person is to be fully respected.[46] Any official action or commitment of the university is to be in accord with its Catholic identity.

§5. A Catholic university possesses the autonomy necessary to develop its distinctive identity and pursue its proper mission. Freedom in research and teaching is recognized and respected according to the principles and methods of each individual discipline, so long as the rights of the individual and of the community are preserved within the confines of the truth and the common good.

Article 3. The Establishment of a Catholic University

§1. A Catholic university may be established or approved by the Holy See, by an episcopal conference or another assembly of Catholic hierarchy, or by a diocesan bishop.

§2. With the consent of the diocesan bishop, a Catholic university may also be established by a religious institute or other public juridical person.

§3. A Catholic university may also be established by other ecclesiastical or lay persons; such a university may refer to itself as a Catholic university only with the consent of the competent ecclesiastical authority, in accordance with the conditions upon which both parties shall agree.

§4. In the cases of Sections 1 and 2, the statutes must be approved by the competent ecclesiastical authority.

Article 4. The University Community

§1. The responsibility for maintaining and strengthening the Catholic identity of the university rests primarily with the university itself. While this responsibility is entrusted principally to university authorities (including, when the positions exist, the chancellor and/or a board of trustees or equivalent body), it is shared in varying degrees by all members of the university community and therefore calls for the recruitment of adequate university personnel, especially teachers and administrators, who are both willing and able to promote that identity. The identity of a Catholic university is essentially linked to the quality of its teachers and to respect for Catholic doctrine. It is the responsibility of the competent authority to watch over these two fundamental needs in accordance with what is indicated in Canon Law.[49]

§2. All teachers and all administrators, at the time of their appointment, are to be informed about the Catholic identity of the institution and its implications, and about their responsibility to promote, or at least to respect, that identity.

§3. In ways appropriate to the different academic disciplines, all Catholic teachers are to be faithful to, and all other teachers are to respect, Catholic doctrine and morals in their research and teaching. In particular, Catholic theologians, aware that they fulfill a mandate received from the Church, are to be faithful to the Magisterium of the Church as the authentic interpreter of Sacred Scripture and Sacred Tradition.[50]

§4. Those university teachers and administrators who belong to other churches, ecclesial communities, or religions as well as those who profess no religious belief, and also all students, are to recognize and respect the distinctive Catholic identity of the university. In order not to endanger the Catholic identity of the university or institute of higher studies, the number of non-Catholic teachers should not be allowed to constitute a majority within the institution, which is and must remain Catholic.

§5. The education of students is to combine academic and professional development with formation in moral and religious principles and the social teachings of the Church; the program of studies for each of the various professions is to include an appropriate ethical formation in that profession. Courses in Catholic doctrine are to be made available to all students.

Article 5. The Catholic University Within the Church

§1. Every Catholic university is to maintain communion with the universal Church and the Holy See; it is to be in close communion with the local Church and in particular with the diocesan bishops of the region or nation in which it is located. In ways consistent with its nature as a university, a Catholic university will contribute to the Church's work of evangelization.

§2. Each bishop has a responsibility to promote the welfare of the Catholic universities in his diocese and has the right and duty to watch over the preservation and strengthening of their Catholic character. If problems should arise concerning this Catholic character, the local bishop is to take the initiatives necessary to resolve the matter, working with the competent university authorities in accordance with established procedures[52] and, if necessary, with the help of the Holy See.

§3. Periodically, each Catholic university to which Article 3, Sections 1 and 2, refers, is to communicate relevant information about the university and its activities to the competent ecclesiastical authority. Other Catholic universities are to communicate this information to the bishop of the diocese in which the principal seat of the institution is located.

Article 6. Pastoral Ministry

§1. A Catholic university is to promote the pastoral care of all members of the university community, and to be especially attentive to the spiritual development of those who are Catholics. Priority is to be given to those means which will facilitate the integration of human and professional education with religious values in the light of Catholic doctrine, in order to unite intellectual learning with the religious dimension of life.

§2. A sufficient number of qualified people—priests, religious, and lay persons—are to be appointed to provide pastoral ministry for the university community, carried on in harmony and cooperation with the pastoral activities of the local Church under the guidance or with the approval of the diocesan bishop. All members of the university community are to be invited to assist the work of pastoral ministry, and to collaborate in its activities.

Article 7. Cooperation

§1. In order better to confront the complex problems facing modem society, and in order to strengthen the Catholic identity of the institutions, regional, national, and international cooperation is to be promoted in research, teaching and other university activities among all Catholic universities, including ecclesiastical universities and faculties.[53] Such cooperation is also to be promoted between Catholic universities and other universities, and with other research and educational institutions, both private and governmental.

§2. Catholic universities will, when possible and in accord with Catholic principles and doctrine, cooperate with government programs and the programs of other national and international organizations on behalf of justice, development, and progress.

TRANSITIONAL NORMS

Article 8

The present Constitution will come into effect on the first day of the academic year 1991.

Article 9

The application of the Constitution is committed to the Congregation for Catholic Education, which has the duty to promulgate the necessary directives that will serve toward that end.

Article 10

It will be the competence of the Congregation for Catholic Education, when with the passage of time circumstances require it, to propose changes to be made in the present Constitution in order that it may be adapted continuously to the needs of Catholic universities.

Article 11

Any particular laws or customs presently in effect that are contrary to this Constitution are abolished. Also, any privileges granted up to this day by the Holy See, whether to physical or moral persons, that are contrary to this present Constitution are abolished.

CONCLUSION

The mission that the Church, with great hope, entrusts to Catholic universities holds a cultural and religious meaning of vital importance because it concerns the very future of humanity. The renewal requested of Catholic universities will make them better able to respond to the task of bringing the message of Christ to man, to society, to the various cultures:

"Every human reality, both individual and social has been liberated by Christ: persons, as well as the activities of men and women, of which culture is the highest and incarnate expression. The salvific action of the Church on cultures is achieved, first of all, by means of persons, families and educators. . . . Jesus Christ, our Savior, offers his light and his hope to all those who promote the sciences, the arts, letters and the numerous fields developed by modern culture. Therefore, all the sons and daughters of the Church should become aware of their mission and discover how the strength of the Gospel can penetrate and regenerate the mentalities and dominant values that inspire individual cultures, as well as the opinions and mental attitudes that are derived from it."[54]

It is with fervent hope that I address this document to all the men and women engaged in various ways in the significant mission of Catholic higher education.

Beloved brothers and sisters, my encouragement and my trust go with you in your weighty daily task that becomes ever more important, more urgent and necessary on behalf of evangelization for the future of culture and of all cultures. The Church and the world have great need of your witness and of your capable, free, and responsible contribution.

Given in Rome, at St. Peter's, on August 15, the solemnity of the Assumption of the Blessed Virgin Mary into heaven, in the year 1990, the 12th of the pontificate.

JOANNES PAULUS PP. II
[*sig.*]

NOTES

1. Cf. the letter of Pope Alexander IV to the University of Paris, April 14, 1255, Introduction: *Bullarium Diplomatum. . .*, vol. III, Turin, 1858, p. 602.

2. St. Augustine, *Confessions*, X, xxiii, 33: "In fact, the blessed life consists in *the joy that comes from the truth*, since this joy comes from you who are Truth, God my light, salvation of my face, my God." *Patrologia Latina* 32, pp. 793–794. Cf. St. Thomas Aquinas, *De Malo*, IX, 1: "It is actually natural to man to strive for knowledge of the truth."

3. John Paul II, Discourse to the Catholic Institute of Paris, June 1, 1980: *Insegnamenti di Giovanni Paolo II*, Vol. 3/1 (1980), p. 1581.

4. John Paul II, Discourse to the Cardinals, November 10, 1979: *Insegnamenti di Giovanni Paolo II*, Vol. 2/2 (1979), p. 1096; cf. Discourse to UNESCO, Paris, June 2, 1980: *Acta Apostolicae Sedis*, 72 (1980), pp. 735–752.

5. Cf. John Paul II, Discourse to the University of Coimbra, May 15, 1982: *Insegnamenti di Giovanni Paolo II*, Vol. 5/2 (1982), p. 1692.

6. Paul VI, Allocution to Representatives of States, October 4, 1965: *Insegnamenti di Paolo VI*, Vol. 3 (1965), p. 508.

7. John Henry Cardinal Newman, *The Idea of a University*, (London: Longmans, Green and Company, 1931), p. XI.

8. Jn 14:6.

9. Cf. St. Augustine, *Serm.* 43, 9: PL 38, 258. Cf. also St. Anselm, *Proslogion*, Ch. 1: PL 158, 227.

10. Cf. John Paul II, Allocution to the International Congress on Catholic Universities, April 25, 1989, n. 3: AAS 18 (1989), p. 1218.

11. John Paul II, Apostolic Constitution *Sapientia Christiana*, concerning the Ecclesiastical Universities and Faculties, April 15, 1979: AAS 71 (1979), pp. 469–521.

12. Vatican Council II, Declaration on Catholic Education *Gravissimum Educationis*, n. 10: AAS 58 (1966), p. 737.

13. Mt 13:52.

14. Cf. *The Magna Carta of the European Universities*, Bologna, Italy, September 18, 1988, "Fundamental Principles."

15. Cf. Vatican Council II, Pastoral Constitution on the Church in the Modern World *Gaudium et Spes*, n. 59: AAS 58 (1966), p. 1080; Declaration on Catholic Education *Gravissimum Educationis*, n. 10: AAS 58 (1966), p. 737. "Institutional autonomy" means that the governance of an academic institution is and remains internal to the institution; "academic freedom" is the guarantee given to those involved in teaching and research that, within their specific specialized branch of knowledge and according to the methods proper to that specific area, they may search for the truth wherever analysis and evidence lead them, and may teach and publish the results of this search, keeping in mind the cited criteria, that is, safeguarding the rights of the individual and of society within the confines of the truth and the common good.

16. There is a twofold notion of culture used in this document: the humanistic and the socio-historical. "The word 'culture' in its general sense indicates all those factors by which man refines and unfolds his manifest spiritual and bodily qualities. It means his effort to bring the world itself under his control by his knowledge and his labor. It includes the fact that by improving customs and institutions he renders social life more human both within the family and in the civic community. Finally, it is a feature of culture that throughout the course of time man expresses, communicates and conserves in his works great spiritual experiences and desires, so that these may be of advantage to the progress of many, even of the whole human family. Hence it follows that human culture necessarily has a historical and social aspect and that the word 'culture' often takes on a sociological and ethnological sense". Vatican Council II, Pastoral Constitution on the Church in the Modern World *Gaudium et Spes*, n. 53: AAS 58 (1966), p. 1075.

17. "The Catholic University in the Modern World," final document of the Second International Congress of Delegates of Catholic Universities, Rome, November 20–29, 1972, Section 1.

18. Ibid.

19. John Paul II, Allocution to the International Congress on Catholic Universities, April 25, 1989, n. 4: AAS 81 (1989), p. 1219. Cf. also Vatican Council II, Pastoral Constitution on the Church in the Modern World *Gaudium et Spes*, n. 61: AAS 58 (1966), pp. 1081–1082. Cardinal Newman observes that a university "professes to assign to each study which it receives its proper place and its just boundaries; to define the rights, to establish the mutual relations and to effect the intercommunion of one and all" (*The Idea of a University*, p. 457).

20. Vatican Council II, Pastoral Constitution on the Church in the Modern World *Gaudium et Spes*, n. 36: AAS 58 (1966), p. 1054. To a group of scientists I pointed out that "while reason and faith surely represent two distinct orders of knowledge, each autonomous with regard to its own methods, the two must finally converge in the discovery of a single whole reality which has its origin in God" (John Paul II, *Address at the Meeting on Galilee*, May 9, 1983, n. 3: AAS 75 [1983], p. 690).

21. John Paul II, Address at UNESCO, June 2, 1980, n. 22: AAS 72 (1980), p. 750. The last part of the quotation uses words directed to the Pontifical Academy of Sciences, November 10, 1979: *Insegnamenti di Giovanni Paolo II*, Vol. 2/2 (1979), p. 1109.

22. Cf. Vatican Council II, Declaration on Catholic Education *Gravissimum Educationis*, n. 10: AAS 58 (1966), p. 737.

23. Vatican Council II, Pastoral Constitution on the Church in the Modern World *Gaudium et Spes*, n. 59: AAS 58 (1966), p. 1080. Cardinal Newman describes the ideal to be sought in this way: "A habit of mind is formed which lasts through life, of which the attributes are freedom, equitableness, calmness, moderation and wisdom " (*The Idea of a University*, pp. 101–102).

24. John Paul II, Post-Synodal Apostolic Exhortation *Christifideles Laici*, December 30, 1988, n. 44: AAS 81 (1989), p. 479.

25. Vatican Council II, Dogmatic Constitution on the Church *Lumen Gentium*, n. 31: AAS 57 (1965), pp. 37–38. Cf. Decree on the Apostolate of the Laity *Apostolicam Actuositatem, passim*: AAS 58 (1966), pp. 837ff. Cf. also *Gaudium et Spes*, n. 43: AAS 58 (1966), pp. 1061–1064.

26. Cf. Vatican Council II, Declaration on Religious Liberty *Dignitatis Humanae*, n. 2: AAS 58 (1966), pp. 930–931.

27. John Paul II, Address to Leaders of Catholic Higher Education, Xavier University of Louisiana, U.S.A., September 12, 1987, n. 4: AAS 80 (1988), p. 764.

28. Vatican Council II, Pastoral Constitution on the Church in the Modern World *Gaudium et Spes*, n. 59: AAS 58 (1966), p. 1080.

29. Cf. Vatican Council II, Dogmatic Constitution on Divine Revelation *Dei Verbum*, nn. 8–10: AAS 58 (1966), pp. 820–822.

30. Cf. Vatican Council H, Dogmatic Constitution on the Church *Lumen Gentium*, n. 25: AAS 57 (1965), pp. 29–31.

31. Cf. Congregation for the Doctrine of the Faith, "Instruction on the Ecclesial Vocation of the Theologian'" May 24, 1990.

32. Cf. John Paul II, Encyclical Letter *Sollicitudo Rei Socialis*, nn. 27–34: AAS 80 (1988), pp. 547–560.

33. Paul VI, Encyclical Letter *Populorum Progressio*, n. 1: AAS 59 (1967), p. 257.

34. "Therefore, in that there has been a pleasing multiplication of centers of higher learning, it has become apparent that it would be opportune for the faculty and the alumni to unite in common association which, working in reciprocal understanding and close collaboration, and based upon the authority of the Supreme Pontiff, as father and universal doctor, they might more efficaciously spread and extend the light of Christ" (Pius XII, Apostolic Letter *Catholicas Studiorum Universitates*, with which the International Federation of Catholic Universities was established: AAS 42 [1950], p. 386).

35. The Code of Canon Law indicates the general responsibility of the bishop toward university students: "The diocesan bishop is to have serious pastoral concern for students by erecting a parish for them or by assigning priests for this purpose on a stable basis; he is also to provide for Catholic university centers at universities, even non-Catholic ones, to give assistance, especially spiritual, to young people" (*CIC*, can. 813).

36. "Living in various circumstances during the course of time, the Church, too, has used in her preaching the discoveries of different cultures to spread and explain the message of Christ to all nations, to probe it and more deeply understand it, and to give it better expression in liturgical celebrations and in the life of the diversified community of the faithful." (Vatican Council II, Pastoral Constitution on the Church in the Modern World *Gaudium et Spes*, n. 58: AAS 58 [1966], p. 1079).

37. Paul VI, Apostolic Exhortation *Evangelii Nuntiandi*, n. 20: AAS 68 (1976), p. 18. Cf. Vatican Council II, Pastoral Constitution on the Church in the Modern World *Gaudium et Spes*, n. 58: AAS 58 (1966), p. 1079.

38. John Paul II, Address to Intellectuals, Students and University Personnel at Medellin, Columbia, July 5, 1986, n. 3: AAS 79 (1987), p. 99. Cf. also Vatican Council II, Pastoral Constitution on the Church in the Modern World *Gaudium et Spes*, n. 58: AAS 58 (1966), p. 1079.

39. Paul VI, Address to the Delegates of the International Federation of Catholic Universities, November 27, 1972: AAS 64 (1972), p. 770.

40. Paul VI, Apostolic Exhortation *Evangelii Nuntiandi*, n. 18ff.: AAS 68 (1976) pp. 17–18.

41. Paul VI, Address to Presidents and Rectors of the Universities of the Society of Jesus, August 6, 1975, n. 2: AAS 67 (1975), p. 533. Speaking to the participants of the International Congress on Catholic Universities, April 25, 1989, I added (n. 5): "Within a Catholic university the evangelical mission of the Church and the mission of research and teaching become *interrelated* and *coordinated*": Cf. AAS 81 (1989), p. 1220.

42. Cf. in particular the Chapter of the Code: "Catholic Universities and Other Institutes of Higher Studies" (*CIC*, can. 807–814).

43. Episcopal conferences were established in the Latin Rite. Other Rites have other assemblies of Catholic hierarchy.

44. Cf. *CIC*, Can. 455, Section 2.

45. Cf. *Sapientia Christiana*: AAS 71 (1979), pp. 469–521. Ecclesiastical universities and faculties are those that have the right to confer academic degrees by the authority of the Holy See.

46. Cf. Vatican Council II, Declaration on Religious Liberty *Dignitatis Humanae*, n. 2: AAS 58 (1966), pp. 930–931.

47. Cf. Vatican Council II, Pastoral Constitution on the Church in the Modern World *Gaudium et Spes*, nn. 57 and 59: AAS 58 (1966), pp. 1077–1080; *Gravissimum Educationis*, n. 10: AAS 58 (1966), p. 737.

48. Both the establishment of such a university and the conditions by which it may refer to itself as a Catholic university are to be in accordance with the prescriptions issued by the Holy See, episcopal conference or other assembly of Catholic hierarchy.

49. Canon 810 of CIC specifies the responsibility of the competent authorities in this area: Section 1: "It is the responsibility of the authority who is competent in accord with the statutes to provide for the appointment of teachers to Catholic universities who, besides their scientific and pedagogical suitability, are also outstanding in their integrity of doctrine and probity of life, when those requisite qualities are lacking they are to be removed form their positions in accord with the procedure set forth in the statutes. Section 2: The conference of bishops and the diocesan bishops concerned have the duty and right of being vigilant that in these universities the principles of Catholic doctrine are faithfully observed." Cf. also Article 5, Section 2 ahead in these "Norms."

50. Vatican Council II, Dogmatic Constitution on the Church *Lumen Gentium*, n. 25: AAS 57 (1965), p. 29; *Dei Verbum*, nn. 8–10: AAS 58 (1966) pp. 820–822; cf. *CIC*, can. 812: "It is necessary that those who teach theological disciplines in any institute of higher studies have a mandate from the competent ecclesiastical authority."

51. Cf. *CIC*, can. 811, Section 2.

52. For universities to which Article 3, Sections 1 and 2, refer, these procedures are to be established in the university statutes approved by the competent ecclesiastical authority; for other Catholic universities, they are to be determined by episcopal conferences or other assemblies of Catholic hierarchy.

53. Cf. *CIC*, can. 820. Cf. also *Sapientia Christiana*, Norms of Application, Article 49: AAS 71 (1979), p. 512.

54. John Paul II, Address to the Pontifical Council for Culture, January 13, 1989, n. 2: AAS 81 (1989), pp. 857–858.

Appendix B:

DRAFT ORDINANCES
National Conference of Catholic Bishops Committee
to Implement the Apostolic Constitution,
Ex corde Ecclesiae

In early May of 1993, the following memorandum, draft ordinances,
and questionnaire were sent to the nation's Archbishops and Bishops as
well as the Presidents of Catholic Colleges and Universities in the United
States.

MEMORANDUM   ***Date:***   May 4, 1993

To: Archbishops and Bishops
          Presidents of Catholic Colleges and Universities
From: Bishop John Leibrecht

In 1990, the president of the National Conference of Catholic Bishops, Archbishop
Daniel Pilarczyk, appointed a Committee to Implement the Apostolic Constitution Ex
corde Ecclesiae promulgated by Pope John Paul II that same year. The Committee of
seven bishops is assisted by eight Catholic college and university presidents as consultors.
Several resource persons also took part in the Committee's deliberations. The task of
the Committee, in response to the Apostolic Constitution itself, is to begin the process
of drawing up national ordinances by applying the Constitution's general norms to
the United States.

The enclosed draft of ordinances is sent as part of a national consultation with
bishops and presidents of Catholic colleges and universities. All bishops in the United
States are invited to submit recommendations on the enclosed draft, especially if there
are Catholic colleges and universities in their archdioceses. They are asked to consult
with any advisors they believe helpful. Presidents are invited to consult with their
boards, faculties and others associated with their colleges and universities. Where
applicable, they are asked to seek comments from provincials of religious communities
which sponsor their institutions.

The Committee sending this draft of ordinances strongly recommends that bishops
and presidents in each diocese meet together in order to benefit from one another's   ***255***

insights before comments are sent back to the Committee. Some bishops and presidents may want to make joint recommendations in addition to individual ones. The Association of Catholic Colleges and Universities has offered to facilitate regional opportunities for dialogue between bishops and presidents.

The draft text is from the bishop members of the Committee. Presidents and resource people participated fully in all discussions prior to the bishop's decisions about the text of the draft. On some matters during discussion, bishops and presidents agreed—both about what particiular issues should be addressed in the ordinances for the United States and the wording of individual ordinances. In some cases, bishops and presidents found themselves unanimously with opposing views on a particular proposal. In some discussions neither the bishops nor presidents were among themselves, unanimous in their opinons. Votes among the bishops were unanimous on the ordinances finally presented in the accompanying draft. This draft is also being sent for comment to Catholic learned societies in the United States.

After recommendations have been received, the Ex corde Eccleasiae Implementation Committee will draw up a revised document to be considered by the full assembly of the National Conference of Catholic Bishops. After NCCB action, the document will be sent for review to the Apostolic See.

The enclosed evaluation form is meant to be of assistance in making your recommendations.

Your recommendations to the Committee are due no later than December 31, 1993.

Please return them to:

Bishop John J. Leibrecht, *Chair*
Ex corde Ecclesiae Implementation Committee
National Conference of Catholic Bishops
3211 4th Street, NE, Washington, DC 20017-1194

Committee Members:
His Eminence, James Cardinal Hickey
Most Rev. James A. Griffin
Most Rev. John J. Leibrecht
Most Rev. Oscar Lipscomb

Most Rev. Adam J. Maida
Most Rev. James W. Malone
Most Rev. Francis B. Schulte

Consultors:
Dr. Dorothy McKenna Brown
Reverend William Byron, S.J.
Brother Raymond Fitz, S.M.
Dr. Norman C. Francis
Karen M. Kennelly, C.S.J.

Reverend Edward A. Malloy, C.S.C.
Reverend J. Donald Monan, S.J.
Dr. Matthew Quinn

Resource Persons:
Rev. Msgr. Frederick R. McManus
Alice Gallin, O.S.U.

Mr. Benito Lopez

NCCB/USCC Staff:
Sharon Euart, R.S.M.
John Liekweg

Reverend Charles Hagan
Lourdes Sheehan, R.S.M.

PROPOSED ORDINANCES FOR CATHOLIC COLLEGES AND UNIVERSITIES IN THE UNITED STATES

Part One: INTRODUCTION

1 In the Introduction to his Apostolic Constitution *Ex corde Ecclesiae* (August 15, 1990), His
2 Holiness Pope John Paul II says, "I desire to share with everyone my profound respect for
3 Catholic Universities" **[No. 2]**. He notes that the Catholic university shares with every other university that
4 *"gaudium de veritate,"* so precious to Saint Augustine, which is that joy of searching for, discovering and
5 communicating truth in every field of knowledge." But the Catholic university, according to the Holy
6 Father, also has the "privileged tash" to unite two orders of reality that too often remain unconnected and
7 "frequently tend to be placed in opposition as though they were antithetical," namely, the orders of faith
8 ("the certainty of already knowing the fount of truth") and reason ("the search for truth") **[No. 1]**.

9   The "honor and responsibility," as Pope John Paul II puts it, of the Catholic university is
10 to "consecrate itself without reserve to the cause of truth" **[No. 4]**. An in doing so, the Holy Father says,
11 the Catholic college or university is serving both the dignity of the human person and the good of the
12 Church.

13   "If it is the responsibility of every university to search ... for meaning," observes the Pope, "a
14 Catholic university is called in a particular way to respond to this need: its Christian inspiration enables it
15 to include the moral, spiritual and religious dimension in its research, and to evaluate the attainments of
16 science and technology in the perspective of the totality of the human person" **[No. 7]**.

17   *Ex corde Ecclesiae* identifies four characteristics that "necessarily" belong to research conducted by
18 a Catholic university: "(a) the search for an integration of knowledge, (b) a dialogue between faith and
19 reason, (c) an ethical concern, and (d) a theological perspective" **[No. 15]**.

1   Of particular interest to the Catholic university, writes the Pope, "is the dialogue between Christian
2 thought and the modern sciences. This task requires persons particularly well versed in the individual
3 disciplines who are at the same time adequately prepared theologically, and who are capable of confronting
4 epistemological questions at the level of the relationship between faith and reason" **[No. 46]**. The apostolic
5 constitution recalls for its readers the purpose of Catholic higher education as articulated in the Second
6 Vatical Council's declaration on Christian education: that "the Christian mind may achieve as it were, a
7 public, persistent and universal presence in the whole enterprise of advancing higher culture..." **[No. 9]**.

8   According to *Ex corde Ecclesiae*, "the objective of a Catholic university is to assure in an
9 institutional manner a Christian presence in a university world confronting the great problems of society
10 and culture" **[No. 13]**. Hence, the Holy Father regards the work of Catholic colleges and univesities as
11 "irreplaceable" **[No. 10]** in the life of the Church. He concludes the apostolic constitution by saying to
12 Catholic college and university educators: "The Church and the world have great need of your witness and
13 of your capable, free, and responsible contribution."

14   The purpose of the following ordinances is to provide implementation guidelines that embody both
15 the vision and the spirit of *Ex corde Ecclesiae*. These ordinances do not apply to ecclesiastical faculties
16 which are governed by the Apostolic Constitution *Sapientia Christiana* (1979), but they do not apply to all the

17 rest of the remarkable set of Catholic institutions of higher learning in the United States to which Pope
18 John Paul II looks for their "capable, free, and responsible contribution" to the future of both church and
19 culture.

Part Two: ORDINANCES

1 The ordinances on Catholic higher education for the dioceses of the United States are
2 complementary to and in harmony with Canons 807–814 of the Code of Canon Law and the
3 general norms of the Apostolic Constitution *Ex corde Ecclesiae* (part II), both of which in their entirety
4 are part of the universal law ofthe Church.

ORDINANCE 1.

5 Catholic colleges and universities are those which, through their governing boards, freely commit
6 themselves to the Christian message as it comes to us through the Catholic church, and together
7 with the bishops, seek to preserve and foster their Catholic character and mission.

ORDINANCE 2.

8 Catholic colleges anduniversities are to identify themselves as belonging to one of the descriptive
9 categories on the list appended to these ordinances (see Appendix) and include the appropriate
10 identification in their governing documents [Gen. Norms, 1:3] or statements of mission [Gen.
11 Norms, 2:3].

ORDINANCE 3.

12 Periodically, and at lease every ten years, each Catholic college or university is to undertake an
13 internal review of the congruence of its research program [Nos. 7, 15, 18, 45], course of instruction
14 [Nos. 16, 17, 19, 20], and service activity [Nos. 21, 31, 32. 34, 36, 37, 38] with the ideals and
15 principles expressed in *Ex corde Ecclesiae"* [Gen. Norms 2 and 5].

ORDINANCE 4.

16 As a manifestation of their common desire to maintain the Catholic identity of the
17 college/university, institutional authorities and the diocesan bishop, according to their own proper
18 roles, will seek to promote the teaching of Catholic theological disciplines in communion with the
19 church [Gen. Norms 4:3].

ORDINANCE 5.

20 The mandate granted to those who teach theology in Catholic colleges and universities should be
21 understood as recognition by the competent ecclesiastical authority of a Catholic professor's
22 suitability to teach theological disciplines ŒobGen. Norms, 4:3].

ORDINANCE 6.

1 Catholic professors of theological disciplines are to be advised by academic officials of the
2 Church's expectation that they request the mandate from the competent ecclesiastical authority,
3 normally the diocesan bishop or his delegate (cf. Canon 812). Accordingly, the bishop is to invite
4 the Catholic professor to request the mandate and, after appropriate review, the bishop is to
5 respond to the request.

ORDINANCE 7.

6 If a dispute arises between the competent ecclesiastical authority and a Catholic college or
7 university, or individuals or groups within such institutions, it is to be resolved according to

8   procedures that respect the rights of persons in the church (for example, Canons 208–223, 224–231,
9   and 273–289), the autonomy of the academic institution (I, n. 12; II, art. 2, par. 5, art.
10 5, par. 2), and the responsibility of church authorities (I nn. 28–29, II art. 4, par. 1; art. 5 par. 2) to
11 assist in the preservation of the institution's Catholic identity. Such procedures are also to follow
12 the principles and, to the extent applicable, the procedures of the documents of the National
13 Conference of Catholic Bishops *On Due Process* (1972) in administrative matters and *Doctrinal*
14 *Responsibilites* (1989) in matters of differences in doctrine.

ORDINANCE 8.
15 Governing Boards, in appropriate collaboration with the administration of the college/university,
16 should provide for an adequately staffed campus ministry program and suitable liturgical and
17 sacramental opportunities under the moderation of the local bishop [Gen. Norms 6: 1–2].

18 The ordinances, as particular law for the dioceses of the United States, become effective at the beginning
19 of the academic year following their enactment by the National Conference of Catholic Bishops and
20 communication from the Congregation for Catholic Education that they have been reviewed by the
21 Apostolic See. (Gen. Norma, 1:2).

Appendix

1 Descriptive Categories of Catholic Colleges and Universities

CATEGORY 1.

2 Ecclesiastical Faculties/Universities.

CATEGORY 2.

3 Canonically Established (by the Holy See).

CATEGORY 3.

4 Established by a Diocese:

5 **a)** governed by a board of trustees with some powers reserved to the diocese; or

6 **b)** independent governing board with no powers reserved to the diocese.

CATEGORY 4.

7 Established by a Religious Community:

8 **a)** governed by a board of trustees with some powers reserved to the religious community; or

9 **b)** independent governing board with no powers reserved to the religious community.

CATEGORY 5.

10 Established by other ecclesiastical or lay initiative:

11 **a)** governed by a board of trustees with some powers reserved to the founding entity; or

12 **b)** independent governing board with no powers reserved.

13 Institutions in this fifth category may call themselves "Catholic" by consent of the competent
14 ecclesiastical authority.

QUESTIONNAIRE

Please respond to the following questions:

Using the scale below, indicate your position on the following: (Please put the number that best responds to your answer on the line next to the question.)

9	8	7	6	5	4	3	2	1
Strongly Agree			*Agree*		*Disagree*		*Strongly Disagree*	

1. ____ **Introduction**

2. **Proposed Ordinances:**

   ____Ordinance 1   ____ Ordinance 3   ___ Ordinance 5   ____Ordinance 7

   ___ _Ordinance 2   ____ Ordinance 4   ___ Ordinance 6   ____Ordinance 8

3. ____ **Appendix**

4. How does the Introduction apply the Apostolic Constitution *Ex corde Ecclesiae* to the Catholic colleges and universities in the United States? (Please check one)

   a._____ Perfectly   **c.** _____ Fairly well

   b._____ Very well   **d.** _____ Not well

5. How well do the Ordinances apply the Apostolic Constitution *Ex corde Ecclesiae* to the Catholic colleges and universities in the United States? (Please check one)

   a. _____ Perfectly   **c.** _____ Fairly well

   b. _____ Very well   **d.** _____ Not well

6. Can you locate your institution(s) in the Appendix within the categories therein described? (Please check one) (To be answered by college presidents and bishops with Catholic colleges or universities in the diocese.)

   a. Yes_____   **b.** _____ No   If No, please indicate what is needed.

7. Please indicate other matters, if any, which should be treated in the Introduction.

8. Please indicate additional matters, if any, which should be treated with the section on Ordinances.

9. What recommendations, if any, do you have on any specific ordinance(s) in this draft?

10. Additional comments (please use reverse of sheet or attachments for Answers to Questions 6, 7, 8, & 9).